T0305939

MANAGING THE DIGITAL WORKPLACE IN THE POST-PANDEMIC

Managing the Digital Workplace in the Post-Pandemic provides a cutting-edge survey of digital organizational behaviour in the post-pandemic workplace, drawing from an international range of expertise. It introduces and guides students and practitioners through the current best practices, laboratory methods, policies and protocols in use during these times of rapid change to workplace practices. This book is essential reading for students, researchers and practitioners in business and management.

The book draws on global expertise from its contributors while being suitable for class and educational use, with each chapter including further reading, chapter summaries and exercises. Tutors are supported with a set of instructor materials that include PowerPoint slides, a test bank and an instructor's manual.

This text covers a wide range of themes in this fast-developing field, including:

- The effect of the pandemic on the digital workplace
- Gender and cyberbullying in the context of the digital workplace
- Digital ergonomics and productivity
- Digital conflict management

Fahri Özsungur graduated from Ataturk University Faculty of Law, Çağ University Department of Private Law – Master of Laws – LL.M., Hacettepe University Department of Family and Consumer Sciences Ph.D., Aksaray University Department of Business Ph.D., Anadolu University Department of Private Law – Doctor of Law (student). He has two associate professorships (associate professor: management and strategy; associate professor: social work). He serves as a Higher Degrees by Research (HDR) Examiner/Ph.D. Examiner. He has more than 120 works (books, chapters, articles, etc.). He is the editor of 24 journals (two SSCI/SCI/SCI-Expanded) and a reviewer of more than 500 journals (25 SSCI/SCI/SCI-Expanded, 45 ESCI).

MANAGING THE DIGITAL WORKPLACE IN THE POST-PANDEMIC

A Companion for Study and Practice

Edited by Fahri Özsungur

Routledge
Taylor & Francis Group

LONDON AND NEW YORK

Cover image: Getty Images

First published 2023
by Routledge
4 Park Square, Milton Park, Abingdon, Oxon, OX14 4RN

and by Routledge
605 Third Avenue, New York, NY 10158

Routledge is an imprint of the Taylor & Francis Group, an informa business

British Library Cataloguing-in-Publication Data
A catalogue record for this book is available from the British Library

ISBN: 978-1-032-25474-6 (hbk)
ISBN: 978-1-032-25387-9 (pbk)
ISBN: 978-1-003-28338-6 (ebk)

DOI: 10.4324/9781003283386

Typeset in Bembo
by Apex CoVantage, LLC

Access the Support Material: www.routledge.com/9781032253879

CONTENTS

CONTRIBUTORS

Furkan Arasli, Auburn University

Huseyin Arasli, Norwegian School of Hotel Management

Gözde Baycur, Boğazici University and Amin Shoari Nejad, Maynooth University

Esra Sipahi Döngül, Aksaray University and Luigi Pio Leonardo Cavaliere, University of Foggia

Mahmoud El Samad, Lebanese International University (LIU), Hani El-Chaarani, Beirut Arab University, Sam El Nemar, AZM University and Lukman Raimi, Universiti Brunei Darussalam

Arturo Luque González, Universidad Técnica de Manabí, Ecuador & Observatorio Euromediterráneo de Espacio Público y Democracia URJC and Cristina Raluca Gh. Popescu, University of Bucharest

Muhsin Halis, Kocaeli University

Duygu Hıdıroğlu, Mersin University and Rustamov Parviz Hajı oğlu, Azerbaijan State University of Economics

Hande Karadağ, MEF University

Gözde Mert, Nişantaşı University and Slimane ED-Dafali, ENCG, Chouaib Doukkali University

Ionica Oncioiu, Titu Maiorescu University

Joanna Paliszkiewicz, Warsaw University of Life Science and Esra Sipahi Döngül, Aksaray University

Sameen Rafi, Aligarh Muslim University

Sumbul Rafi, Aligarh Muslim University

Lukman Raimi, Universiti Brunei Darussalam and Muhammad Usman Tariq, Abu Dhabi School of Management

Sneha Saha, CHRIST (Deemed to be University and Ridhima Shukla, CHRIST (Deemed to be University

Richa Sahay, Usha Martin University and Anupama Verma, Usha Martin University

Muhammad Usman Tariq, Abu Dhabi School of Management and Lukman Raimi, Universiti Brunei Darussalam

Simona Vasilache, Bucharest University of Economic Studies and Mihaela Sava, Bucharest University of Economic Studies

Aytan Zeynalli, Azerbaijan State Oil and Industry University

Latif Zeynalli, The Academy of Public Administration Under The President of The Republic of Azerbaijan

PART I

Digital workplace management

1

DIGITAL ERGONOMICS AND PRODUCTIVITY

Muhsin Halis

Introduction

Digital ergonomics is a subfield of ergonomics that explores increasing efficiency and minimizing possible risks to humans to maximize human effort using information technologies. Therefore, it covers all aspects of human–computer interaction. Human–computer interaction is a field of study related to human behaviour, psychology, cognitive sciences, computer technologies and software engineering, as well as fields such as ergonomics, graphics and industrial design, sociology, anthropology and educational sciences due to its focus on interaction between humans and computers. Computer–human interaction is a field of study that deals with the design, evaluation and implementation of interactive computer systems for human use and the investigation of other factors surrounding them (Whitworth et al., 2006). There are four main components of the human–computer interaction (HCI) system: user, task, tool and context. In human computer interaction, the observation obtained when a user performs certain tasks with certain tools is evaluated, and this data is used in the process of developing interactive systems.

According to Booth and Marshall (1989), the framework for HCI studies consists of the following six topics:

1   What are the characteristics that affect people's use of technology?
2   What are the aspects of technology that affect people's use of technology?
3   How do people acquire and conceptualize their interactive abilities?
4   How do we match people's needs with technical facilities?
5   How can usable technologies be designed?
6   How does technology affect organizations?

DOI: 10.4324/9781003283386-2

Technological developments come up with new inventions every day. These technological developments continue to affect our business and private lives with different reflections of virtual reality. Especially in the digital field, developments are changing many of our habits. In this context, many new concepts to be considered in the relationship of the human element with the machine, which mediated the transformation of virtual elongation into reality with its cognitive and sensory abilities, describe this change.

One of these concepts is virtual reality. The word "virtual" is derived from the Latin word "*virtus*", which means power or strength, and has become the word "*virtualis*", which is not a real entity in philosophy but has potential. Accordingly, what is virtual is the one that tends to be real, without any certainty. Anything can take place in virtual reality without being subjected to physical limitations. In this sense, the virtual concept defines the real but intangible (Milovanovic et al., 2017). Virtual reality, on the other hand, is the combination of reality and fantasy with fiction created using technology. Technically, the term "virtual reality" is used for computer-generated 3D environments where individuals experience the feeling of being there. Technology users can participate in virtual environments through various peripherals. For users to really experience this, virtual reality designs need to be ergonomically flawless, otherwise, poor perception of reality will adversely affect the sensory and cognitive performance of the user in this virtual environment.

It has now become possible, through computers, that many ideas and thoughts that have a tendency to be real can be realized without the need for physical space and that many activities can be carried out in cyberspace in parallel with what has traditionally existed. The construction of virtual spaces and relationships in the virtual universe have also changed the way they do business (Manovich, 2016).

Milgram (Milgram & Kishino, 1994), who made the first studies on the concept of reality in a digital environment, developed a diagram on the distinction of the *virtual reality, augmented reality* and *physical reality* concepts that have been referenced many times in the literature. According to this diagram, *augmented reality* is part of mixed reality, which includes all realities. Augmented reality (AR) belongs to the physical side of this diagram.

AR, as a type of reality, is the subject of bringing the interaction established in the virtual environment to the physical environment. Unlike virtual reality, AR uses physical reality in spatial terms. The environment is perceived by superimposing virtual attachments on physical reality using computer and imaging technologies (Azuma et al., 2001, p. 34; Henderson & Feiner, 2010; Krevelen & Poelman, 2010). AR relies on the digitization of real-time views. Every day, a large number of start-ups enter the world of augmented reality. In this respect, AR opens up new opportunities for many business areas. Companies aim to make their shopping experiences more intuitive, friendly and satisfying by integrating technologies such as augmented reality into their existing e-commerce sites in order to be able to make innovative solutions and developments on issues such as customer satisfaction, brand awareness and sales process efficiency.

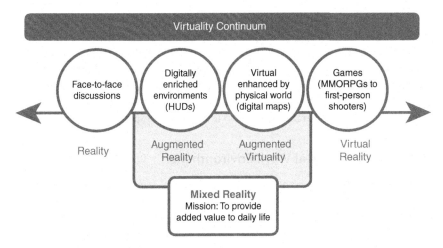

FIGURE 1.1 Milgram's Confused Reality Diagram

One of the important elements in human–computer interaction is wearable information-equipped technologies. Wearable technologies can be utilized in the form of a computer-enabled clothing or accessory (Huang, 2002). Wearable computers will allow many activities to be done with computers as well as extending business applications to business areas. Wearable technologies eliminate the necessity of business and entertainment being dependent on location (Makimoto, 2013).

Traditional business environments are transforming to respond to the new possibilities of the information age, and the concept of space in human–business relationships is undergoing a transformation. Augmented reality has turned into computer-aided spaces that characterize the stable structure of traditional business architecture, an interactive environment with constantly updated and new messages (Manovich, 2016). Simultaneously with technology, space designs are constantly transforming. One of the important problems in terms of ergonomics is the design problem of this interaction area. Human technology compatibility with new spaces shaped by digital technologies and this interaction interface is an important design problem.

Developing information technologies have enabled spatial functions to be realized in cyberspace. The physical space-dependent functions of banking, librarianship, commerce, business and entertainment have been digitized and have started to be performed in cyberspace and virtual spaces (Baykan, 2002). Information technologies also change the spatial and temporal acceptance of objects (Kan, 1999, p. 55). Now, public spaces are becoming private, private spaces are gradually turning into public spaces, and the functions of private spaces can become public.

For this reason, dependency on space has decreased and some workplaces have become mobile with wearable computers (Makimoto, 2013). These mobile spaces have caused the boundaries of business environments to evaporate. The ability of unrelated spaces to fulfil their functions at the same time through information technologies has caused any space to have a variable functional structure, and the relationship between space and its function has weakened. Mass data transfer increased the amount of space-independent work and turned fixed spaces into mobile cellular spaces. Physical spaces with visible, identifiable boundaries and a volume in space are deformed and transformed into invisible cloud spaces (Manovich, 2016).

Ergonomics in Digital Work Environments

Ergonomics: in the face of organic and psychosocial stresses (pressures) that may occur under the influence of all factors in the industrial work environment, taking into account the anatomical (physical muscle characteristics, body structure characteristics) and anthropometric characteristics (dimensional characteristics of the human body, height, weight, physiological capacity and tolerances of the skeletal system), the system is a multidisciplinary field of research and development that seeks to demonstrate efficiency and the basic laws of human–machine–environmental harmony.

Because of information technologies' effects on our lives, the working area of today's people has shifted from the labour-intensive field to the information-intensive field. This situation makes it even more important to consider the cognitive and affective characteristics of the employees in human–system integration designs. The productivity problems of employees with digital interfaces will lead managers to new search avenues. User interfaces designed in accordance with ergonomic principles emerge as an important work area in increasing productivity.

Meanwhile, not only ergonomic principles but also individual cognitive abilities that are suitable for the characteristics of the work should be considered in human–computer interaction in the process of job design. Although this is undoubtedly a special field of study of applied psychology, it is more appropriate to examine it within the framework of cognitive sciences, which is an interdisciplinary field of study. It constitutes psychology, linguistics, computer science and the common working area of studies in the field of artificial intelligence. In terms of software systems, the trust is complex and requires good knowledge of the brain's learning mechanisms and prioritized consideration of how individuals use their cognitive abilities.

The ergonomic subfield, which focuses on ergonomic designs for the more efficient operation of human beings on the human–computer interface, can be called digital ergonomics. Digital ergonomics focuses heavily on mental processes in human–information technology interaction. The interaction of humans and other elements of the system with elements such as detection, memory, reasoning, motor response, etc. are considered as basic issues. Digital ergonomics *has an important common area with software ergonomics*. In addition to making decisions, the digital ergonomics mental workload deals with topics such as human–computer interaction (HCI). It also takes care of issues such as human reliability, the business system and acquiring the skills associated with human system design. HCI consists of the design of the methods, specifications, guidelines and principles necessary to develop the available software, which enables software that communicates with the way people think and process information.

In HCI, it is understood how important digital ergonomics is given the development of information technologies. Digital ergonomics is particularly interested in the design of complex and high-tech systems related to computing to enable the person to interact with information, tools and the environment. HCI can also be considered in the process of designing systems in the field of digital ergonomics.

HCI is an interdisciplinary field of study that deals with the design, development, evaluation and implementation of interactive technologies. The most important issue of HCI is *availability*. Availability is defined as the ability of a specific group of users to perform certain tasks effectively and efficiently in a specific context. With the development of the design terms "usability", "ease of use" and "user-friendly" with the development of the design terms of software and interface (such as web page, which allows computer software to be run by the user, including various pictures, graphics and texts) the terms have started to be equated.

In order to ensure effective compliance in HCI, it is important to consider the following four dimensions in ergonomic designs:

- Anthropometric compatibility: The likelihood of seeing the external area, considering the physical dimensions of the person, the location of the operator during operation, etc.
- Sensory-motor compatibility: Taking into account the speed of the person's motor operations and their sensory response to various types of stimuli.
- Energy compatibility: Considering a person's power abilities when determining efforts for control.
- Psychophysiological compatibility: To consider the person's reaction to colour, colour range, frequency range of the signals provided, shape of the machine and other aesthetic parameters.

The proliferation of computers requires more attention to the design of interfaces to help eliminate or reduce the stress that a person experiences while working with the computer. The user interface (UI) is understood as a series of elements that allow the user of the programme to control its operation and achieve the necessary results. This is a system of rules and tools that regulates the interaction of the programme with the user. When designing interfaces, the main task is to facilitate the process of detecting and processing information.

Software quality is another important aspect in digital ergonomic designs. One of the important indicators of software quality is ease of use. UI availability is an indicator of its quality, which determines overall ease when using software, such as simplicity and consistency in the regulation of controls. Availability is an ergonomic feature. Availability in the ergonomic requirements document for office operation with visual terminals according to ISO 9241–11 (Bevan et al., 2015), the international quality standard for interfaces, is defined by certain users as the degree of availability of a product in order to achieve its goals effectively, economically and satisfactorily.

It is important that the interface is designed in accordance with ergonomic principles so that any user can easily use the programme. These policies are developed based on UI design experience, considering users' requests. These principles allow us to see the user of the software product and the software product as a single system. The person is considered part of the working system. Proper design of work systems allows for reduced risks and therefore reduced stress in the workplace and increased workforce productivity.

Good UI design means that the programme meets the user's expectations of how to behave. The main advantage of a good user interface is that the user feels that he or she has control over the software. To create such a sense of satisfaction for the user, the interface must have several features, including:

Naturalness: A natural interface is one that does not force the user to significantly change the way they get used to it. This means that the messages and results generated by the application should not require further explanation. The use of concepts and images familiar to the user provides an intuitive interface when performing tasks.

Consistency: Consistency should not waste time in users understanding the differences in the use of certain controls, commands and similar elements. It should allow them to transfer existing knowledge to new tasks and learn new features quickly so they can focus on the task at hand. Consistency is important for an interface, including command names, visual presentation of information and behaviour of interactive elements.

Consistency within the product: The same command must perform the same functions wherever it occurs and in the same way.

Consistency in the operating environment: The application should be able to improve the user's knowledge and the skills previously acquired when working with other applications while maintaining consistency with the interface provided by the operating system.

Consistency in the use of metaphors: If the behaviour of a software object is often outside the scope of what is meant by the corresponding metaphor, the user may have difficulty working with such an object.

User-friendly: An efficient interface should only allow appropriate actions at each stage of the process and alert users to situations where they could damage the system or data. Also, the user should be able to undo or correct the actions taken. Users can make some mistakes even with a well-designed interface. These errors can be physical (wrong choice of command or data by mistake) or logical (wrong decision to select command or data). An effective interface should be able to prevent situations that are likely to result in errors.

Feedback policy: There should always be feedback for user actions. Each user action must receive visual and/or audible confirmation that the software accepts the command entered. The type of reaction, if possible, should consider the nature of the action performed. It is desirable that the response time is comparable to human reaction. A typical user can only last a few seconds waiting for a response from their electronic counterpart. Latency can often be hidden from the user through multitasking, which allows other work to be done while background calculations are in place. In any case, the user needs to know that the programme is not suspended but continues to work.

Simplicity: The interface should make it easier to learn and use from simplification. In addition, the interface must provide access to the entire list of functionalities provided by this application. Providing access to rich functionality and ease of use is at odds with each other. In the design of an effective interface, these goals are balanced. A possible way to keep this simple is to display the minimum information required for the user to complete the next step on the screen.

Flexibility: The flexibility of the interface is that it can consider the level of training and productivity of the user. Flexibility refers to the ability to change the structure of dialogue and/or input data.

Aesthetics: Designing visual components is an important part of developing a programming interface. Accurate visual representation of the objects used ensures that crucial additional information is transferred about the behaviour and interaction of various objects. At the same time, it should be noted that every visual element that appears on the screen potentially requires the user's attention. It is necessary to create an environment on the screen that not only facilitates the understanding of the information presented by the user, but also allows it to focus on the most important aspects.

It is difficult to assess the quality of the interface with quantitative features, but an objective assessment can be obtained based on the partial indicators given here.

- The time it takes for a specific user to reach a certain level of knowledge and skills when working with the application.
- Recording the work skills gained after a while (for example, after a week off, the user must be able to complete a specific sequence of operations within a certain period).
- The speed at which you solve the problem using this application; in this case, it is not the speed of the system that should be evaluated or the speed of data entry from the keyboard, but the time it takes to achieve the purpose of the solved problem.
- Subjective user satisfaction when working with the system.

Human-Centred Design Standards

Human-centred design is a method of developing interactive systems based on ergonomic principles, aiming to create useful systems based on the users' characteristics and needs. This approach increases the effectiveness, efficiency, availability and durability of systems, user satisfaction and productivity, and prevents the potential negative effects of system use on human health and safety. There is a lot of research on ergonomics and usability that can be useful for human-centred design. Interstellar systems have also been developed that guide the human-centred design of computer interactive systems. But mostly these standards are designed for professionals involved in system development. Some of the standards are:

- ISO 1503:2008, Spatial orientation and direction of movement
- ISO 6385:2004, Ergonomic principles in the design of business systems
- ISO 10075, Ergonomic principles regarding mental workload
- ISO 11064–1:2000, Ergonomic design of control centres
- ISO 14915–2:2003, Software ergonomics for multimedia user interfaces
- ISO/IEC 15288:2008, Systems and software engineering
- ISO/TR 16982:2002, Ergonomics of human–system interaction
- ISO/PAS 18152:2003, Ergonomics of human–system interaction
- ISO/TR 18529:2000, Ergonomics – Ergonomics of human–system interaction
- ISO 20282–1:2006, Ease of use of everyday products
- ISO/IEC/TR 25060, Software product quality requirements and evaluation
- ISO/IEC/TR 29138–1:2009, Information technology
- IEC 62508(2010), Guidance on the human aspects of reliability

Standards address ways to improve human–system interaction through hardware and software components of interactive systems. Here it is useful to determine the limits of the concept for a more accurate understanding of computer interactive systems: Computer interactive systems differ in size and complexity. Examples include software, office systems, process control systems, automated banking systems, websites and applications and consumer products, such as vending machines, mobile phones and digital television. In this international standard, such systems are referred to as systems or services, but sometimes computer interactive systems is used in the name of simplicity.

It is seen that the standards developed for this purpose provide an overview of the activities in the field of human-centred design. Detailed descriptions of human-centred design methods or all details of project management are not included in these standards. Some of the standards also do not address health or safety issues.

These systems, developed for the managers responsible for the planning and development of systems, enable managers to understand the role of human factors and ergonomics in the overall design process. In this regard, standards such as ISO 9241 and ISO 6385 and GOST R 1.0, which determine the general principles of ergonomics, can be examined in detail (Bevan et al., 2015).

Adopting a human-centred approach to design and development brings significant economic and social benefits to users, employers and suppliers. Products and systems with high availability tend to be technically more advanced and more commercially successful. Most of the time in the consumer product range, buyers are willing to pay more for a well-designed product or system. The cost of technical support is reduced when users can understand and use products without additional help. In most countries, employers and suppliers have a legal obligation to protect users from disease risk. Human-centred and safety practices can reduce this risk (e.g., risk of exposure to the musculoskeletal system). Systems developed using human-centred methods are of better quality, for example, due to the following:

1   Increase user productivity and productivity in organizations
2   Ease of comprehension and ease of use resulting in reduced training and support costs
3   Improve accessibility by improving availability for a wide range of users
4   Consideration towards the user experience
5   Reduce user dissatisfaction and stress
6   To gain a competitive advantage by improving the brand image, for example
7   To contribute to the organization's sustainable development goals

The overall benefit of adopting a human-centred design approach can be determined by considering the cost of the entire life cycle of a product, system or service, including concept, design, implementation, support, use, maintenance and decommissioning. The adoption of a human-centred design approach also benefits other aspects of system design, such as making it easier to define and formulate functional requirements. Adopting a human-centred approach also increases the likelihood of successfully completing a project on time and within budget. Using appropriate human-centred methods may reduce the risk of the product not meeting stakeholder and user requirements (ISO/IEC/TR 25060).

Regardless of design processes and allocation of responsibilities and functions, a human-centred approach should consider the following principles:

1   The design should be based on a precise definition of the targeted users, tasks and environment.
2   Users must be included in design and development.
3   A human-centred assessment should be made to improve the design.
4   Design improvement must be iterative.
5   The design must consider the user experience.
6   The design team should include people with knowledge and skills in various fields.

Products, systems and services must be designed to consider the impact on all parties involved. Therefore, all important user groups and stakeholders should be defined. Creating systems based on misunderstanding or under-understanding of user needs is one of the main sources of system failure. The degree of conformity and availability depends on the terms of use. That is, defined users perform tasks defined under defined conditions of use (Bevan et al., 2015).

Involving system users in the system design is important for the effectiveness of the system. For this purpose, designers can increase efficiency by bringing the system and users together. Active participation of users is an important data source that can be useful for important design. This is something that decision makers should consider. The features of the users in the design should be presented as input to the system development process.

User feedback is an important source of information in human-centred design. Evaluating a design with user involvement and improving it based on user feedback is an effective way to minimize the risk of a system not meeting the needs of users or customer organization (including requirements that are difficult to find). Such an assessment ensures that pre-design solutions are checked against real conditions, which allows for gradual improvement of the project. The user evaluation of the project should be part of verifying that the project requirements have been met after acceptance. Feedback from users when using the system exposes long-term problems and is the basis for subsequent system upgrades.

Optimal interactive system design can often not be developed at once. Therefore, it is important to repeat a series of actions until the desired result is achieved in terms of maturing the system. In development methods consisting of small development cycles, human-centred design iterations can be performed first on individual parts of the system and then at the macro level for the product, system or service. An iterative approach allows to gradually eliminate the ambiguity of interactive systems. To minimize the risk of the developed system not meeting user requirements, each iteration reviews descriptions, features and examples and improves as new information is obtained.

The complexity of human–computer interaction means that it is not possible to fully and accurately identify every detail of each aspect of this interaction at the beginning of development. Most of the needs and expectations of users and other stakeholders that affect the design of human–computer interactions arise only in the design process, since developers improve their understanding of users and their tasks, and users define their desires in response to the presented design.

Repeating design decisions, including user feedback, is a way to reduce the risk of incompatibility with user requirements.

The user experience is a combination of brand image, presentation, functionality, system performance, interactive features and system auxiliary features that can include both hardware and software. The user experience covers the user's previous experience, habits, skills and personality. There is a widespread misconception that availability means that only one product is easy to use. According to ISO 9241, availability should be understood more broadly, considering the emotional and perceptual aspects normally associated with the user's experience, as well as the user's personal goals, including job satisfaction and lack of monotony.

When determining what functions a user should perform and which system or product they should perform, users' capabilities, limitations, preferences and expectations should be considered.

Modern society needs projects that consider sustainable development and strike a balance between economic, social and environmental problems. Sustainable development, according to the ISO definition, includes "meeting the needs of the present generation without compromising the ability of future generations to meet their own needs". In this respect, it is important to develop "standards for a sustainable world".

Human-centred design also ensures that environmental requirements are met throughout the life of the project. It specifies that the consequences of the use of the system for users and the environment should be considered. This approach enables the creation of available products.

Working and business styles have started to change radically, especially with the influence of information technologies. The result of the Industrial Revolution is classic because of the shifting labour-intensive to knowledge-intensive workforce; ergonomic approaches have been replaced by cognitive ergonomic approaches that prioritize mental abilities over muscle strength.

Especially computers, which are indispensable tools of the information process, are also in the situation of adapting to human abilities along with software and hardware components. This adaptation problem must be considered both in the determination of cognitive and psychological qualities in the recruitment of the individual, in the design of computer systems and ultimately in business designs based on all kinds of information systems. In terms of software, sensitivity to human qualities is more pronounced and difficult to design.

References

Azuma, R., Baillot, Y., Behringer, R., Feiner, S., Julier, S., & MacIntyre, B. (2001). Recent advances in augmented reality. *IEEE Computer Graphics and Applications, 21*(6), 34–47. https://doi.org/10.1109/38.963459

Bevan, N., Carter, J., & Harker, S. (2015, August). ISO 9241–11 revised: What have we learnt about usability since, 1998? In *International conference on human-computer interaction* (pp. 143–151). Springer.

Booth, P. A., & Marshall, C. J. (1989). Usability in human-computer interaction. In *An introduction to human-computer interaction* (pp. 103–136). Lawrence Erlbaum Associates.

Henderson, S., & Feiner, S. (2010). Exploring the benefits of augmented reality documentation for maintenance and repair. *IEEE Transactions on Visualization and Computer Graphics, 17*(10), 1355–1368. https://anticipatingarrevolution.wordpress.com/what-is-augmented-reality/. https://doi.org/10.1109/TVCG.2010.245

Huang, P. (2002). Promoting wearable computing. In *Enabling society with information technology* (pp. 367–376). Springer.

Kan, G. (1999). *Cyberspace, as a generator concept for the architecture of the future* [Doctoral dissertation, Izmir Institute of Technology].

Makimoto, T. (2013). The age of the digital nomad: Impact of CMOS innovation. *IEEE Solid-State Circuits Magazine, 5*(1), 40–47. https://doi.org/10.1109/MSSC.2012.2231498

Manovich, L. (2016, April). Computer simulation and the history of illusion.

Milgram, P., & Kishino, F. (1994). A taxonomy of mixed reality visual displays. *IEICE Transactions on Information and Systems, 77*(12), 1321–1329.

Milovanovic, J., Moreau, G., Siret, D., & Miguet, F. (2017, July). Virtual and augmented reality in architectural design and education. In *17th* international *conference, CAAD futures 2017.* https://www.researchgate.net/publication/319665970_Virtual_and_ Augmented_Reality_in_Architectural_Design_and_Education_An_Immersive_ Multimodal_Platform_to_Support_Architectural_Pedagogy

Van Krevelen, D. W. F., & Poelman, R. (2010). A survey of augmented reality technologies, applications and limitations. *International Journal of Virtual Reality*, *9*(2), 1–20. https://doi. org/10.20870/IJVR.2010.9.2.2767

Whitworth, B., Ahmad, A., Soegaard, M., & Dam, R. F. (2006). Encyclopaedia of human computer interaction. *von C. Ghaoui. Hershey: Idea Group Reference. Kap. Socio-technical Systems*, 533–541.

2

DIGITAL OCCUPATIONAL HEALTH AND SAFETY

Hande Karadağ

Introduction

With the rapid advances in information and communication technologies, the digitalization of several tasks became routine in a majority of public and private organizations, while digital transformation processes were employed in larger institutions. Digital devices brought various advantages and opportunities to workplaces, including the transfer of unsafe or physically demanding work to electronic systems and robots, immense data-processing availabilities and productivity increase through the increased use of computers and helping the building of a healthy work–life balance for employees (Ahlers, 2016). The digitalization at the workplace also brought the liberation of choosing the time and place for completing a certain task, which had a major impact, even changing the way of work in a revolutionary manner for the workforce, particularly for white-collar occupations.

Despite the vital advantages and opportunities of the digital age, the increased use of computers and shifting from office to remote work environments had some serious negative consequences. For instance, with the new demands stemming from the digitalization processes at workplaces, majority of the employees found themselves under heavy stress related to job security concerns, both due to the new skills and knowledge required for excelling in new technologies, as well as the automatization of several tasks, causing a complete extinction of certain jobs. Another major issue that had to be addressed in the discussion of digitalization was how the reforming digital age would affect occupational safety and health (OSH) in work environments, particularly under unexpected and crisis-like circumstances.

The emergence of COVID-19 severely affected social lives on a global scale, and several major precautions were taken by the governments, including closing national borders, enforcing personal isolation, canceling crowded events, and closing workplaces, to prevent the virus from spreading (Al-Mansour & Al-Ajmi,

DOI: 10.4324/9781003283386-3

2020). COVID-19 is unique and different from other crises; therefore, its measures and precautions do not match those of the 2008 financial crisis, World War 2, or the 9/11 attack. The pandemic is an immense health threat impacting the globe, requiring different actions and mechanisms, including personal isolation and social distancing (Knitter et al., 2021). While the impact of this new and worldwide crisis on the world economy was experienced in various dimensions, such as disruption of the supply chain, temporary and permanent layoffs, and decreasing consumer demand in many sectors (Meier & Pinto, 2020), protecting the health of the workforce became one of the most important topics addressed by regulators, employers, and workers. With COVID-19, most traditional workplaces had to employ new digital practices, and the already digitalized companies and institutions increased their levels of digital work, thus during the pandemic, the OSH risks formerly identified and investigated concerning digital working environments became prominent for a lot of organizations, requiring in-depth analyses and close-up examinations from various angles on this important issue.

Occupational Health Issues Related to Digital Work

Occupational health lies at the intersection of medicine, psychology, engineering, and management (Macik-Frey et al., 2007) and is closely related to public health and preventive medicine (Last & Tyler, 1998). Prior research identified several risk factors impacting occupational health, such as secondhand smoke, vibrations, noise, and being exposed to toxic chemicals, as well as psychosocial health risk factors. While this is the case, a review of extant literature shows that scientific research studies to date have mainly concentrated on work stress and the outcomes of stressful work conditions, e.g., burnout, coping, and loss of organizational commitment (Macik Frey et al., 2007). Another important topic closely related to occupational health is occupational safety, which prioritizes the improvement of physical workplace conditions for decreasing injury and accident risks for employees (Geller, 1996). Scholars investigating OSH cases have discussed that, while a majority of occupational health problems to date are investigated concerning the medical costs incurred, other occupational aspects have to be considered, such as diminishing productivity or absenteeism in workplaces.

Recently, potential negative consequences of technological changes and digital transformation were largely focused on the field of occupational health, as digitalization in the workplace reached new heights, bringing novel health problems to the employees. With the increasing pace of digitalization and technological change both in private- and public-sector organizations, the line of research investigating the outcomes of digitalization on the health of workers became popular. Research has shown that computerized work has been increasing at an immense pace in workplaces, amounting to 87% of all employees in Germany using a stationary and/or mobile computer (Bitkom, 2013). The segment of occupational health research focusing on the risk factors caused by digitalized work, namely, *digital occupational health* (DOH) concentrates on the effects of improvement in remote working conditions and the development of applications for this on people's psychological and mental health. The scholars working on technology and occupational health introduced the concept of *virtual work* to the literature, which is described as "work in which people interact in an interdependent relationship using various electronic or technology-based means of communication with little or no face-to-face contact" (Lipnack & Stamps, 2000).

With the increasing interest in DOH, initial research studies conducted to address the potential negative OSH factors associated with new technologies have indicated several physical occupational health problems, which mainly stem from being exposed to excessive computer and other digital platform screens and with loss of human interaction (Benedotto et al., 2014; Aaras et al., 2000; Dillon & Emurian, 1996). These studies showed that workers, particularly those working excessively over computers, are experiencing various physical problems caused by unhealthy working environments. For instance, a report by the National Institute for Occupational Safety and Health (NIOSH) stated that over 80% of workers who spend long hours over computers suffer from musculoskeletal or eye syndromes (Richter et al., 2013).

Since the beginning of computer-intensive workplace settings, musculoskeletal pain and vision challenges are the most commonly reported physical health problems of computer workers (Woods, 2005; Aaras et al., 2000), which directly influence the loss of workdays (Ahib & Dutta, 1998). The name *work-related musculoskeletal disorders* (WMSDs) was given as a general category to this certain group of physical health problems experienced at workplaces (Triphathy et al., 2015). In the literature, WMSDs are described as

> disordersand diseases of the musculoskeletal system which are suspected to have been caused and exacerbated by a wide extent of work-related risk factors such as abominable work conditions, disorganized working process, shift work and long work hours, excessive force and sustained postures, etc.
>
> *(Wang & Lau, 2013)*

The WMSDs are in general considered major health risks in organizations, as they can affect employee performance negatively through an increasing rate of errors that directly influence organizational performance. Several empirical studies were performed to understand the effects of these syndromes on the employees and their overall physical well-being and performance at work. Among these, the results of the empirical study conducted by Hakala et al. (2006) suggested that, for adolescents, increased computer usage is a major risk factor for neck and shoulder pain (NSP) and lower back pain (LBP). Studies further indicated that the factors associated with physical working environments which are reported to cause musculoskeletal pain and visual discomfort are mainly poor seating and being required to sit in the same position during long working hours to complete the given tasks (Woods, 2005).

Besides WMSDs, employees who work for long hours over computers and perform typing and mouse scrolling are also reported to experience several repetitive stress syndromes and injuries, such as tendonitis or carpal tunnel syndrome, general tissue pain, tenosynovitis (inflammation of affected tendons), and epicondylitis (tennis elbow) (Kao & Hwang, 2013; Stedt, 1992). Prior studies indicated that psychosocial stressors, combined with increased work demands, such as pressures of deadline and performance, may cause the lengthening of digital working hours, which in turn accelerate the employee behaviors that raise the factors of risk for musculoskeletal symptoms related to work (Griffiths et al., 2007).

It is also well documented that remote work may have harmful effects on the psychological well-being of employees, apart from physical health problems (Ekberg et al., 1995; Sparks et al., 2001). With the advances in information technology, the amount of information that has to be absorbed and processed by the workers grew at an immense pace, causing a significant increase in workplace stress (Thomee, 2012). Another important outcome of technological developments was the loss of barriers between work and non-work hours, which also helped with worsening health conditions of employees due to stress-related illnesses. The main psychosocial risk factors associated with digitalized work environments were listed as increasing intensity of work, monitoring of behavior and performance by the employer and or manager, competition among workers, and decreasing possibilities for attaining work–life balance (Ahlers, 2016). Studies on occupational health issues as the outcomes of virtual work indicated social isolation as another major threat (Cascio, 2000; Kirkman et al., 2002). Other factors suggested to be associated with virtual work included lack of belonging and not getting adequate personal support (Harpaz, 2002). Despite that, studies show that virtual work and the perceptions of social isolation may be moderated by personal coping styles and being skillful with communication technologies (Macik-Frey, 2006), which provided a more positive perspective on the elaboration of stress-related health threats in digital working environments.

OSH During the COVID-19 Pandemic

Research studies show that a vast 42% of all workers shifted from office work to working from home full time as of May 2020, the occupations experiencing the largest transformation being management, education, administrative support, computers and mathematics, finance, and law (Bloom, 2020). With the emergence of COVID-19, a majority of private companies and public organizations accelerated their digital transformation projects, and remote work practices increasingly had to be employed in a revolutionary manner due to serious isolation restrictions and health concerns resulting from the pandemic. The new working conditions involving digital technologies in the post-pandemic period are expected to affect both regular and flexible employees, as most of them are expected to stay and become *the new normal* after the pandemic (Spurk & Straub, 2020). The new ways of work during the pandemic also changed the human resources function inside the organization and shifted it to an integral role (Collings et al., 2021).

During the COVID-19 pandemic, most of the health issues related to digital and virtual work became frequent, mainly due to an increase in remote work practices. For instance, while loneliness caused by loss of social relations was addressed as a negative factor in traditional workplaces, the pandemic caused this to be a common issue for many employees, as working from home was implemented by nearly half of the workplaces during this period. Conducting the risk analysis regarding different risk factors also was important during the pandemic. For instance, research studies showed that workers who were older than 50 years of age were under a greater risk of being affected by COVID-19, as these adults belonged to the riskiest age group (Ayalon et al., 2020), requiring special care and risk mitigation techniques. Similarly, the productivity of female employees is reported to decrease significantly with the pandemic conditions when compared to males (Lyttelton, et al. 2022; Yavorsky et al., 2021), which is another finding indicating that specific gender-related measures must be taken at digital or remote workplaces.

Preventive Strategies Against Occupational Hazards in Digitalized Working Environments Before and During COVID-19

Traditionally, setting written, accurate, and accessible managerial goals for the reduction of injuries and making this an integral part of corporate policy have been proposed for decreasing the rate of accidents and situations that pose a great risk for workplace safety (Ross, 1991). Recently, scholars have been calling for a holistic approach to reduce the risk factors, integrating organizational, psychosocial, and physical work factors and finding systematic solutions to occupational health issues (Woods, 2005). Therefore, before the formulation and evaluation of alternative strategies, particularly for solving the digital occupational health-related challenges of employees, managers of the organizations should first acknowledge the biomechanical and psychosocial risk factors linked with the increasing rate of computerized tasks (Griffiths et al., 2007). For instance, to minimize the hazard of WMSDs, understanding how the working environment can generate or accelerate these health hazards and how these risks can be measured and mitigated should become a part of the overall management strategy of the organization.

Adding occupational health safety measures to the performance management system of the organization through the Balanced Scorecard tool can be a potential strategy for every type of organization for reducing harmful incidents in the workplace. Here, the four dimensions of a classical Balance Scorecard can be modified for this area of operations, e.g., the financial dimension could include the costs related to safety-measure improvements, the customer dimension can be applied to creating a safety culture for internal customers (in this case employees), the internal process dimension can be formulated concerning checking and refining health and safety procedures and guidelines, and finally, learning and growth dimension can call for strengthening the skills, information, and knowledge in the workplace and skills for OSH (Mearns et al., 2003).

In the digital age, taking advantage of the recent developments in new technologies, such as the Internet of Things (IoT), artificial intelligence (AI), machine learning, and big data, and utilizing these methods in combination with various smart devices can be an important potential strategy for organizations that are undergoing a digital transformation and thus can improve the environments of digital work a great deal (Podgorski, 2020). For instance, AI systems can be used to provide support to processes of occupational health management by screening and reporting the stress levels and cognitive loads of digital workers in real time, by using the non-invasive tool of electroencephalography (Neu et al., 2019). As an example of the practical use of new technologies in this regard, a major project involving AI in creating a flexible and healthy working environment particularly targeting the elder employees working from home was introduced as the EU-funded Aging@work project, where the workers aimed to improve their physical working conditions parallel to ideal ergonomic principles (Giakoumis et al., 2019).

For addressing the physical risks and hazards in digital workplaces, and more specifically minimizing the physical symptoms caused by excessive use of computers on the human body, researchers suggested various solutions, such as innovative ergonomic designs that increase work satisfaction to a large extent (Hedge, 2013; Marmaras & Nathanael, 2005). The utilization of simulation models of physical work activities and body postures to conduct a thorough evaluation of the WMSDs that decrease both individual and organizational performance was another method proposed for identifying and coping with negative physical outcomes of computer-related jobs (Wang & Lau, 2013). In addition to them, using specially designed resting devices that improve the angle and posture of the wrists and palms thus helping to reduce the muscle pain of computer users was also suggested by OSH researchers Kao and Hwang (2013). An important finding of workplace security is that provision of informative feedback on safety behavior was not found to be as impactful on the prevention of safety violations as persuasive designed feedback (Hartwig & Windel, 2013). Thus, companies can utilize the advanced technologies effectively for designing such feedback mechanisms, taking human psychology to the core.

With the breaking pandemic, the human resources (HR) departments of many organizations faced significant challenges about how to lead their workforce with the new remote working conditions and aid them, when necessary, for the continued effectiveness of business operations (Collings et al., 2021). The most important HR practice that emerged as a direct outcome of COVID-19 is the rising trend in remote work practices. Research studies suggest that the working conditions of many workers worsened during the pandemic. The increases in remote work practices required finding solutions to new challenges from various aspects, which include the difficulties in setting boundaries between work and non-work when working from home, the new technology-related employee skills required for facilitating communication, and the impact of remote work on organizational goals, such as productivity, innovation, and creativity (Kniffin et al., 2021). This role of the HR department necessitated understanding the impact of the digital transformation processes in greater detail, including the redefinition of jobs, introduction of new work designs and flows, and planning digital skill development programs for the employees (Shankar, 2020).

The problematic areas requiring particular action from the regulators thus calling for the planning of protective measures against digitalized remote or mobile work risks were identified before COVID-19 (Ahlers, 2016), however, became urgent and vitally important with the pandemic, when a large percentage of full-time office work had to be transformed into full-time work from home. In this regard, the first main issue in and after the COVID-19 period to address is the management of flexible working hours, which is very hard to calculate when working full time from home. Thus, the legislators must take the necessary initiatives for preventing the excessive monitoring of employees. Secondly, the psychosocial needs of workers who now must work alone instead of in traditional crowded working environments have to be identified, such as participation, belonging, and motivation. Another important issue in digitalized remote work is the intensity of work that is associated with increased physical and mental health risks for workers. Thus, regulators must take action to protect digital employees against overworking under demanding conditions.

While the managers of private and public organizations and the legislators strive to find solutions to these problematic areas, challenging issues are stemming from the changing nature of work. For instance, under remote working conditions, it is very hard to take action against workplace hazards. Traditionally, risk mitigation techniques were employed at the organizational level for the increased safety of employees. However, when employees work full time from home or other physical locations, monitoring and maintaining occupational safety is very challenging to execute in practice. Thus, HR executives must communicate the guidelines of OSH clearly to the employees, together with their responsibilities and obligations when working outside of the office premises.

For addressing the pandemic-related psychological and physiological problems experienced by the employees, several alternative strategies were mentioned by the researchers, such as allocating technological and psychological organizational resources, including information, assistance programs, therapy, and counseling (Kniffin et al., 2021). While these measures are suggested, a low percentage of workplaces have been reported to traditionally implement risk assessments against psychosocial risks that employees are facing (Ahlers, 2011, 2015), mainly due to inadequate training, underrepresentation of employees in risk management, and cost concerns regarding actions to be taken. Thus, an important challenge in and after the COVID-19 period would be the shift of risk assessment and mitigation perspectives of managers.

Another important change in OSH strategies in digitalized working environments would be to include OSH in performance management systems, as this issue has become a major risk factor with the pandemic, where overworking for meeting the deadlines under blurred working times and places became the new work routine for most workplaces. Here, conducting the staffing fairly and carefully by the HR department might provide a natural solution to this important problem.

Besides these challenging issues, some positive aspects can be regarded as "good news" for human resources management after the COVID-19 period. For instance, while older workers are regarded as the riskiest group concerning COVID-19, empirical research studies presented important findings of the adaptability of these workers to preventive measures against the virus (Losada-Baltar et al., 2020), as well as engaging in several strategies of self-regulation targeting the continuation or alteration of the person–environment fit (Kooij, 2020; Taneva & Arnold, 2018).

Conclusion

The COVID-19 period changed the way of work in an unchangeable fashion. As stated by Papanikolaou and Schmidt (2020), the pandemic created "essentially the largest global experiment in telecommuting in human history" (p. 4). With the outbreak of COVID-19, it became evident that the most important and urgent issue for managers in every type of organization must be the well-being and health of their organization's workforce, which requires an important mindset change to the traditional cost-centered approach to human resource management (Eklund, 2021).

Apart from this major shift in the managerial approach to organizational priorities, the pandemic has also dramatically altered the core responsibilities of the HR function itself. The future of work will be shaped by finding plausible answers to important questions, such as the impact of remote work on organizational-level (e.g., innovation) and individual-level performance indicators (e.g., well-being and productivity) and building a balance between office work and working from home (Collings et al., 2021). The pandemic revealed that, while the work environments are becoming more remote, thanks to digitalization, there are some vital regulatory actions required for balancing the priorities and targets of organizations and the physical and psychological well-being of employees. Taking the right measures for building this balance could help to minimize the potential exploitation of employees and the associated work-related risks; however, it would necessitate collective actions and initiatives from the employees, organizations, and regulators.

References

Aarås, A., Horgen, G., & Ro, O. (2000). Work with the visual display unit: Health consequences. *International Journal of Human-Computer Interaction, 12*(1), 107–134. https://doi.org/10.1207/S15327590IJHC1201_5

Abib, A. H., & Dutta, S. P. (1998). Epidemiological investigation of workdays lost due to VDT related injuries. *Occupational Ergonomics, 1*(4), 285–290. https://doi.org/10.3233/OER-1998-1404

Ahlers, E. (2011). Wachsender Arbeitsdruck in den betrieben [Growing work pressure in the workplace]. In N. Kratzer, W. Dunkel, K. Becker, & S. Hinrichs (Eds.), *Arbeit und Gesundheit im Konflikt: Analysen und Ansätze für ein partizipatives Gesundheitsmanagement* [Work and health in conflict: Analyses and approaches for a participative health management] (pp. 35–60). Sigma.

Ahlers, E. (2015). Leistungsdruck, Arbeitsverdichtung und die (ungenutzte) Rolle von Gefährdungsbeurteilungen [Pressure, work compaction and the (unused) role of risk assessments]. *WSI-Mitteilungen, 68*(3), 194–201. https://doi.org/10.5771/0342-300X-2015-3-194

Ahlers, E. (2016). Flexible and remote work in the context of digitization and occupational health. *International Journal of Labour Research, 8*(1–2), 85–99.

Al-Mansour, J. F., & Al-ajmi, S. A. (2020) Coronavirus 'COVID-19' – Supply chain disruption and implications for strategy, economy, and management. *Journal of Asian Finance, Economics and Business, 7*(9), 659–672. https://doi.org/10.13106/jafeb.2020.vol7.no9.659

Ayalon, L., Chasteen, A., Diehl, M., Levy, B., Neupert, S. D., Rothermund, K., & Wahl, H. W. (2020). Aging in times of the COVID-19 pandemic: Avoiding ageism and fostering intergenerational solidarity. *Journals of Gerontology: Series B., 76*(2), 49–52.

Benedetto, S., Carbone, A., Drai-Zerbib, V., Pedrotti, M., & Baccino, T. (2014). Effects of luminance and illuminance on visual fatigue and arousal during digital reading. *Computers in Human Behavior, 41*, 112–119. https://doi.org/10.1016/j.chb.2014.09.023

Bitkom. (2013). Arbeit 3.0: Arbeiten in der Digitalen Welt [Work in the digital world] (Berlin). In *Flexible and remote work in the context of digitization and occupational health.* http://www.bitkom.org/noindex/Publikationen/2013/Studien/Studie-Arbeit-3-0/Studie-Arbeit-30.pdf

Bloom, N. (2020). *How working from home works out.* Stanford University Institute for Economic Policy Research. https://siepr.stanford.edu/research/publications/how-working-home-works-out.

Cascio, W. F. (2000). Managing a virtual workplace. *Academy of Management Perspectives, 14*(3), 81–90. https://doi.org/10.5465/ame.2000.4468068

Collings, D. G., Nyberg, A. J., Wright, P. M., & McMackin, J. (2021). Leading through paradox in a COVID-19 world: Human resources comes of age. *Human Resource Management Journal, 31*(4), 819–833. https://doi.org/10.1111/1748-8583.12343

Dillon, T. W., & Emurian, H. H. (1996). Some factors affecting reports of visual fatigue resulting from use of a VDU. *Computers in Human Behavior, 12*(1), 49–59. https://doi.org/10.1016/0747-5632(95)00018-6

Ekberg, K., Eklund, J., Tuvesson, M., Örtengren, R., Odenrick, P., & Ericson, M. (1995). Psychological stress and muscle activity during data entry at visual display units. *Work and Stress, 9*(4), 475–490. https://doi.org/10.1080/02678379508256894

Eklund, M. A. (2021). The COVID-19 lessons learned for business and governance. *SN Business and Economics, 1*(1), 25. https://doi.org/10.1007/s43546-020-00029-2

Geller, E. S. (1996). *Working safe: How to help people actively care for health and safety.* CRC Press.

Giakoumis, D., Votis, K., Altsitsiadis, E., Segkouli, S., & Paliokas, I. (2019, June 5–7). Smart, personalized and adaptive ICT solutions for active, healthy and productive ageing with enhanced workability. In *PETRA19. Proceedings of the 12th ACM international conference on Pervasive technologies related to assistive environments, Rhodes, Greece* (pp. 442–447). The Association for Computing Machinery.

Griffiths, K. L., Mackey, M. G., & Adamson, B. J. (2007). The impact of a computerized work environment on professional occupational groups and behavioural and physiological risk factors for musculoskeletal symptoms: A literature review. *Journal of Occupational Rehabilitation, 17*(4), 743–765. https://doi.org/10.1007/s10926-007-9108-x

Hakala, P. T., Rimpelä, A. H., Saarni, L. A., & Salminen, J. J. (2006). Frequent computer-related activities increase the risk of neck-shoulder and low back pain in adolescents. *European Journal of Public Health, 16*(5), 536–541. https://doi.org/10.1093/eurpub/ckl025

Harpaz, I. (2002). Advantages and disadvantages of telecommuting for the individual, organization and society. *Work Study, 51*(2), 74–80. https://doi.org/10.1108/00438020210418791

Hartwig, M., & Windel, A. (2013, July). Safety and health at work through persuasive assistance systems. In *International conference on digital human modeling and applications in health, safety, ergonomics and risk management* (pp. 40–49). Springer. https://doi.org/10.1007/978-3-642-39182-8_5

Hedge, A. (2013, July). Evaluating ergonomics risks for digital radiologists. In *International conference on digital human modeling and applications in health, safety, ergonomics and risk management* (pp. 50–58). Springer. https://doi.org/10.1007/978-3-642-39182-8_6

Kao, G. H., & Hwang, T. K. P. (2013, July). Hand and arm support for computer workstation. In *International conference on digital human modeling and applications in health, safety, ergonomics and risk management* (pp. 232–238). Springer. https://doi.org/10.1007/978-3-642-39182-8_27

Kirkman, B. L., Rosen, B., Gibson, C. B., Tesluk, P. E., & McPherson, S. O. (2002). Five challenges to virtual team success: Lessons from Sabre, Inc. *Academy of Management Perspectives, 16*(3), 67–79. https://doi.org/10.5465/ame.2002.8540322

Kniffin, K. M., Narayanan, J., Anseel, F., Antonakis, J., Ashford, S. P., Bakker, A. B., . . . Vugt, M. V. (2021). COVID-19 and the workplace: Implications, issues, and insights for future research and action. *American Psychologist, 76*(1), 63–77. https://doi.org/10.1037/amp0000716

Kooij, D. T. A. M. (2020). The impact of the Covid-19 pandemic on older workers: The role of self-regulation and organizations. *Work, Aging and Retirement, 6*(4), 233–237. https://doi.org/10.1093/workar/waaa018

Last, J. M., & Tyler, C. W., Jr. (1998). Public health methods. In R. B. Wallace & B. N. Doebbeling (Eds.), *Maxcy Rosenau-Last public health & preventive medicine* (14th ed.) (pp. 1–66). Appleton & Lange.

Lipnack, J., & Stamps, J. (2000). *Virtual teams: People working across boundaries with technology* (2nd ed.). John Wiley.

Losada-Baltar, A., Jiménez-Gonzalo, L., Gallego-Alberto, L., PedrosoChaparro, M. D. S., Fernandes-Pires, J., & Márquez-González, M. (2020). "We're staying at home." Association of self-perceptions of aging, personal and family resources and loneliness with psychological distress during the lock-down period of COVID-19. *The Journals of Gerontology: Series B*. https://doi.org/10.1093/geronb/gbaa048.

Lyttelton, T., Zang, E., & Musick, K. (2022). Telecommuting and gender inequalities in parents' paid and unpaid work before and during the COVID-19 pandemic. *Journal of Marriage and Family, 84*(1), 230–249.

Macik-Frey, M. (2006). *Virtual work: Loneliness, isolation, and health outcomes.* Paper presented at the Academy of Management Meeting, Atlanta, GA.

Macik-Frey, M., Quick, J. C., & Nelson, D. L. (2007). Advances in occupational health: From a stressful beginning to a positive future. *Journal of Management, 33*(6), 809–840. https://doi.org/10.1177/0149206307307634

Marmaras, N., & Nathanael, D. (2005). Workplace design. In G. Salvendy (Ed.), *Handbook of human factors and ergonomics* (3rd ed.) (pp. 368–382). John Wiley & Sons.

Mearns, K., Whitaker, S., Flin, R., Gordon, R., & O'Connor, P. (2003). Benchmarking human organizational factors in offshore safety. In *Factoring the human into safety: Translating research into practice* (Vol. 1). Research Report 059. Health and Safety Executive. Retrieved January 2022, from www.hse.gov.uk/research/rrpdf/rr059.pdf.

Meier, M., & Pinto, E. (2020). Covid-19 supply chain disruptions. *Covid Economics, 48*, 139–170.

Neu, C., Kirchner, E. A., Kim, S. K., Tabie, M., Linn, C., & Werth, D. (2019). Cognitive work protection -A new approach for occupational safety in human–machine interaction. In F. Davis, R. Riedl, J. vom Brocke, P. M. Léger, & A. Randolph (Eds.), *Information systems and neuroscience: Lecture notes in information systems and organization* (Vol. 29). Springer. Retrieved January 2022, from https://link.springer.com/chapter/10.1007/978-3-03 0-01087-4_26#citeas.

Papanikolaou, D., & Schmidt, L. D. W. (2020). *Working remotely and the supply-side impact of COVID-19*. http://www.nber.org/system/files/working_papers/w27330/w27330.pdf. National Bureau of Economic Research

Podgórski, D. (Ed.). (2020). *New opportunities and challenges in occupational safety and health management*. CRC Press.

Richter, H. O., Zetterberg, C., & Forsman, M. (2013, July). Temporal dependence of trapezius muscle activation during sustained eye-lens accommodation at near. In *International conference on digital human modeling and applications in health, safety, ergonomics and risk management* (pp. 269–275). Springer. https://doi.org/10.1007/978-3-642-39182-8_32

Ross, C. W. (1991). *Computer systems for occupational safety and health management* (2nd ed.). CRC Press. ISBN 9780824784799.

Shankar, R. (2020). The impact of COVID-19 on IT services industry-expected transformations. *British Journal of Management, 31*(3), 450–452. https://doi.org/10.1111/1467-8551.12423

Sparks, K., Faragher, B., & Cooper, C. L. (2001). Well-being and occupational health in the 21st century workplace. *Journal of Occupational and Organizational Psychology, 74*(4), 489–509. https://doi.org/10.1348/096317901167497

Spurk, D., & Straub, C. (2020). Flexible employment relationships and careers in times of the COVID-19 pandemic. *Journal of Vocational Behavior, 119*, 103435. https://doi.org/10.1016/j.jvb.2020.103435

Stedt, J. D. (1992). Interpreter's wrist: Repetitive stress injury and carpal tunnel syndrome in sign language interpreters. *American Annals of the Deaf, 137*(1), 40–43.

Taneva, S. K., & Arnold, J. (2018). Thriving, surviving and performing in late career: A mixed-method study of pathways to successful aging in organizations. *Work, Aging and Retirement, 4*(2), 189–212. https://doi.org/10.1093/workar/wax027

Thomée, S. (2012). *ICT use and mental health in young adults. Effects of computer and mobile phone use on stress, sleep disturbances, and symptoms of depression.* Institute of Medicine. Department of Public Health and Community Medicine.

Tripathi, B., Rajesh, R., & Maiti, J. (2015). Ergonomic evaluation of billet mould maintenance using hierarchical task analysis, biomechanical modeling and digital human modeling. *Computer-Aided Design and Applications, 12*(3), 256–269. https://doi.org/10.1080/16864360.2014.981453

Wang, L., & Lau, H. Y. K. (2013, July). Digital human modeling for physiological factors evaluation in work system design. In *International conference on digital human modeling and applications in health, safety, ergonomics and risk management* (pp. 134–142). Springer. https://doi.org/10.1007/978-3-642-39182-8_16

Woods, V. (2005). Musculoskeletal disorders and visual strain in intensive data processing workers. *Occupational Medicine, 55*(2), 121–127. https://doi.org/10.1093/occmed/kqi029

Yavorsky, J. E., Qian, Y., & Sargent, A. C. (2021). The gendered pandemic: The implications of COVID-19 for work and family. *Sociology Compass, 1*, 1–13.

3

MENTAL HEALTH AND STRESS IN THE DIGITAL WORKPLACE

Sumbul Rafi and Sameen Rafi

Introduction

In the past couple of years, the world has witnessed massive deviations worldwide, predominantly in the corporate world, physical work environment, every aspect of organization get into some or the other changes as pandemic knockouts everyone across the globe. The most compression can be seen on entrepreneurs, employees, and human resource management. As the pandemic made working from home a new trend and a hasty conversion of the physical workplace into the digital workplace, it brought new challenges to the plate and drawbacks that needed to be faced and handled to keep the pace in work and its outcomes.

The COVID-19 pandemic has brought the globe to its knees in a way it has never seen before. Governments were driven to impose total lockdowns and social distancing rules, wreaking havoc on every facet of human life. Enterprises worldwide were compelled to scramble for business process continuity, and a unifying clarion cry for remote labour was issued. Even then, in several industries, such as retail, manufacturing, and health care, we were unable to integrate remote working fully and were forced to operate within the limitations of the social–disadvantage regulations (Varrier, 2021). While workplace digitization began well before 2020, there is no doubt that COVID-19 hastened the trend. Recent data indicates that digital company adoption accelerated by five years in just eight weeks in May 2020 and is showing no signs of slowing. Businesses today have the task of implementing an integrated technological framework, or digital workplace platform, in order to exploit the full potential of that unprecedented pace of adoption (Baig et al., 2020).

Digital Workplace

A digital workplace is a secure cloud-based platform that enables and empowers organization to empower and enable their workforce to be productive regardless

DOI: 10.4324/9781003283386-4

of whether they work remotely, on site, or a combination of the two. These platforms are securely available from any device, at any time, and from any location in the world and include everything employees need to perform their jobs efficiently, including apps, data, content, files, tools, software, and documents. Naturally, people's requirements significantly differ between job titles, departments, organisations, and sectors. A digital workplace solution enables the consolidation of all information into a single virtual platform available from any place, at any time, and from any device (McIntyre, 2021).

The purpose of a digital workplace is to enable remote work. This is pertinent at the moment, as hybrid work models gain popularity in response to employee demand and preferences. To achieve a balance between corporate objectives and employee preferences, organisations must use solutions that improve communication, collaboration, project management, transparency, problem solving, automation, and culture development (Hoyland, 2021).

Digital Workplace Framework

There are no hard and fast rules for designing a digital workplace, but there are several best practices that can be used. For example, the following digital workplace framework gives businesses a tool to analyse their present digital workplace and discover areas of opportunity to support a better way of doing business by assisting you in thinking holistically about the technologies you use in your workplace (Herrera et al., n.d.).

The digital workplace framework includes four layers covering the following components:

1 Use: Collaborate, Communicate, Connect

The digital workplace is all about people being able to perform their jobs effectively through collaboration, communication, and connection with one another. The objective is to foster beneficial business relationships both within and outside of natural workgroups, as well as to facilitate information sharing across the firm.

2 Technology: The Digital Toolbox

The digital workplace is enabled by technology. Each organization already has a toolkit for the digital workplace, which includes a variety of technologies; that required required to enable your digital workplace will vary according to your industry and business needs. The trick is to provide your employees with the tools they need to accomplish their tasks effectively.

3 Control: Governance, Risk, and Compliance

Appropriate controls support the effective use of technology in the digital workplace. This means that you must provide suitable governance structures and management processes to support the digital workplace. Additionally, the flow and usage of information must adhere to your organisation's standards and industry regulations.

4 Business Drivers: Measurable Business Value

For any major project, the digital workplace must be driven by the demands of the business. Your digital workplace should be aligned with your organisation's strategic goals in order to achieve the desired outcomes (Hoyland, 2021).

Organisations Need a Digital Workplace

1   **No switching between apps:** Every day, workers need access to a slew of programmes in order to stay on top of their tasks. However, too many tools may generate employee confusion and overburden. They will have to switch between applications to perform a single task. Over two-thirds of workers spend up to 60 minutes per day switching applications (RingCentral, 2018). It saves time and enhances employee satisfaction to have a single platform for all business data and apps.

2   **More visibility and more control:** Because all team members can monitor the status of any project or activity, there are fewer email follow-ups and more work done in a digital workplace. The team leader can set deadlines for all tasks to be completed. Employees feel more accountable and responsible with more visibility. It also avoids superfluous meetings and allows team members to focus on their main jobs.

3   **Automation:** Processes like document approvals and data entry that take up a lot of time in a traditional office can be automated in a digital workplace. As a result, individuals are better able to focus on more complicated tasks that demand imaginative thinking and problem solving. Even more importantly, automating tedious tasks allows individuals to be more enthusiastic about their work.

4   **Support for remote employees:** Although most workers were supposed to be remote by 2025, the coronavirus pandemic accelerated the pace of remote work. Firms rushed to design solutions for remote workers to manage their jobs. Remote work is here to stay, no matter how long the pandemic lasts. Creating a digital workplace will enable your staff to perform at their peak whether they are in the office or working from home (Prashant, 2021).

Stress in the Digital Workplace

For broad swaths of workers, digital working became an essential mode of operation in 2020, which has been dubbed "the world's largest work-from-home experiment" (Banjo et al., 2020). In recent years, the term "digital workplace" has become a familiar and rapidly emerging concept. The new and effective trend of working from home has become the norm for many professionals, and while it has many compensations, it also comes with a number of stressors that must be acknowledged and actions that must be taken to keep them under control so that an efficient process can take place and a productive result can be expected.

- *Precarious work and the gig economy*: When it comes to new businesses, they are known for their ability to adapt and overcome hurdles. Employee rights, such as the amount of time spent on the job, the unstable nature of zero-hour contracts, and the hazards involved, such as long periods of driving or cycling, are one of these impediments.
- *Humans and machines*: A second factor is the advancement of high-tech gadgets, such as augmented reality programmes and robotics, that can help ease some of the physical strain involved with particular vocations. However, the usage of machines is perceived to have some effect on the health of users, such as psychosocial concerns. One such challenge is balancing the "worker's own visual and sensory experiences with those generated by an augmented reality system." When this balance gets disrupted, it can have a negative influence on both safety and performance.
- *Blurring of time and geography*: A third component is a location, which affects how workers perform tasks such as programming, translation, editing, and providing legal services. This increased competition but also resulted in a reduction in quality in some circumstances, as operations in one country offered services to another for which they were not competent. Additionally, digital nomadism has an effect on where and when employees work.
- *Technostress*: Craig Brod, a novelist from the early 1980s, created the word technostress. He classified it as amodern sickness of adaptation caused by an inability to cope in a healthy manner with new computing technology (Chiappetta, 2017). Another definition states that technostress comprises "any negative impact on attitudes, beliefs, behaviours, or psychology generated directly or indirectly by technology." Technostress can occur in the workplace as a result of a variety of technological consequences, including rapid change, constant connectivity, concern about one's capability and ability to use technology, and an overflow of information and inputs. It can result in fatigue, focus issues, frustration, motivation loss, decreased job satisfaction, and burnout (Sandle, 2018).
- *Information overload*: The sheer volume of information available to us digitally can surpass our ability to cognitively digest it. It is defined by Cenfetelli and Schwarz (2011) as an individual state in which overwhelming information is delivered beyond the user's needs. Overflowing inboxes, interruptions via instant messaging, and information repositories with large amounts of content and low signal-to-noise ratio can all contribute to information overload during the workday (Marsh, 2019).

Factors That Help to Reduce Stress in the Digital Workplace

Over the last few decades, new technology has dramatically revolutionized the workplace, and new tools for boosting our performance and efficiency are being produced at a breakneck pace. We are surrounded by productivity tools and are more connected than at any previous point in history. There are, however, drawbacks to this. With communication tools and platforms enabling the majority of office workers to simply check in from anywhere, it's becoming increasingly difficult to entirely disconnect once the workday is gone. You may find yourself responding to emails right before going to bed or even performing a small job or two while on vacation.

Following are some factors that could help workers to reduce their digital stress at the office as well as at home:

Communication: Technology can frequently overwhelm us. It's easy to overlook the value of face-to-face communication. Many workers use phones. Working on vacation can become a nasty habit. Remind staff to turn off notifications after hours. Allow your employees to voice their concerns and thoughts by using the most effective methods. Working from home requires constant communication with supervisors and peers. Improve the working environment.

Company culture: Employers must ensure that employees like coming to work. Summer barbecues and frequent socialising can help build team relationships and reduce stress. Creating a secure and friendly workplace allows employees to express what works. Employees must feel comfortable to express issues about their jobs, and the organisation must support them (Mind, 2013).

Streamline your digital systems: Your digital tools should help, not hinder. Ask your staff what works best to identify a flawed system. They may need to change programmes or teams. Your current system may require workers to input or record. A tight deadline is stressful. In addition, it will benefit your workforce.

Flexible working: Flexibility is not the same as remote work. While many of us now work remotely, not everyone has this option. Adapting your work life to your personal needs may help you reduce stress in all areas. The benefits of flexible working should be managed carefully to avoid aggravating the "always-on" mentality.

Encourage good physical health: Stress leads the body to produce cortisol. While small amounts of cortisol are good to human health, excessive amounts can induce fatigue, headaches, irritability, weight gain, digestive difficulties, anxiety, and depression. Exercise helps reduce stress by sweating out excess cortisol. Giving your staff access to a gym or exercise courses may help them move more. The good news is that exercise reduces stress and increases resilience (Hashemi, 2020).

What Is Stress?

Stress has been studied by psychologists for decades. There are two ways to deal with stress: alter the unpleasant event or adapt to its effects (Baum, 1990). You get stressed out when anything requires your attention or action. However, how you handle stress has a big impact on your overall health (Scott, 2020). The first study focused on stressors, which are situations that induce anxiety or discomfort. When one individual sees a threat to their job, another sees an opportunity to gain new skills and change careers. The perception of a potential stressor is determined by the individual experiencing it (Taylor, 2012).

Early Approaches to Stress

Walter Cannon and Hans Selye were both physiologists who had a significant impact on the popularisation of stress. Cannon coined the term "fight or flight" as a response to stress. The fight-or-flight reaction is a coordinated physiological response that mobilises the body to either attack or flee a threat. There are two ways of responding to stress, one of which is to fight, and the other of which is to flee. However, on the other hand, the organism's ability to respond swiftly to a threat is facilitated by the fight-or-flight response. In contrast, stress can be damaging since it interferes with emotional and physiological functioning, and when stress persists unchecked, it sets the stage for health problems (Cannon, 1932).

General adaptation syndrome was coined by Hans Selye (Selye, 1956). "Adaptability and resistance to stress are key criteria for life, and every vital organ participates in them," he noted (Selye, 1950). He believed that regardless of the stressor, the basic physiological response was always the same and that comprehending this phenomenon required knowledge of numerous fields of physiology, biochemistry, and medicine. However, it comprises three stages:

- *Alarm.* The normal response of the body to stress is the release of stress hormones to prime it for action (fight or flight).
- *Resistance.* Stress hormones remain elevated if the stress continues for a long period of time. However, throughout this time, the individual appears to have adapted to the stressor, but he or she is still more susceptible to sickness.
- *Exhaustion.* An overburdened body will eventually succumb to disease and perhaps death if the stress is prolonged.

Contemporary Approaches to Stress

A significant contemporary stress theory, developed by McEwen and Stellar, builds on Selye's work to explain how long-term stress might induce sickness (McEwen & Stellar, 1993). This technique aims to provide a comprehensive physiological explanation of the numerous bodily systems that may be influenced by stress and how different stressful conditions may affect health. McEwen argued that the long-term impact of stress, known as allostatic load, affects the body at the cardio-vascular, metabolic, neurological, behavioural, and cellular levels (McEwen, 1998). The autonomic nervous system, cardiovascular, metabolic, and immunological systems are all examples of systems that may adjust to stressors within and outside the body in order to maintain homeostasis. In medical terms, this phenomenon is called allostasis. But if the activation of these systems is repeated and sustained, the stress hormones, immune cells, brain activity, and cardiovascular response are allostatically loaded (McEwen, 2007).

Psychological Appraisal of Stress

Primary and secondary appraisals of a stressor are particularly significant in this context. A stressor's degree of potential injury or threat to one's well-being is assessed in a *primary appraisal*. The prospect of harm, loss, or other negative consequences would certainly make a stressor seem like a threat; on the other hand, a stressor could be seen as a challenge that could lead to personal growth. The promotion would be perceived as a larger danger by an employee if he believed it would lead to an increase in work demands than if he considered the promotion as an opportunity to learn new skills and further his professional career. *Secondary appraisal* begins at the same time as a person's main appraisal of a stressful situation. One's resources and ability to cope are evaluated in the secondary appraisal, which examines whether the harm, threat, and challenges posed by the event will be met. When it comes down to it, the subjective experience of stress involves a balance between primary and secondary assessments. Stress is felt when there is a high level of danger and the person's ability to cope is low. Stress can be reduced if a person's ability to cope is high.

Stress in the Workplace

Workplace stress can be caused by a number of factors or by a single event. It can affect both employees and employers. The constant pressure to perform at the highest level can cause workplace unhappiness, staff turnover, inefficiency, and illness. Unavailable or alcoholic employees, "petty internal politics," apathy or ingenuity are all signs of a stressed-out workplace (Cartwright et al., 2002). Factors causing stress in the workplace include:

- **Work and sedentary lifestyle**: People who worked in agricultural sector before the Industrial Revolution had to labour hard. Individuals get less exercise at work, as more people work in offices or other jobs that don't need much physical exertion (House & Smith, 1985). Even physically demanding activities like construction and firefighting may contain enough stress to negate the benefits of exercise. Because physical activity is linked to health, a change in job duties may increase the risk of sickness.

- **Work overload**: It's a major contributor to the high levels of workplace stress. As a result of being overworked, workers are more likely to engage in unhealthy behaviours and experience more health risks than their peers who are not overworked (Repetti, 1993). Cardiovascular disease may be exacerbated by persistent activation of the neuroendocrine and cardiovascular systems as a result of overcommitment (Steptoe & Marmot, 2003; Von Känel et al., 2009).

- **Ambiguity and role conflict**: Being uncertain about what is expected of them and how their performance will be evaluated can lead to role ambiguity. Information regarding a person's job tasks or expectations might cause role conflict. High blood pressure and higher heart rate have been connected to role conflict and uncertainty (French & Caplan, 1973). Stress levels are reduced when people are given accurate information regarding their performance (Cohen & Williamson, 1988).

- **Social relationships**: Social isolation at work has been linked to stress at work (House, 1981; Buunk et al., 1993) as well as to a lack of both physical and mental wellness (Landsbergis et al., 1992). In the workplace, having a bad connection with one's supervisor is linked to job stress and an increased risk of coronary heart disease (Davis et al., 1995). Conversely, men and women who are able to form socially supportive relationships at work are better at coping in daily life (Loscocco & Spitze, 1990).

- **Control**: Stress and illness indicators, such as elevated catecholamine secretion, job dissatisfaction, absenteeism, and the development of coronary artery disease (Bosma et al., 1997), as well as the risk of death from all causes, have been linked to lack of control over work (Amick et al., 2002). It has been found that a sense of job control can help workers cope with stressful situations in the workplace (Shimazu et al., 2008). Changing one's job control can have a direct impact on one's health (Smith et al., 2008).

Mental Health in the Workplace

The World Health Organisation (WHO) defines mental health as a condition of well-being in which an individual recognises his or her own skills, is capable of coping with regular life challenges, is capable of productive and fruitful employment, and is capable of contributing to his or her community (WHO, n.d.). It is an essential component of health and well-being that underlies our individual and communal capacity to make decisions, form connections, and influence the environment in which we live. Mental health is a fundamental human right. It is also essential for personal, communal, and socioeconomic growth (WHO, 2018). In organisational behaviour, mental health has been a major focus of research (Harnois & Gabriel, 2000). Mental well-being is essential for both the personal efficacy of employees and the overall performance of organisations. Furthermore, the concept of mental health has experienced radical transformations in terms of its definition, interpretation, and practical application (Herrman et al., 2005). Mental well-being is commonly understood to include "subjective well-being, perceived self-efficacy, autonomy, competence, intergenerational reliance, and self-actualisation of one's intellectual and emotional capacity, amongst other things" (WHO, 2002). Mental health studies must be seen positively, emphasising what an individual may do rather than what they lack. As a result, mental health is now different from mental illness. Because most people spend a large percentage of their waking hours at work, workplace satisfaction is an important aspect in determining total life satisfaction. Contextual factors are very essential in the research of mental health (Briner, 2000).

Nearly everyone throughout the world has had difficulty with COVID-19. It has had a toll on employees' mental health, especially those whose sole escape from a troubled home was work, as people are now more likely to work remotely. Many others, on the other hand, lamented their exhaustion as a result of working long hours. Because of the COVID-19 pandemic, WHO estimated that crucial mental health services were disrupted and even halted in up to 93% of countries (Biswas, 2021).

Factors That Negatively Impact Mental Health

The impact of technology on our mental health may be overlooked due to our familiarity with it. As a result of COVID-19, more people are using digital technology at work. Thanks to digital technologies, employers and employees can now engage more efficiently. But spending so much time online has clear drawbacks. Weak mental health is caused by excessive use of technology, such as the "always-on" mentality.

> *Communication and collaboration*: Because virtual communication doesn't provide us with a whole picture, it can have a lot of bad consequences on us. When communicating by email or instant chat, it's difficult to tell if the other person is being positive or negative, for example. Video calls, in particular, have sparked a lot of debate. Even though video conferencing has numerous advantages, overreliance on technology by some organisations can lead to employee tiredness and burnout.
>
> *Hyper-focused work conversation*: While it is claimed that digital technology allows workers to communicate even while they are not at work, this is not confirmed. When there are no informal or casual talks in the office, people tend to remain doing work-related emails, video calls, and instant chats. We can no longer discuss our weekends, which can help us relax, because everything is work related. As a result, employers may miss signs of employee stress or need for support.
>
> *Flexibility*: Technological advancements and the ability to work from anywhere may be counterproductive. Even if allowed to work from home, many

employees feel obligated to keep "regular hours," consequences of an "always-on" mentality. Employees may believe they must be available 24 hours a day, 7 days a week due to remote working and job instability. A break from work to avoid burnout is often criticised. Employers can't always tell when and why employees are overworked (Bishop, 2020).

How Digital Tools Help to Improve Mental Health

It is estimated that more than half of the people in middle- and high-income countries would be affected by some form of mental problems at some point in their lives (Rehm et al., 2016). Around 42% of employees worldwide have reported a decline in mental health since the onset of the COVID-19 pandemic (Greenwood & Krol, 2020). According to press reports, burnout is becoming more common among both employees and managers (Edward Segal, 2021).

Digital tools offerings are classified into three categories:

1 **Wearables and digital biomarker apps**: In numerous methods, they can acquire physiological data. Smartwatches and cell phones that monitor mental wellness could help employees. Long-term unsatisfied employees may be advised to take time off or receive individualised coaching or counselling. Offers can include these new data-harvesting tools. Only an employer with anonymised aggregated data knows about an employee. Employers can utilise these data to identify and manage workplace concerns, as well as gauge employee satisfaction on an individual, team, or organisational level.
2 **Prevention and treatment solutions**: The theme is mental health and resilience. These solutions offer CBT, meditation, hypnosis, and human interaction ranging from proactive chatbots to in-person counselling. Some companies only measure mental health, while others assess both, and then offer anything from resilience training to clinical support. Smaller companies may provide employees a wellness budget to spend on their preferred support. Employee surveys and third-party solution supplier success data may be examples.
3 **Analytic tools**: With wearables and digital biomarkers, these tools frequently collect distant data. They can tell employees when they need a break or supervisors when their teams appear stressed. To quantify workplace well-being on a bigger scale, solution providers can link findings to productivity. Employers can use analytics technologies to identify potentially dangerous employees and direct them to internal or external support services (Brassey et al., 2021).

Practices to Use in a Digital Workplace to Improve Mental Health

• **Firm to switch off**: Many workers struggle to "turn off" after a long day at work. As expected, a third of workers had trouble limiting their work time after the office closed for the day. Informed distant or hybrid employees find it difficult to shut down computers. Workmates who send out-of-hours emails can disrupt concentration even if many of us log off at the end of the day. For 39% of those polled, technology makes it difficult to switch from work to home life. Managers and HR can help by setting "core hours." Only allow someone to contact you if it is absolutely necessary.

- **Limit non-essential communications**: Excessive communication also harms employees' digital well-being. Email is a common offender. Unnecessary job stress affects two-thirds of workers as much as the quantity of communications received. Email takes up the most of that time, roughly 17% of the typical workday. Teamwork and respect for differences should be taught to employees by minimising non-essential communication.

- **Avoid meeting fatigue**: While video conferencing can be quite useful in today's digital workplace, it's no surprise that video call weariness has set in. It is possible to save time and recreate face-to-face communication with video chats that have a defined purpose. As a result, they can be exhausting for those who have to be "on." Of those polled, 80% said they'd like a virtual meeting–free day once a week in order to avoid digital overwhelm.

- **Respect co-workers' status**: When using a digital platform such as Microsoft Teams, individuals can control when they are available or busy at any given time. A "do not disturb" setting is available in Teams, preventing the user from receiving any notifications at all. Workers should be encouraged to show consideration for their co-workers' busy schedules. People will be able to focus on their work more effectively this way. Nonetheless, not every question can be put off indefinitely.

- **Integrate well-being sessions on Teams**: When it comes to digital well-being, the office should be more than just a place to do work. There are a lot of communications, shared documents, and continuous notifications on Microsoft Teams. Using unique workshops, HR and managers may add a softer side to the platform. Talk about anything but work at regular coffee dates. External speakers can be brought in to lead seminars on mindfulness, meditation, or even yoga for the whole team.

- **Add well-being content to the intranet**: A company intranet is a great way to keep important information accessible to employees and to encourage a healthy relationship with technology. Provide employees with access to an HR intranet page that has information on health and well-being, company-sponsored services, national helplines, and contact information for anyone with whom they can get in touch.

- **Create a digital well-being workspace**: All of these best practices can be gathered and stored on the workplace intranet to promote digital well-being. For each company, pick rules tailored to their needs, then develop interesting material and store it in the digital workplace where employees will see it (Harris, 2021).

Conclusion

The workplace is a platform where many processes happen simultaneously and could have productive effects and be detrimental. In order to keep up with the rate of change in the working sector, we need to keep upgrading our skills for personal growth and organisational development so that the desired outcome can be achieved. Thanks to digital workplace, organisations can face new challenges even in the most uncertain business environments. Digital workplace can help businesses become more agile and produce more tangible results because they provide greater efficiency, flexibility, and cooperation. Along with this, stressors and well-being give primary concern to HR. Stress is a negative emotion caused by many factors in the workplace. Physiological and psychological processes work simultaneously when a person experiences stress. The impact of stress on mental health is relatively negative and leads to physiological illness and psychological disturbances. Mental health can be improved by using many digital tools and can monitor their daily activities; if any error is encountered, it could be corrected immediately. Many new innovations come to the digital world that could help employees adopt the new standard, different working methods and coordinate with the swiftly modifying world.

References

Amick, B. C., III, McDonough, P., Chang, H., Rogers, W. H., Pieper, C. F., & Duncan, G. (2002). Relationship between all-cause mortality and cumulative working life course psychosocial and physical exposures in the United States labor market from 1968 to 1992. *Psychosomatic Medicine, 64*(3), 370–381. https://doi.org/10.1097/00006842-200205000-00002

Baig, A., Hall, B., Jenkins, P., Lamarre, E., & McCarthy, B. (2020, December 14). *The COVID-19 recovery will be digital: A plan for the first 90 days.* McKinsey & Company. Retrieved December 20, 2021, from http://www.mckinsey.com/business-functions/mckinsey-digital/our-insights/the-covid-19-recovery-will-be-digital-a-plan-for-the-first-90-days.

Banjo, S., Yap, L., Colum, M., & Vinicy, C. (2020, February 3). The coronavirus outbreak has become the world's largest work-from-home experiment. *Time.* https://time.com/5776660/coronavirus-work-from-home.

Baum, A. (1990). Stress, intrusive imagery, and chronic distress. *Health Psychology, 9*(6), 653–675. https://doi.org/10.1037//0278-6133.9.6.653

Bishop, A. (2020, October 9). Increased use of digital technology at work and mental health. *BritishRedCross.* Retrieved January 4, 2022, from https://blog.redcrossfirstaidtraining.co.uk/how-does-the-increased-use-of-digital-technology-at-work-impact-our-mental-health

Biswas, D. (2021, October 13). Initiatives by tech firms on employee mental health in India. *Analytics India Magazine.* Retrieved December 29, 2021, from https://analyticsindiamag.com/initiatives-by-tech-firms-on-employee-mental-health-in-india/

Bosma, H., Marmot, M. G., Hemingway, H., Nicholson, A. C., Brunner, E., & Stanfeld, S. A. (1997). Low job control and risk of coronary heart disease in Whitehall II (prospective cohort) study. *British Medical Journal, 314,* 285.

Brassey, J., Güntner, A., Isaak, K., & Silberzahn, T. (2021, July 28). *Using digital tech to support employees' mental health and resilience.* McKinsey & Company. Retrieved January 4, 2022, from http://www.mckinsey.com/industries/life-sciences/our-insights/using-digital-tech-to-support-employees-mental-health-and-resilience.

Briner, R. B. (2000). Relationships between work environments, psychological environments and psychological well-being. *Occupational Medicine, 50*(5), 299–303. https://doi.org/10.1093/occmed/50.5.299

Buunk, B. P., Doosje, B. J., Jans, L. G. J. M., & Hopstaken, L. E. M. (1993). Perceived reciprocity, social support, and stress at work: Th e role of exchange and communal orientation. *Journal of Personality and Social Psychology, 65*(4), 801–811. https://doi.org/10.1037/0022-3514.65.4.801

Cannon, W. B. (1932). *Th e wisdom of the body.* Norton.

Cartwright, K., Lewis, D., Roberts, C., Bint, A., Nichols, T., & Warburton, F. (2002). Workload and stress in consultant medical microbiologists and virologists: A questionnaire survey. *Journal of Clinical Pathology, 55*(3), 200–205. https://doi.org/10.1136/jcp.55.3.200

Cenfetelli, R. T., & Schwarz, A. (2011). Identifying and testing the inhibitors of technology usage intentions. *Information Systems Research, 22*(4), 808–823.

Chiappetta, M. (2017, April 11). The technostress: Definition, symptoms and risk prevention. *Researchgate.* Retrieved December 21, 2021, from http://www.researchgate.net/publication/325031719_The_Technostress_definition_symptoms_and_risk_prevention

Cohen, S., & Williamson, G. M. (1988). Perceived stress in a probability sample of the United States. In S. Spacapan & S. Oskamp (Eds.), *The social psychology of health* (pp. 31–67). SAGE.

Davis, M. C., Matthews, K. A., Meilahn, E. N., & Kiss, J. E. (1995). Are job characteristics related to fibrinogen levels in middle-aged women? *Health Psychology, 14*(4), 310–318. https://doi.org/10.1037//0278-6133.14.4.310

French, J. R. P., Jr., & Caplan, R. D. (1973). Organizational stress and the individual strain. In A. J. Marrow (Ed.), *Th e failure of success.* Amacon.

Greenwood, K., & Krol, N. (2020, August 7). 8 ways managers can support employees' mental health. *Harvard Business Review.* hbr.org.

Harnois, G., & Gabriel, P. (2000). *Mental health and work: Impact, issues and good practices.* World Health Organization.

Harris, Y. (2021, November 18). Digital wellbeing and the digital workplace. *Powell Software.* Retrieved January 5, 2022, from https://powell-software.com/resources/blog/digital-wellbeing-and-the-digital-workplace/

Hashemi, C. (2020, August 25). How to reduce stress in the digital workplace. *Recruitment Revolution.* http://www.recruitmentrevolution.com/blog/how-to-reduce-stress-in-the-digital-workplace/

Herrera, F., Chan, G., Legault, M., Kassim, R. M., & Sharma, V. (n.d.). *The digital workplace: Think, share, do transform your employee experience.* Retrieved December 26, 2021, from https://www2.deloitte.com/content/dam/Deloitte/mx/Documents/human-capital/The_digital_workplace.pdf. Deloitte.

Herrman, H., Saxena, S., Moodie, R., World Health Organization, Victorian Health Promotion Foundation, & University of Melbourne (Eds.). (2005). *Promoting mental health: Concepts, emerging evidence, practice.* World Health Organization.

House, J. A. (1981). *Work stress and social support.* Addison-Wesley.

House, J. S., & Smith, D. A. (1985). Evaluating the health effects of demanding work on and off the job. In T. F. Drury (Ed.), *Assessing physical fitness and physical activity in population-base surveys* (pp. 481–508). National Center for Health Statistics.

How app overload is reshaping the digital workplace. (2018, January). *RingCentral*. Retrieved December 28, 2021, from https://netstorage.ringcentral.com/documents/connected_workplace.pdf.

Hoyland, N. (2021, December 2). What is hybrid working? *Huler*. Retrieved December 20, 2021, from https://huler.io/blog/what-is-hybrid-working

Landsbergis, P. A., Schnall, P. L., Deitz, D., Friedman, R., & Pickering, T. (1992). The patterning of psychological attributes and distress by "job strain" and social support in a sample of working men. *Journal of Behavioral Medicine*, *15*(4), 379–405. https://doi.org/10.1007/BF00844730

Loscocco, K. A., & Spitze, G. (1990). Working conditions, social support, and the well-being of female and male factory workers. *Journal of Health and Social Behavior*, *31*(4), 313–327. https://doi.org/10.2307/2136816

Marsh, E. (2019, January 10). Is your organisation's digital workplace causing technostress? *LinkedIn*. http://www.linkedin.com/pulse/your-organisations-digital-workplace-causing-elizabeth-marsh/

McEwen, B. S. (1998). Protective and damaging effects of stress mediators. *New England Journal of Medicine*, *338*(3), 171–179. https://doi.org/10.1056/NEJM199801153380307

McEwen, B. S. (2007). Physiology and neurobiology of stress and adaptation: Central role of the brain. *Physiological Reviews*, *87*(3), 873–904. https://doi.org/10.1152/physrev.00041.2006

McEwen, B. S., & Stellar, E. (1993). Stress and the individual. Mechanisms leading to disease. *Archives of Internal Medicine*, *153*(18), 2093–2101

McIntyre, C. (2021, November 19). What is A digital workplace? *Huler*. Retrieved December 20, 2021, from https://huler.io/blog/what-is-a-digital-workplace

Prashant, S. (2021, November 23). Digital workplace definition and everything you need to know about it. *Kissflow*. Retrieved December 28, 2021, from https://kissflow.com/digital-workplace/everything-about-digital-workplace/

Rehm, J., Trautmann, S., & Wittchen, H.-U. (2016, September). The economic costs of mental disorders: Do our societies react appropriately to the burden of mental disorders? *EMBO Reports*, *17*(9), 1245–1249. embopress.org. https://doi.org/10.15252/embr.201642951

Repetti, R. L. (1993). The effects of workload and the social environment at work on health. In L. Goldberger & S. Bresnitz (Eds.), *Handbook of stress* (pp. 368–385). Free Press.

Sandle, T. (2018, January 3). New types of workplace stress in the digital era. *Digital Journal*. http://www.digitaljournal.com/life/new-types-of-workplace-stress-in-the-digital-era/article/511297.

Scott, E. (2020, August 3). What is stress? *Verywell Mind*. Retrieved December 6, 2021, from http://www.verywellmind.com/stress-and-health-3145086

Segal, E. (2021, February 17). Leaders and employees are burning out at record rates: New survey. *Forbes*. Forbes.com.

Selye, H. (1950). Stress and the general adaptation syndrome. *British Medical Journal*, *1*(4667), 1383–1392. https://doi.org/10.1136/bmj.1.4667.1383

Selye, H. (1956). *The stress of life*. McGraw-Hill.

Shimazu, A., de Jonge, J., & Irimajiri, H. (2008). Lagged effects of active coping within the demand-control model: A three-wave panel study among Japanese employees. *International Journal of Behavioral Medicine*, *15*(1), 44–53. https://doi.org/10.1007/BF03003073

Smith, P., Frank, J., Bondy, S., & Mustard, C. (2008). Do changes in job control predict differences in health status? Results from a longitudinal national survey of Canadians. *Psychosomatic Medicine*, *70*(1), 85–91. https://doi.org/10.1097/PSY.0b013e31815c4103

Steptoe, A., & Marmot, M. (2003). Burden of psychosocial adversity and vulnerability in middle age: Associations with biobehavioral risk factors and quality of life. *Psychosomatic Medicine, 65*(6), 1029–1037. https://doi.org/10.1097/01.psy.0000097347.57237.2d

Taylor, E. (2012). *Health psychology* (Vol. 8). McGraw-Hill Companies.

Varrier, R. (2021, April 9). The digital workplace in the post-pandemic era. *BW Businessworld*. Retrieved December 20, 2021, from http://www.businessworld.in/article/The-Digital-Workplace-in-the-Post-Pandemic-Era/09-04-2021-386138/

Von Känel, R., Bellingrath, S., & Kudielka, B. M. (2009). Overcommitment but not effort-reward imbalance relates to stress-induced coagulation changes in teachers. *Annals of Behavioral Medicine, 37*(1), 20–28. https://doi.org/10.1007/s12160-009-9082-y

Work is biggest cause of stress in people's lives. (2013, October 9). *Mind, the Mental Health Charity – Help for Mental Health Problems*. Retrieved December 19, 2021, from http://www.mind.org.uk/news-campaigns/news/work-is-biggest-cause-of-stress-in-peoples-lives/

World Health Organization (n.d.). *Mental Health*. PAHO/WHO | Pan American Health Organization. Retrieved June 23, 2022, from https://www.paho.org/en/topics/mental-health#:%7E:text=The%20World%20Health%20Organization%20(WHO,to%20his%20or%20her%20community%E2%80%9D.

World Health Organization. (2002). *The World Health Report: Mental health: New understanding, new hope (repr)*. World Health Organization.

World Health Organization (2018, March 30). *Mental health: Strengthening our response*. World Health Organization. Retrieved December 20, 2021, from http://www.who.int/news-room/fact-sheets/detail/mental-health-strengthening-our-response.

4

ONLINE WORK MANAGEMENT

ICT, IoT, and IIoT management

Ionica Oncioiu

Introduction

As integrated full network processes, the new interaction between technical systems and human labor, as well as the development of new business models, are all topics that are currently being covered by the slogans Production 4.0 and Work 4.0 (Coker, 2011). In the foreseeable future, the use of smart systems will lead to new work processes in the field of simple to medium administrative activities and employment in all office jobs, where today there is neither the quantity nor the quality of the requirements for the remaining human workforce, as it must be specifically defined (Kässi & Lehdonvirta, 2018). However, it can be predicted that everything that can be replaced in terms of human labor will be replaced with equipment and computer systems for reasons of opportunity and cost, as well as the aspect of profit maximization.

Nowadays, companies are realizing that the younger generation is increasingly expecting flexibility and the opportunity for mobile work to become more and more important for attracting good employees (Deal et al., 2010). At a time when there is a shortage of skilled workers, it is also time to recruit and attract experts who are relieved of the need to move while working from home (Lister & Harnish, 2019). Slowly but steadily, more and more home office arrangements are being made by creating the necessary technical premises. As in any process of change, not only the tools are enough, but all participants must learn how to deal with them and especially how to work and lead in online work. This takes time, practice and a lot of confidence. In this regard, many questions and developments remain unanswered at the level of the company. It is expected that the developments that occur and take place at the company level will often not be able to be mastered alone because their origin and solution will be the result of negotiations between employees and companies (Stanford, 2017).

DOI: 10.4324/9781003283386-5

Studies show that productivity usually increases rather than decreases when an employee is given the freedom, for example, to write a concept or report that is undisturbed at home (more) than at the office, among many colleagues (Vittersø et al., 2003; Lister & Harnish, 2019; Golden, 2021). With good leadership based on trust, and support based on needs instead of control, this can be achieved with the right organization of teamwork.

Online work management with all its facets

The term "Work 4.0" describes the future of work in the digital age (Bondarouk et al., 2017). The fund mainly consists of the opportunities (but also the problems) that result from the increasing use of technology on the labor market and in the general structures of companies. Thus, the future requires new ways of working, learning and doing business (Bailey & Kurland, 2002). Leadership style, personnel management and staff development become the central and decisive parameters of a new sustainable corporate culture (Contreras et al., 2020).

The world of work is now also largely digitized, and together with the international spread of artificial intelligence systems, further major changes are imminent, with the potential to jeopardize Europe's established social and economic systems due to the disruptive nature of new business models and value-creation processes (Balacescu et al., 2021). The more operational work processes are penetrated by information technology work equipment and IT systems, the less important the physical force argument becomes. Corporate work in the digital society has completely changed quality and other stressful features (Day et al., 2012). Therefore, both the evaluation criteria and the management style, as well as the organization of operational work, need to be adapted more and more to these changed processes. Digitized work processes and work equipment are spreading not only in the world of work today, but in all areas of life pertaining to work, family and society (Kellogg et al., 2020).

On the other hand, the COVID-19 pandemic is likely to remain a major point in the development of the coming years, and as a result companies have been suddenly forced to set their home offices and work together virtually (Shi et al., 2020). The other aspects, such as Work 4.0, outsourcing and the benefit of technology, have significantly contributed to the establishment of new virtual working models for years. Despite these factors, virtual teams and home offices are still considered niche topics and are difficult to establish.

Productive work at home requires not only the right IT equipment but also a good data connection, access to software and data, and proper management and work methods (Lepak & Snell, 1998). At the same time, the digital transformation is changing our understanding of work, which leads to a change in products, processes and business models, as well as organizational structures and management concepts (Graham et al., 2017). These developments require a pronounced ability to adapt and learn from individuals and the entire organization. Existing activities and tasks are changing, ceasing to exist or becoming more demanding, while new activities and job profiles are emerging. Equally, management must adapt to the new world of work (Duggan et al., 2020). The workforce is aging and has to deal with digitalization. In addition, most organizations must face newly arising ethical issues. Generally, the organization should understand digital human resource management as a success factor (Babic et al., 2017).

As for companies, there are concerns from managers that employees who work online are less efficient and their work cannot be controlled, which is why approval is often not granted (Lewis et al., 2019). Even with employees working online, setting up their own office, providing an Internet connection with a sufficient data transfer rate, and organizing the necessary family and work environment can be problematic.

Studies have shown that team members can often gain creativity by networking with other experts (Martins et al., 2004; Hertel et al., 2005; Dulebohn & Hoch, 2017). After all, due to the high level of self-management and better compatibility between family and work, they are often more satisfied at work. Companies get more resources and improved responsiveness through the use of virtual machines.

There are a number of methods for the various triggers of virtual team development that not only professional consultants and team developers can use (Chang et al., 2014). Managers must have moderation and training skills for some of the methods, or else they must use external experts (external consultants or internal human resources experts) to support and implement a method (Marlow et al., 2017). The following applies: the more insecure the manager feels and the more conflicting the area of activity to be treated, the more recommendable the external support becomes. However, this does not mean that the solution is to delegate it to a professional advisor.

Virtual team development always takes place when teams work together on future issues, goals and challenges (Hertel et al., 2005). However, this does not guarantee that a team identity will develop. Development measures provide a good basis for them and can be a key element for team identity, as they discuss and develop common goals, generally binding actions and rules of cooperation that apply to all (Powell et al., 2004). This provides security in everyday life because employees who work online know what is important. However, a true virtual team identity only emerges when such knowledge of commonalities is based on a deeper layer than in the problematic situations in the four areas of action for team development (Dulebohn & Hoch, 2017).

On top of that, when employees work online, strategic thinking is not just reserved for top management, but must also take place at the team level (Ng et al., 2012). It is not just about implementing corporate strategy but also about effective strategic thinking in your own management area. Each system (company, team) is based on assumptions about the future and strategies for dealing with it. Without such assumptions, the survival of a digitized system is left to chance. Even if these assumptions are often not expressly formulated at all, they are still implicitly or unconsciously there (Burchell et al., 2014).

Another important thing to remember is that due to the digitization, automation and robotization of standardized activities, intelligent machines, algorithms and artificial intelligence (AI) are taking on more and more tasks (Bondarouk et al., 2017). In the future, monotonous, difficult and dangerous production processes will take place largely without human intervention. But if there are deviations from the standard process, people can react flexibly and creatively and develop a new strategy. Only people can be creative and open up new ground (so far). People are also irreplaceable in activities that require social skills, empathy and relationship orientation – such as customer service, marketing, counseling and leadership. Therefore, the strengths of human intelligence – compared to artificial ones – are often generic skills such as social skills (in customer management) or creativity, i.e., skills in which people still have a comparative advantage over machines (Graham et al., 2017). In the end, this is not meant to become a comparison between human and artificial intelligence, but rather a cooperative relationship in which the respective strengths of humans and machines are optimally combined. These challenging tasks in the digital world of work impose new skill requirements on people.

The implications of online work on the development of digital skills

The digitization of the world of work requires constant updating and development of employee skills. A person's ability to act appropriately is usually based on knowledge, experience, intuition and self-organization (Beauregard et al., 2019). Skills enable people to act effectively and efficiently in specific situations and are useful only in the interaction between individuals, groups and organizations because they need an appropriate framework in which to develop.

Competence in addressing digital technologies and social networks is self-evident (Meijerink & Keegan, 2019). Not everyone can be able to program, but at least everyone should have a basic understanding of programming languages and how technology will work in the future. First and foremost, however, comes the pure use of technology and media. Problem-solving and optimization skills are also needed: if standardized tasks are automated and algorithmic, employees need to focus on developing and optimizing technology and acting in a problem-oriented manner. In addition, some studies emphasize the importance of social skills for the digital world of work (Lowenthal et al., 2017; Lister & Harnish, 2019). The introduction of new technologies is obviously not a purely technical issue.

In order to properly define the competency requirements for employees working from home and to design appropriate further training, HR managers should reflect and anticipate the digitization processes and associated changes in their company's work tasks (Santana & Manuel, 2020). This can only be done in cooperation with managers and employees in specialized fields who can best assess their future developments and needs. Interdisciplinary and inter-hierarchical online workshops – in which agile methods and creative techniques are used – are particularly suitable. Competency requirements specific to the field and to the position are usually developed in a participatory way, with the online participation of employees and managers, which promotes the implementation and learning motivation of all the participants involved.

On the other hand, there is a new division of labor between humans and technology: robots, algorithms and AI are increasingly able to perform standardized and routine tasks quickly and cheaply, and humans can rely on their strengths, such as strategic, creative and research-and-development activities, as well as social-communicative focus (Lister & Harnish, 2019). However, new tasks require new types of skills from employees, which are to be shared or promoted as part of the digital transformation. Thus, the existing knowledge and skills acquired by employees become obsolete and must be continuously developed for new tasks.

In addition to ensuring team motivation as a result of attending training courses, it is necessary to ensure that tasks are performed in the virtual space (Aloisi, 2016). To do this, in practice, software tools are used in a targeted manner. Managers often try to lead employees who work online using conventional methods of daily office work (Samani, 2015). This does not work with virtual teams, as they are spatially distributed and the information must be communicated specifically on the intranet, chat or in regular daily meetings. Using technology for team management creates more transparency and dynamism.

In addition to personnel management software, digital personnel files or personnel control systems, people analysis; digital requirements for employees, such as work schedule; digital recruitment, including candidate experience or employer branding by marketing on social networks, are becoming more and more established in practice (Stanford, 2017). Moreover, abstract, logical-analytical activities of programming, administration, organization, work in information processes, software development and services determine new value chains. The capacity for complex mental and intellectual work moves to the center of operational work, which is permeated in all areas of information technology. New organizational forms of operational work and, therefore, an innovative corporate culture, are developing in connection with the requirements of new management concepts.

The best practices presented by companies whose employees work online show that investment in continuing education is worthwhile in the long run and that a balance between the interests of the company (greater competitiveness, flexibility and productivity) and those of employees (better work capacity and employment as well as job satisfaction) is feasible. This task cannot be standardized and must be approached in a personalized way by the personnel (personal development) department of a company.

As a result, qualifying employees for new jobs is one of the most important keys to ensuring long-term functionality and employability of employees and to effectively convert opportunities for digital transformation into increased productivity and innovation in companies (Ng et al., 2012).

Opportunities and risks of work processes in the context of ICT, IoT and IIoT management

The distinctive character of the turbulent development phase we are in can be properly identified by the term "digital society", as all industries, professions, companies and fields of public and private life are moving increasingly more toward information technology (Balacescu et al., 2021). Information technology services will thus create, in the near future, new markets with new services that no one has thought of before or did not seriously dare to believe. The only constant remains the permanent change of society, along with the world of work and work processes.

When considering opportunities and risks of work processes in the context of ICT, IoT and IIoT management, both sides of the same coin must be considered: the chances and largely untapped potential of information technology that can be widely used, plus the digital technology in business and many other new opportunities for the flexible organization of work and life that need to be actively used (Day et al., 2012). Therefore, it is important to use the new design options in the company's business to develop innovative forms of work, with an emphasis on an improved work–life balance and, last but not least, equal treatment of all employees, regardless of personal characteristics.

Information technology makes it possible to work all over the world, regardless of place, time and existing national borders, regulations and national laws. The risks associated with increased networking of data flows and the resulting disadvantages for employees need to be identified and mitigated, especially when it comes to disruptive business models that override all national laws and regulations by processing data in the cloud. It is therefore essential to establish an encrypted communication that is regularly monitored.

Another risk, especially for managers, is to keep the motivation high enough (Xiao et al., 2021). Due to cultural differences and relatively impersonal collaboration, many members of online teams find it difficult to build a trusting relationship with other specialists. In a worst-case scenario, this can lead to isolation or a lack of identification of individual employees when working on project tasks. The resulting lack of communication can ultimately affect the quality of the end result. In addition, it may happen that individual employees are overworked and this is only noticed late by the remote manager.

At the moment, it seems that the imminent danger of labor shortages due to getting to work online will be counteracted by the expected increases in productivity (Santana & Manuel, 2020). Productivity gains are not just about losing the jobs available today that require physical presence. They also point out that it is likely for a declining need for human labor to become the norm in the future. On the one hand, this means that the projected quantitative shortage of young professionals due to demographic change is unlikely to occur. Rather, it can be assumed that – with constant efforts to replace human labor – there will be a declining need for labor (Golden, 2021). All of this is needed to develop, maintain and master the complex and innovative business models and IT systems of the future.

When it comes to the skilled workers of the future, there is not only a need to create family-friendly working conditions for all employees (such as working online), but also an urgent need for action to improve training opportunities to provide employees with the possibility of international jobs (Beauregard et al., 2019). Therefore, the international network of systems is associated with an increasing complexity of processing and business processes, which imposes high demands on the remaining human workforce, often even the so-called hybrid qualifications (Kellogg et al., 2020).

Another opportunity for greater flexibility is the reorganization of production and organizational structures, which not only allows independent design when running the company but also opens up many innovative design options for work–family compatibility (Golden et al., 2006). In some companies, this potential for future work is already being realized today. And this is not a dream in terms of strategic resources, in the transfer of decision-making powers in terms of time, work and work organization, but also in terms of content decisions to define operational goals and use of financial resources.

The abolition of regular and fixed-term employment contracts, the loss of protection against dismissal and other socially relevant regulations is a step backward in society and certainly a major threat to employees. And yet, many opportunities for employees, companies and society resulting from comprehensive computerization and job flexibility are not being recognized and exploited in the context of developing innovative service models. In the future, it will be important to develop more and more innovative and acceptable forms of work in the company, as part of the new business models, with cooperative forms of participation and management, which will allow the modeling of an unstoppable change in a profitable way for companies, employees and society.

Conclusion

In conclusion, an important feature of this structural change that is based on online work is the questioning of the classic roles and tasks of employers, management and employees. Used properly, it could prove to be an opportunity for information technology–induced change in the world of work. A completely new design of gender, family and work relations is possible only by creating a greater compatibility between family and work, or a closeness between work and family, which were previously considered only separately.

The existence of an appropriate leadership style can be implemented through appropriate awareness training and guidance through advanced training for managers. Just as stress can be alleviated and absorbed through a proper management style, better online working conditions can be created through a proper managerial culture that takes the employees' personal concerns seriously and tolerates their family conditions, needs and emergencies, personal freedom or even personal concerns.

At the same time, through the use of information technology in the network as a result of the promotion of online work and the approach to diversity management, company and employee equality are massively promoted and the company's working relationships are improved. Last but not least, the new options for creating a good work culture, a pleasant working atmosphere and efficient employee management are among the opportunities offered by digitalization.

In order to perceive this change as a threat but as an opportunity to help shape it, a new way of working together is needed. Thanks to digital technologies, communication and cooperation are becoming more and more interconnected not only between employees but also between different corporate divisions and with customers. In addition, machines and objects can communicate more and more with each other physically and virtually. Therefore, in the digital world of work, the development and training of staff and further education in organizations must contribute to the education and promotion of employees so that people can ultimately help shape the digital world of work and organizations competently and successfully.

References

Aloisi, A. (2016). Commoditized workers: Case study research on labor law issues arising from a set of on-demand/gig economy platforms. *Comparative Labor Law and Policy Journal*, *37*(3), 653–690.

Babic, A., Stinglhamber, F., Bertrand, F., & Hansez, I. (2017). Work-home interface and well-being: A cross-lagged analysis. *Journal of Personnel Psychology*, *16*(1), 46–55. https://doi.org/10.1027/1866-5888/a000172

Bailey, D. E., & Kurland, N. B. (2002). A review of telework research: Findings, new directions, and lessons for the study of modern work. *Journal of Organizational Behavior*, *23*(4), 383–400. https://doi.org/10.1002/job.144

Balacescu, A., Patrascu, A., & Paunescu, L. M. (2021). Adaptability to teleworking in European countries. *Amfiteatru Economic*, *3*, 683–699.

Beauregard, T. A., Basile, K. A., & Canonico, E. (2019). Telework: Outcomes and facilitators for employees. In R. Landers (Ed.), *The Cambridge handbook of technology and employee behavior* (pp. 511–543). Cambridge University Press.

Bondarouk, T., Parry, E., & Furtmueller, E. (2017). Electronic HRM: Four decades of research on adoption and consequences. *International Journal of Human Resource Management*, *28*(1), 98–131. https://doi.org/10.1080/09585192.2016.1245672

Burchell, B. J., Sehnbruch, K., Piasna, A., & Agloni, N. (2014). The quality of employment and decent work: Definitions, methodologies, and ongoing debates. *Cambridge Journal of Economics*, *38*(2), 459–477. https://doi.org/10.1093/cje/bet067

Chang, H. H., Hung, C. J., & Hsieh, H. W. (2014). Virtual teams: Cultural adaptation, communication quality, and interpersonal trust. *Total Quality Management and Business Excellence*, *25*(11–12), 1318–1335. https://doi.org/10.1080/14783363.2012.704274

Coker, B. L. S. (2011). Freedom to surf: The positive effects of workplace internet leisure browsing. *New Technology, Work and Employment*, *26*(3), 238–247. https://doi.org/10.1111/j.1468-005X.2011.00272.x

Contreras, F., Baykal, E., & Abid, G. (2020). E-leadership and teleworking in times of COVID-19 and beyond: What we know and where do we go. *Frontiers in Psychology*, *11*, 1–11.

Day, A., Paquet, S., Scott, N., & Hambley, L. (2012). Perceived information and communication technology (ICT) demands on employee outcomes: The moderating effect of organizational ICT support. *Journal of Occupational Health Psychology*, *17*(4), 473–491. https://doi.org/10.1037/a0029837

Deal, J. J., Altman, D. G., & Rogelberg, S. G. (2010). Millennials at work: What we know and what we need to do (if anything). *Journal of Business and Psychology*, *25*(2), 191–199. https://doi.org/10.1007/s10869-010-9177-2

Duggan, J., Sherman, U., Carbery, R., & McDonnell, A. (2020). Algorithmic management and app-work in the gig economy: A research agenda for employment relations and HRM. *Human Resource Management Journal, 30*(1), 114–132. https://doi. org/10.1111/1748-8583.12258

Dulebohn, J. H., & Hoch, J. E. (2017). Virtual teams in organizations. *Human Resource Management Review, 27*(4), 569–574. https://doi.org/10.1016/j.hrmr.2016.12.004

Golden, T. D. (2021). Telework and the navigation of work-home Boundaries. *Organizational Dynamics, 50*(1), 100822. https://doi.org/10.1016/j.orgdyn.2020.100822

Golden, T. D., Veiga, J. F., & Simsek, Z. (2006). Telecommuting's differential impact on work-family conflict: Is there no place like home? *Journal of Applied Psychology, 91*(6), 1340–1350. https://doi.org/10.1037/0021-9010.91.6.1340

Graham, M., Hjorth, I., & Lehdonvirta, V. (2017). Digital labour and development: Impacts of global digital labour platforms and the gig economy on worker livelihoods. *Transfer, 23*(2), 135–162. https://doi.org/10.1177/1024258916687250

Hertel, G., Geister, S., & Konradt, U. (2005). Managing virtual teams: A review of current empirical research. *Human Resource Management Review, 15*(1), 69–95. https://doi. org/10.1016/j.hrmr.2005.01.002

Kässi, O., & Lehdonvirta, V. (2018). Online labour index: Measuring the online gig economy for policy and research. *Technological Forecasting and Social Change, 137*, 241–248. https://doi.org/10.1016/j.techfore.2018.07.056

Kellogg, K. C., Valentine, M. A., & Christin, A. (2020). Algorithms at work: The new contested terrain of control. *Academy of Management Annals, 14*(1), 366–410. https://doi. org/10.5465/annals.2018.0174

Lepak, D. P., & Snell, S. A. (1998). Virtual HR: Strategic human resource management in the 21st century. *Human Resource Management Review, 8*(3), 215–234. https://doi. org/10.1016/S1053-4822(98)90003-1

Lewis, A. C., Cardy, R. L., & Huang, L. S. R. (2019). Institutional theory and HRM: A new look. *Human Resource Management Review, 29*(3), 316–335. https://doi.org/10.1016/ j.hrmr.2018.07.006

Lister, K., & Harnish, T. (2019). Telework and its effects in the United States. In *Telework in the 21st century*. Edward Elgar Publishing.

Lowenthal, P. R., Dunlap, J. C., & Snelson, C. (2017). Live synchronous web meetings in asynchronous online courses: Reconceptualizing virtual office hours. *Online Learning, 21*(4), 177–194. https://doi.org/10.24059/olj.v21i4.1285

Marlow, S. L., Lacerenza, C. N., & Salas, E. (2017). Communication in virtual teams: A conceptual framework and research agenda. *Human Resource Management Review, 27*(4), 575–589. https://doi.org/10.1016/j.hrmr.2016.12.005

Martins, L. L., Gilson, L. L., & Maynard, M. T. (2004). Virtual teams: What do we know and where do we go from here? *Journal of Management, 30*(6), 805–835. https://doi. org/10.1016/j.jm.2004.05.002

Meijerink, J. G., & Keegan, A. (2019). Conceptualizing human resource management in the gig economy: Toward a platform ecosystem perspective. *Journal of Managerial Psychology, 34*(4), 214–232. https://doi.org/10.1108/JMP-07-2018-0277

Ng, E., Lyons, S. T., & Schweitzer, L. (Eds.). (2012). *Managing the new workforce: International perspectives on the millennial generation*. Edward Elgar Publishing.

Powell, A., Piccoli, G., & Ives, B. (2004). Virtual teams: A review of current literature and directions for future research. *ACM SIGMIS Database, 35*(1), 6–36. https://doi. org/10.1145/968464.968467

Samani, S. (2015). The impact of personal control over office workspace on environmental satisfaction. *Journal of Social Science and Humanities, 1*, 163–175.

Santana, M., & Cobo, M. J. (2020). What is the future of work? A science mapping analysis. *European Management Journal, 38*, 846–862.

Shi, X., Moudon, A. V., Lee, B. H. Y., Shen, Q., & Ban, X. J. (2020). Factors influencing teleworking productivity-A natural experiment during the COVID-19 pandemic. *Findings*, *18195*. https://doi.org/10.32866/001c.18195

Stanford, J. (2017). The resurgence of gig work: Historical and theoretical perspectives. *Economic and Labour Relations Review*, *28*(3), 382–401. https://doi.org/10.1177/1035304617724303

Vitterso, J., Akselsen, S., Evjemo, B., Julsrud, T. E., Yttri, B., & Bergvik, S. (2003). Impacts of home-based telework on quality of life for employees and their partners. Quantitative and qualitative results from a European survey. *Journal of Happiness Studies*, *4*(2), 201–233. https://doi.org/10.1023/A:1024490621548

Xiao, Y., Becerik-Gerber, B., Lucas, G., & Roll, S. C. (2021). Impacts of working from home during COVID-19 pandemic on physical and mental well-being of office workstation users. *Journal of Occupational and Environmental Medicine*, *63*(3), 181–190. https://doi.org/10.1097/JOM.0000000000002097

5

GENDER AND CYBERBULLYING IN THE CONTEXT OF THE DIGITAL WORKPLACE

Simona Vasilache and Mihaela Sava

Introduction

Since this material serves, primarily, as a textbook, we find appropriate, in the first place, a clarification of the concepts we are operating with. Thus, we will address the following terms:

- *Digital workplace*
- *Cyberbullying*
- *Gender-based bullying*

Digital workplace, as a concept, dates back to 1993 (Grantham and Nichols). The two authors were concerned with the moves it takes to turn a traditional workplace into a digital one and the respective impact on human resources and customers. Nowadays, this transformation is certainly accelerated by work-from-home pandemic constraints (Marsh et al., 2022). Marsh et al. (2022) provide a more concise definition, where the key point is the independence from a physical location: "the broad set of technologies and practices involved in employees' digital workplace experience irrespective of physical location."

In a 2021 thesis, Paulmair identifies six definitions of the digital workplace, as follows:

- Deloitte (2014, p. 4): "all the technologies people use to get work done in today's workplace – both the ones in operation and the ones yet to be implemented. It ranges from your HR applications and core business applications to e-mail, instant messaging and enterprise social media tools and virtual meeting tools."

DOI: 10.4324/9781003283386-6

- Tubb (2014): "the collection of all of the digital tools provided by an organization to allow its employees to do their jobs."
- Perks (2015): "collection of all the digital tools in an organization that allow employees to do their jobs. Those tools include intranets, communication tools, e-mail, CRM, ERP, HR system, calendar and other enterprise processes or tools which assist in the general day-to-day functioning of a business."
- Dery et al. (2017, p. 136): "the physical, cultural and digital arrangements that simplify working life in complex, dynamic and often unstructured working environments."
- Avanade Inc. (2017): "an environment that empowers employees – regardless of their location – to drive business advantage by using digital tools and intelligent context."
- Byström et al. (2017, p. 2): "an environment which occurs when an organization's workforce collectively carry out their work in digital, rather than physical work spaces."

It may be seen that some of these definitions send to other concepts, for instance, *digital tools*. But it is common sense to say that employees make use of digital tools in a physical workplace as well. Essential to us, following some of the quoted definitions, for speaking of a digital workplace, is the fact that *location becomes irrelevant*. And, of course, employees may benefit from all their workplace facilities due to digital tools.

We should note, however, that opinions in literature are far from converging into a generally accepted definition. In 2020 research, Lagus interviewed employees from six industries, admitting that they work in a digital workplace, and found out that their definitions are different. For one respondent, for instance, a digital workplace means to have access to information from multiple devices; for another one the digital workplace is technology that works for him and provides him with the resources he needs, without bothering to understand how it functions.

Cyberbullying is typically associated with adolescents and children (Nocentini et al., 2010; Corcoran et al., 2015; Kofoed & Staksrud, 2018; Menin et al., 2021). Obviously, cyberbullying is a form of bullying that emerged as the large-scale use of new technologies exploded. Olweus (1994), who has long been preoccupied about the topic, advanced the main criteria for a behavior to be labeled as bullying:

1   To be aggressive, with an obvious intention of doing harm
2   To repeat over time
3   To appear in an interpersonal relationship where power is unbalanced (i.e., the aggressor dominates the victim)

However, these criteria are not necessarily valid in the case of cyberbullying. In the online environment, a single post may last and be visible long enough to harm, even if it is not repeated (Slonje & Smith, 2008). Also, the aggressor may not be visible, or may have a fake identity, which makes it hard to discuss the power imbalance.

As in the case of the digital workplace, there is no widely accepted definition of cyberbullying (Peter & Peterman, 2018). The two researchers review, in their article, 24 definitions of the term, over a period of six years (2012–2017)! We quote, next, some older definitions, as well as some more recent approaches:

> Smith et al., 2008, p. 376: "aggressive intentional act carried out by a group or individual, using electronic forms of contact, repeatedly and over time against a victim who cannot easily defend him or herself."
> Tokunaga, 2010, p. 278: "any behavior performed through electronic or digital media by individuals or groups that repeatedly communicates hostile or aggressive messages intended to inflict harm or discomfort on others."
> Barlinska et al., 2013, p. 38: "violence committed by perpetrators and bystanders using information and communication technologies and various functionalities of the Internet, especially messaging software and social networking services."
> Bottino et al., 2015, p. 464: "an intentional act of aggression towards another person online."
> Hutson, 2016, p. 67: "willful and repeated harm inflicted through aggressive actions through the use of computers, cell phones, and other electronic devices."
> Watts et al., 2017, p. 272: "any electronic means to repeatedly harass, intimidate, or embarrass another person."

It may be seen that most of the definitions refer to the intentional and aggressive character of the cyberbullying. Some mention the electronic means of communication as the vehicle of the bullying, others refer to the physical support, such as computers, phones, etc.

In summary, cyberbullying can be seen as an intentional aggression in the digital environment, having as effects the humiliation or intimidation of the victim.

Gender-based bullying is a type of bias-based bullying, probably the most prevailing (Mulvey et al., 2018). According to Mishna et al. (2016), gender-based bullying, early in school, is a socialization process intended to familiarize girls with gender-based stereotypes and with gender-based violence. According to Meyer (2009), gender bullying is a type of behavior that maintains and asserts dominant gender norms of heterosexual masculinity and femininity. We may also speak about sexual bullying, which consists of "unwanted sexual attention that makes the recipient feel uncomfortable, demeaned, or humiliated" (Sullivan, 2011, p. 54). Namely, girls are given increased attention (i.e., harassed), as compared to boys, who are left unnoticed.

Swanson and Anton-Erxleben (2016) also link gender-based bullying to gendered violence. In their view, boys learn early in their lives that aggression and dominance are masculine attributes, while submission and shame are gender roles for girls. The pattern of aggressions in the virtual world, in the form of cyberbullying, suits these preconceptions from the physical world.

However, gender-based bullying is not restricted, in literature, only to school environments (with their online extensions). DeJordy and Barrett (2014) discuss gender-based bullying as a form of institutional control, building on the experiences of women working in highly masculine organizational cultures. Thus, bullying, and especially gender-based bullying, although it starts in school, in the early ages, must be studied, as well, as an organizational problem, affecting the gender equality in the workplace and, ultimately, the status and performance of the employees being bullied.

Literature review

Most of the studies addressing bullying in the workplace refer to its prevalence (Privitera & Campbell, 2009; Matthiesen & Einarsen, 2010; Ciby & Raya, 2015; Iftikhar et al., 2020). However, some of these works discuss risk groups, which are likely to serve as a victim for bullying or cyberbullying (Forssell, 2020).

Among the first to introduce the gender issue, Salin (2003) draws attention to the severe consequences bullying has on the workforce and on the organization. Hence, the need for prevention strategies.

Choi (2018) discusses cyberbullying as a cybercrime. As compared to traditional bullying, cyberbullying does not observe a work schedule, the aggressor having virtually unlimited access to the victim (Pettalia et al., 2013), who is harassed day and night. Also, cyberbullying often implies the anonymity of the aggressor (Calvete et al., 2010) and the instant access to a very large audience (Slonje & Smith, 2008). Thus, the prejudice to the victim is fast and hardly reparable, their reputation being damaged in the eyes of people who cannot easily verify the truth, as they are not face to face with either the victim or the aggressor. Barlett (2019) advocates that cyberbullying may have as an effect the disconnecting of the victim from technology in order to escape the attacks, which has severe consequences, in the context of online work, which doesn't leave much space for choice.

According to Vranjes et al. (2017), cyberbullying in the workplace occurs in three forms: work related, person related, and intrusive. Behaviors that target the person refer to gossiping, or spreading rumors, while those targeting work may refer to not disclosing relevant information in order to put someone in a position of inferiority (Einarsen et al., 2009). Intrusive behavior refers to sharing information regarding the personal life of a coworker, information that is more easily accessible in an online environment (Vranjes et al., 2017) – like, for instance, reposting private photos, forwarding messages that were intended only for a particular person and that contain sensitive information, etc. Also, hacking accounts and delivering compromising information belongs to this third component of cyberbullying.

Peled (2019) identifies the following forms of cyberbullying: fraping, which means changing the online identity of the victim in order to affect their reputation;

trolling, which means repeatedly insulting the victim to provoke a response; and catfishing, meaning to take another identity in order to attract the victim into a romantic relationship.

A study by Loh and Snyman (2020) reveals that even the perceptions of cyberbullying in the workplace are gendered, female employees reporting higher levels of stress and job dissatisfaction when exposed to this phenomenon. One explanation may be that they are more exposed to this type of stress; another is that they tend to be more vulnerable to the stressors in the online environment.

Weber et al. (2018) study the behavior of bystanders in bullying incidents, drawing the conclusion that when the watchers take the part of the victim, their perceptions are subject to gender stereotypes. Their results show that female victims are treated with more empathy, as compared to male victims of cyberbullying in the workplace, who are expected to fight for themselves.

During the COVID-19 pandemic, citizens have become netizens (Yang, 2021), and the accelerated digital migration led to new challenges. Most of the negative emotions of the people compelled to stay behind their doors were released online (Wong et al., 2020). As we don't yet have a measurable extension of the phenomenon of cyberbullying during pandemics, some of its manifestations include the stigmatization of those who are vaccinated/those who refuse the vaccine, those who observe the restrictions/those who do not, racism (cyberbullying against Chinese/Asians), and homophobia (Yang, 2021).

According to Karmakar and Das (2021), cyberbullying during the COVID-19 pandemic is mainly prevalent on the social networks, where people express their opinions and are often harassed for that.

In the workplace, cyberbullying takes more often the form of offensive emails or messages (on social networks, WhatsApp, etc.) that contain inappropriate words, jokes with a sexual background, spreading gossip about coworkers, and being uncivilized in social media comments (Kowalski & Robbins, 2021). The discrepancy in power between the victim and the aggressor, which is a common trait of traditional bullying, appears in the case of workplace cyberbullying in the form of superiors bullying their subordinates (Kim & Choi, 2021). Additionally, as Gardella et al. (2017) outline, low-position and low-wage workers are more likely to endure cyberbullying and less likely to act legally to protect their rights.

Case study of Romania

We will present, in brief, the case of a female employee working as the general secretary of a city hall from Romania, Vaslui County, who was exposed to a form of cyber-harassment after she retook her attributions at the end of her maternal leave. The mayor did not agree that she should come back to work and tried to intimidate his employee through a series of bullying tactics, among which were an article published on a local website, which included personal information about the employee; photos disclosed on WhatsApp; calumnies transmitted live on Facebook; and more.

Chronology of the facts[1]

By provision nr. 120/02.05.2018, the applicant's service relations were suspended upon request, pursuant to art. 91, para. (1), lit. a), of Law nr. 188/1999 on the Statute of civil servants, republished, for parental leave up to two years.

On 29.08.2018, the applicant requested in writing, registered in the City Hall register, addressed to Mr. ZL, as legal representative, the resumption of service relations, starting on 01.10.2018. The mayor, ZL, referred to the article that appeared on 20.08.2018 in the online edition of the local newspaper, containing defamatory details regarding the applicant's private life, and advised her not to return to work, as it would spoil the image of the institution.

The mayor also asked her to tell in detail the aspects invoked regarding her private life and also to detail her sources of income, recommending her to deal with the child-raising allowance, and if she did not manage, to ask her husband for money.

By address no. 7280/26.09.2018, the applicant officially answered that she could not resume her service relations, as she had personal problems likely to affect the prestige of the employing institution. It was specified that after solving personal problems she was entitled to formulate a new request for reintegration into work.

Following the formulation of a criminal complaint for abuse of office, which led to the opening of a criminal prosecution against the mayor, on 12.12.2018 the applicant resumed her service relations. A series of threatening emails followed, in which the applicant was told that she would be subject to defamation in the media. Also, the mayor informed her that he owned the applicant's telephone conversations index and that he would use this information, if necessary.

Also, the applicant's daily activity was monitored by means of a surveillance camera oriented to her office, and the other employees were questioned about the time they spent in the office and the cases they had to solve with the applicant.

The applicant was blocked from accessing the institution's email, the password being changed, and the other colleagues were forbidden to communicate it to her. Also, she was denied access to the general register of entrances-outputs in electronic format, although, in terms of the function she owned, she is a leading civil servant.

On 02.07.2020, the applicant had an open conflict with the mayor, who entered her office and offended her child, whom he called 'bastard,' 'flower child,' etc. Subsequently, the mayor took footage from the surveillance camera with the incident, which he posted on his WhatsApp profile in order to be seen by all colleagues. The videos and pictures were kept on the WhatsApp profile for 24 hours, during which the applicant was contacted by numerous colleagues who informed her of the situation.

On 13.08.2020, when, being on her lunch break, the applicant went to the local store to buy some food, and in front of the store she stopped to talk to a few citizens, the mayor followed her and took out his mobile phone and took pictures of her, although it was not during working hours.

On 18.08.2020, the mayor, ZL, was present in a show broadcast live on Facebook, denigrating the applicant and requesting that she be monitored permanently via video and audio recordings. The show had 3,062 views and was distributed 121 times, reaching a relatively large audience.

On 20.08.2020, the local newspaper published, in the online version, an open letter of the city hall officials, which denounced the faults of the civil servant in a generic way. The article was illustrated, however, with the photo taken of the applicant by the mayor on 13.08.2020, to make readers associate the portrait of the civil servant, from the article, with a real person. In the comments section of the article numerous denigrating comments were posted regarding the applicant, her child, and her family situation.

Legal action

The applicant requested the court to find the repeated actions of harassment to which she was subjected, obliging the respondent to pay the sum of 50,000 lei (10,000 euros) as moral damages, for the psychic trauma that was caused to her, knowingly, and with the obvious purpose of making her give up her job, to resign.

The court, corroborating the documents in the file and the statements of the witnesses, held that the respondent had carried out a real surveillance action of the applicant. The court also noted that all the manifestations of the respondent, ZL, met the conditions of moral harassment, provided by art. 5, para. 5, ind.1 of GO 137/2000.

Although respondent ZL relied in his defense on the applicant's conduct, the court noted that no form of professional or personal conduct of an employee may authorize the employer to act systematically in order to harm the dignity of the employee, all the more so as he invoked private personal circumstances that had no relevance in the professional activity of the employee.

Thus, the court ordered the respondent to pay the sum of 30,000 lei (6,000 euros) in damages and at the same time obliged him to cease the acts of moral harassment exercised on the applicant.

The court did not admit that the application by which the applicant requested the publication of a dismissing, in the online edition of the local newspaper, of the fact that the open letter of 20.08.2020 was not signed by the officials of the city hall, as the direct involvement of the mayor in this endeavor could not be proved.

Legal means to fight gender-based cyberbullying

The legal framework in Romania contains several provisions against harassment in the workplace, as well as cybernetic violence.

Moral harassment in the workplace has, recently, a dedicated law, Law no. 167/7.08.2020, which completes Government Ordinance 137/2000 regarding the sanctioning of all forms of discrimination, as well as art. 6 from Law 202/2002 regarding the equality of chances between men and women.

Through the Civil Decision no. 1439/2020, the Cluj Court of Appeal held that the first condition for discussing moral harassment at work refers to the repeated or systematic character of the incriminated behaviors, as well as to their intentional character. It is not enough to talk of one exceptional episode in order to qualify that behavior of a colleague or superior as harassment.

Also, the Iasi Court of Appeal, by Civil Decision no. 338/2018, underlined the repeated character of the pressures that had been made by a superior on a subordinate to resign.

Concerning international provisions, Romania has adhered to the Convention on the Elimination of All Forms of Discrimination against Women (CEDAW Convention), to the EU Strategy on Gender Equality: Towards a Union of Equality 2020–2025, as well as to the UN Agenda 2030, Sustainable Development Goal 5.

Cybernetic violence against women, which was introduced as a form of domestic violence by Law 174/2018, which completes Law 217/2003 regarding domestic violence, is further sanctioned, in a broader context, by Law 106/2020, which defines cybernetic violence as

> cyberbullying, gender-based hate speech online messages, online tracking, online threats, non-counter-confessional publication of intimate information and graphic content, unlawful access to intercept private communications and data, and any other form of misuse of information and communication technology through computers, smart mobile phones or other similar devices using telecommunications or connecting to the internet and transmitting and use social or email platforms with the aim of embarrassing, humiliating, scaring, threatening, silencing the victim.

However, cybernetic violence is still linked to violence between actual or ex-partners. We propose, as an initiative *de lege ferenda*, that cybernetic violence is discussed in a more comprehensive framework, including situations of harassment in the workplace. Thus, a better legal framework will support the initiatives of the victims to defend their rights in justice.

Conclusion

In conclusion, we may say that, although both the definitions of the terms we discussed in this chapter, as well as legal framework, are still lacking consistency and coherence, important steps have been taken for acknowledging a reality that becomes more and more present due to COVID-19 pandemic conditions.

Although we do not yet have released statistics measuring the spread of cyberbullying in the new digital environment, and especially the gender bias of this phenomenon, we may estimate that existing problems, at least in Romania, are likely to deepen.

This calls for the need for a coherent, clear, and adequate legal framework in order to be able to appropriately control and prevent the occurrence of gendered cyberbullying.

Note

1 Retrieved January 16, 2022, from www.clujust.ro/angajata-unei-primarii-a-obtinut-daune-morale-de-30-000-de-lei-pentru-hartuire-la-locul-de-munca/

References

Avanade, Inc. (2017). Retrieved from Global Survey: Companies are Unprepared for the Arrival of a True Digital Workplace. http://www.avanade.com/-/media/asset/research/digitalworkplace-global-study.pdf

Barlett, C. P. (2019). *Predicting cyberbullying: Research, theory, and intervention.* Elsevier Academic Press.

Barlińska, J., Szuster, A., & Winiewski, M. (2013). Cyberbullying among adolescent bystanders: Role of the communication medium, form of violence, and empathy. *Journal of Community and Applied Social Psychology, 23*(1), 37–51. https://doi.org/10.1002/casp.2137

Bottino, S. M. B., Bottino, C. M. C., Regina, C. G., Correia, A. V. L., & Ribeiro, W. S. (2015). Cyberbullying and adolescent mental health: Systematic review. *Cadernos de Saúde Pública, 31*(3), 463–475. https://doi.org/10.1590/0102-311X00036114

Byström, K., Ruthven, I., & Heinström, J. (2017). Work and information: Which workplace models still work in modern digital workplaces? *Information Research, 22*(1), 1–16.

Calvete, E., Orue, I., Estévez, A., Villardón, L., & Padilla, P. (2010). Cyberbullying in adolescents: Modalities and aggressors' profile. *Computers in Human Behavior, 26*(5), 1128–1135. https://doi.org/10.1016/j.chb.2010.03.017

Choi, J. O. (2018) Influence of cyber bullying victimization on cyber bullying: Mediating effects of anxiety and moderation effects of stress coping strategy. *Crisisonomy, 11,* 195–214.

Ciby, M., & Raya, R. P. (2015). Workplace bullying: A review of the defining features, measurement methods and prevalence across continents. *IIM Kozhikode Society and Management Review, 4*(1), 38–47. https://doi.org/10.1177/2277975215587814Corcoran, L., Guckin, C. M., & Prentice, G. (2015). Cyberbullying or cyber aggression?: A review of existing definitions of cyber-based peer-to-peer aggression. *Societies, 5*(2), 245–255. https://doi.org/10.3390/soc5020245

DeJordy, R., & Barrett, F. (2014). Emotions in institutions: Bullying as a mechanism of institutional control. In *Emotions and the organizational fabric (research on emotion in organizations, Vol. 10)* (pp. 219–243). Emerald Group Publishing Limited. https://doi.org/10.1108/S1746-979120140000010017

Deloitte. (2014). *The digital workplace: Think, share, do.* Retrieved January 7, 2022, from https://www2.deloitte.com/content/dam/Deloitte/mx/Documents/humancapital/The_digital_workplace.pdfTubb

Dery, K., Sebastian, I. M., & van der Meulen, N. (2017, June). The digital workplace is key to digital innovation. *MIS Quarterly Executive, 16*(2), 135–152.

Einarsen, S., Raknes, B. I., & Matthiesen, S. B. (2009). Bullying and harassment at work and their relationships to work environment quality: An exploratory study. *European Work and Organizational Psychologist, 4*(4), 381–401. https://doi.org/10.1080/13594329408410497

Forssell, R. C. (2020). Cyberbullying in a boundary blurred working life: Distortion of the private and professional face on social media. *Qualitative Research in Organizations and Management, 15*(2), 89–107. https://doi.org/10.1108/QROM-05-2018-1636

Gardella, J. H., Fisher, B. W., & Teurbe-Tolon, A. R. (2017). A systematic review and meta-analysis of cyber-victimization and educational outcomes for adolescents. *Review of Educational Research, 87*(2), 283–308. https://doi.org/10.3102/0034654316689136

Grantham, C. E., & Nichols, L. D. (1993). *The digital workplace. Designing groupware platforms.* Van Nostrand Reinhold. https://doi.org/10.1016/j.chb.2009.11.014

Hutson, E. (2016). Cyberbullying in adolescence. A concept analysis. *ANS. Advances in Nursing Science, 39*(1), 60–70. https://doi.org/10.1097/ANS.0000000000000104

Iftikhar, M., Waheed, Z., Um-E-Laila, Yousafzai, S. K., & Qureshi, M. I. (2020). Traditional bullying and cyber bullying: Prevalence, effects and workplace spirituality as an antibullying policy. *International Journal of Management, 11*(11), 2165–2186.

Karmakar, S., & Das, S. (2021). Understanding the rise of twitter-based cyberbullying due to COVID-19 through comprehensive statistical evaluation (January 4, 2021). In *Proceedings of the 54th Hawaii International Conference on System Sciences.* Maui, Hawaii (Virtual), Retrieved from SSRN: https://ssrn.com/abstract=3768839 or http://dx.doi.org/10.2139/ssrn.3768839

Kim, K. Y., & Choi, J. S. (2021, Nov–Dec). Cyberbullying, student nurses' ethical awareness and the Covid-19 pandemic. *Nursing Ethics, 28*(7–8), 1258–1268. https://doi.org/10.1177/09697330211010280

Kofoed, J., & Staksrud, E. (2018). We always torment different people, so by definition, we are no bullies: The problem of definitions in cyberbullying research'. *New Media and Society, 21*(3). https://doi.org/10.1177/1461444818810026

Kowalski, R. M., & Robbins, C. (2021). The meaning, prevalence, and outcomes of cyberbullying in the workplace. In L. R. Salazar (Ed.), *Handbook of research on cyberbullying and online harassment in the workplace* (pp. 1–27). IGI Global.

Lagus, M. (2020). *Implementation of a digital workplace from the perspective of employees.* Retrieved December 17, 2021, from http://www.theseus.fi/handle/10024/337949

Loh, J., & Snyman, R. (2020). The tangled web: Consequences of workplace cyberbullying in adult male and female employees. *Gender in Management: An International Journal, 35*(6), 567–584. https://doi.org/10.1108/GM-12-2019-0242

Marsh, E., Vallejos, E. P., & Spence, A. (2022). The digital workplace and its dark side: An integrative review. *Computers in Human Behavior, 128,* 107–118. https://doi.org/10.1016/j.chb.2021.107118

Matthiesen, S. B., & Einarsen, S. (2010). Bullying in the workplace: Definition, prevalence, antecedents and consequences. *International Journal of Organization Theory and Behavior, 13*(2), 202–248. https://doi.org/10.1108/IJOTB-13-02-2010-B004

Menin, D., Guarini, A., Mameli, C., Skrzypiec, G., & Brighi, A. (2021). Was that (cyber) bullying? Investigating the operational definitions of bullying and cyberbullying from adolescents' perspective. *International Journal of Clinical and Health Psychology, 21*(2), 100221. https://doi.org/10.1016/j.ijchp.2021.100221

Meyer, E. J. (2009). *Gender, bullying, and harassment: Strategies to end sexism and homophobia in schools.* Teacher's College Press.

Mishna, F., McInroy, L. B., Lacombe-Duncan, A., Bhole, P., Van Wert, M., & Schwan, K., . . . Johnston, D. (2016). Prevalence, motivations, and social, mental health and health consequences of cyberbullying among schoolaged children and youth: Protocol of a longitudinal and multi-perspective mixed method study. *JMIR Research Protocols, 5,* e83.

Mulvey, K. L., Hoffman, A. J., Gönültaş, S., Hope, E. C., & Cooper, S. M. (2018). Understanding experiences with bullying and bias-based bullying: What matters and for whom? *Psychology of Violence, 8*(6), 702–711. https://doi.org/10.1037/vio0000206

Nocentini, A., Calmaestra, J., Schultze-Krumbholz, A., Scheithauer, H., Ortega, R., & Menesini, E. (2010). Cyberbullying: Labels, behaviours and definition in three European countries. *Australian Journal of Guidance and Counselling, 20*(2), 129–142. https://doi.org/10.1375/ajgc.20.2.129

Olweus, D. (1994). Bullying at school. Long-term outcomes for the victims and an effective school-based intervention program. In L. Rowell Huesmann (Ed.), *Aggressive behavior. Current perspectives* (pp. 97–130). Springer Publishing Company.

Paulmair, T. (2021, January). *The impact of virtual collaboration on firm competitiveness: A case study of accounting companies.* Institute of Strategic Management. Retrieved January 19, 2022, from https://epub.jku.at/obvulihs/download/pdf/5767440?originalFilename=true.

Peled, Y. (2019). Cyberbullying and its influence on academic, social, and emotional development of undergraduate students. *Heliyon, 5*(3), e01393. https://doi.org/10.1016/j.heliyon.2019.e01393

Perks, M. (2015). *Everything you need to know but were afraid to ask: The Digital Workplace.* Retrieved January 7, 2022, from http://www.unily.com/media/23747/the-digitalworkplace-guide-whitepaper.pdf

Peter, I. K., & Petermann, F. (2018). Cyberbullying: A concept analysis of defining attributes and additional influencing factors. *Computers in Human Behavior, 86,* 350–366. https://doi.org/10.1016/j.chb.2018.05.013

Pettalia, J. L., Levin, E., & Dickinson, J. (2013). Cyberbullying: Eliciting harm without consequence.

Privitera, C., & Campbell, M. A. (2009). Cyberbullying: The new face of workplace bullying? *Cyber Psychology and Behavior,* 395–400. http://doi.org/10.1089/cpb.2009.0025

Salin, D. (2003). Ways of explaining workplace bullying: A review of enabling, motivating and precipitating structures and processes in the work environment. *Human Relations, 56*(10), 1213–1232. https://doi.org/10.1177/00187267035610003

Slonje, R., & Smith, P. K. (2008). Cyberbullying: Another main type of bullying? *Scandinavian Journal of Psychology, 49*(2), 147–154. https://doi.org/10.1111/j.1467-9450.2007.00611.x

Smith, P. K., Mahdavi, J., Carvalho, M., Fisher, S., Russell, S., & Tippett, N. (2008). Cyberbullying: Its nature and impact in secondary school pupils. *Journal of Child Psychology and Psychiatry, and Allied Disciplines, 49*(4), 376–385. https://doi.org/10.1111/j.1469-7610.2007.01846.x

Sullivan, K. (2011). *The anti-bullying handbook* (2nd ed.). SAGE.

Swanson, J. H., & Anton-Erxleben, K. (2016). Bullying from a gender-based violence perception. In *Ending the torment: Tackling bullying from the schoolyard to cyberspace.* UNICEF Report.

Tokunaga, R. S. (2010). Following you home from school: A critical review and synthesis of research on cyberbullying victimization. *Computers in Human Behavior, 26*(3), 277–287. https://doi.org/10.1016/j.chb.2009.11.014

Tubb, C. (2014, January 21). *Which of these 8 definitions of "digital workplace" works best for you?* Digital Press Workplace Group. Retrieved December 17, 2021, from https://digitalworkplacegroup.com/2014/01/21/whats-employees-view-of-digitalworkplace/.

Vranjes, I., Baillien, E., Vandebosch, H., Erreygers, S., & De Witte, H. (2017). The dark side of working online: Towards a definition and an Emotion Reaction model of workplace cyberbullying. *Computers in Human Behavior, 69,* 324–334. https://doi.org/10.1016/j.chb.2016.12.055

Watts, L. K., Wagner, J., Velasquez, B., & Behrens, P. I. (2017). Cyberbullying in higher education: A literature review. *Computers in Human Behavior, 69,* 268–274. https://doi.org/10.1016/j.chb.2016.12.038

Weber, M., Koehler, C., & Schnauber-Stockmann, A. (2019). Why should I help you? Man up! Bystanders' gender stereotypic perceptions of a Cyberbullying incident. *Deviant Behavior, 40*(5), 585–601. https://doi.org/10.1080/01639625.2018.1431183

Yang, F. (2021, February 15). Coping strategies, cyberbullying behaviors, and depression among Chinese netizens during the COVID-19 pandemic: A web-based nationwide survey. *Journal of Affective Disorders, 281,* 138–144. https://doi.org/10.1016/j.jad.2020.12.023

PART II

Digital organization functions and workplace

6

DIGITAL HUMAN RESOURCES MANAGEMENT

Gözde Mert and Slimane ED-Dafali

Introduction

One of the business functions most affected by digital transformation is human resources management (HRM). With a people-oriented approach, the transition from personnel management to HRM has been adopted, and a strategic human resources approach has become dominant by adding a strategic perspective to this understanding. Digitalization has become very important in HRM with the advancement of technology today.

Industry 4.0 literature sees digitalization as the technical way to cope with difficulties. Systems that do not include people in the solution cannot achieve sustainable success. Knowledge, which is the basic dynamic of today is human, that as the only production factor that has the ability to produce, process and develop knowledge. Stenmark (2001) states that since the source of the information produced is the person, awareness and interest in this field are created. In the information age, organizations that are equipped with human resources and knowledge of human resources play an important role in obtaining a sustainable competitive advantage. In this respect, the most important function of the human resources department should be the acquisition and/or development of human capital, which enables the business to become more competitive, work for maximum efficiency and fulfill its business strategy at the highest level (Lepak & Snell, 1998).

Digitization is seen as a disruptive innovation. The main reason for this is that while digitalization creates new business and social opportunities, it also challenges traditional business design. This challenge requires change of both people and organizations. Employees have to develop new competencies and abilities based on technological expertise, data analysis and social, emotional and creative skills (Colbert et al., 2016, p. 733). As a result of this, organizations should redesign their structures and processes (Kane & Ransbotham, 2016). From this point

DOI: 10.4324/9781003283386-8

of view, human resources managers need to take on new responsibilities for rapid technological developments and include them in their processes.

Digitization has very important effects on HRM processes (Stone & Dulebohn, 2013). The use of technology has contributed to critical transformation among different functions of the organization such as human resources (Mohiuddin et al., 2022). These technologies are used to exert various activities, e.g., the collection, storage, use and extraction of information about employees and candidates (Stone et al., 2015).

Digital Transformation

The concept of digitalization is one of the topics most focused on in all sectors in recent years. Digitization has major implications for corporate success. Brynjolfsson and McAfee (2014, p. 58) state that researchers are increasingly interested in digitalization. Due to the successes achieved with information technology applications in all processes of institutions with Industry 4.0, it has also led to digitalization in management processes. Information technologies, as a driving force, have caused great changes and transformations in products and services in all sectors.

The radical change and transformation that comes with the digital age causes a great change in all processes to continue without slowing down. Markus and Loebbecke (2013, p. 650) attribute this to the fact that digitalization has become too widespread in all sectors. The digital age has brought forth important innovations in two basic structures in the digitalized business ecosystem:

- First, effective and efficient management of all processes in ecosystems, the design, production, sales and marketing processes of new products/services having significant effects on the value of the business.
- Second, enabling the establishment of integrated structures by creating new structures between upper ecosystems or sub-ecosystems.

The first signs of digital transformation emerged with the invention of the computer in the middle of the 20th century. Then, the internet gained speed with the invention and spread of personal computers and mobile phones. With its technological access power, digital transformation also provides access to the basic needs of the masses, such as health, education, micro-finance and communication, without requiring too much infrastructure investment (Gush et al., 2006; Mitra & Dangwal, 2010). In order to keep up with the digital age, digitalization improves the business processes of organizations, brands and structures by adding value to their organizational structures, ecosystems and customers. Digitization facilitates organizations to increase their knowledge and skills and their transition to new ways of doing business and thinking (Mert, 2020, p. 51). Digital transformation develops approaches that will affect all sectors and organizations for the national economy. Without applying these approaches, it becomes difficult to continue organizational activities.

Digital transformation plays an important role in the future plans, programs, policies and strategies, development, investment and practices of organizations (Fırat & Fırat, 2017).

Transition From Personnel Management to Human Resources Management

It is possible to encounter examples of practices that can be associated with human resources in the early periods of history. Hunting, fishing, gathering, leadership power, endurance, skill, loyalty to the clan, age and gender discrimination in doing business and the effectiveness of traditions can be evaluated in this context. Likewise, in the late Neolithic, Bronze and Iron Ages, apprenticeship, hereditary occupation, simple record keeping and payments can be seen as early examples of HRM (Bass, 1994, pp. 3–5).

Today's international competition and globalization process directs the working norms, management and human factor toward new targets and policies. All these relations affect the relations and management techniques of the enterprise and help the development of the modern HRM approach, which determines the future of the enterprise (Wayne, 1995, p. 14).

When the historical development of HRM is examined, it is seen that although "personnel management", "personnel management and industrial relations" and other related concepts have been widely used since the 1980s, new searches have started since the 1950s (Baysal, 1993, p. 64). Advances in branches such as psychology, sociology and anthropology also affected the field of management in the 1950s. Most of the literature studies in the field of HRM started in this period; It has been done by psychologists such as Shartle (1950), Brown (1952) and Harrell (1953). In these studies, the psychology of the employees was emphasized and the issues of increasing motivation and training for the employee were discussed (Cingöz, 2011, p. 31).

In the 1960s, due to the intensification of legal regulations and social legislation, it caused organizations to make changes in their personnel departments. These changes, such as the growth of organizations with technological developments, the increase in national and international competition, and the changes in the workforce due to education, have caused the transition from personnel management to human resources management to become mandatory. The continuation of changes in organizations, and especially the introduction of strategic planning and strategic target concepts in the early 1980s, has found application for HRM (Jackson & Mathis, 1997, p. 19).

In the late 1970s and early 1980s, great advances were made in new technologies. This has led to changes in the nature and content of many tasks and has also affected traditional personnel and organizational systems. The reason for this is a higher degree of integrating different production processes and allocating production responsibilities to lower levels of the organization. This has increased the importance of human contribution (Smith, 1987, pp. 80–91). In other words, it is the increase in the importance of the remaining tasks due to the computerization of many jobs (Beirneve & Ramsay, 1992, pp. 11–30).

The Effect of Digitization on HRM

Digital transformation deeply affects different areas of society, economy and business models. It is an element that enables the digitalization of services, processes and value chains (Schallmo & Daniel, 2018, pp. 1–2). It is important for businesses to be ready and proactive toward change, resources/capabilities and their use, and how they anticipate and cope with the uncertainties brought about by change. In the business world, where aggressive competition conditions exist, one of the key elements for change management is human resources (El-Dirani et al., 2019, p. 1).

HRM systems are realized with the support of digital transformation, which provides tools that facilitate the acquisition, recording and updating of data related to the existing knowledge, skills and abilities of the personnel in the enterprises and accessing the relevant data if necessary. Thus, it is effective in making faster and more effective decisions for businesses (Hopkins & Markham, 2003, pp. 57–58).

The use of technology simplifies existing human resources functions, but digitization affects HRM more than just facilitating day-to-day administrative work. Digitalization has effects on functions such as human resource planning, recruitment and selection, performance management, reward management, health and safety, employee relations and job design. However, digitalization has also added new tasks to the human resources function. Digitization has added the responsibility of ensuring that human resources in the organization are capital in harmony with the strategic needs of the digital age (Fenech et al., 2019, p. 168). One of the most important effects of digitalization on human resources is that it allows flexible working. Regardless of time and place, through online platforms, employees can perform their jobs and managers can monitor and control them. This is a positive contribution of digitalization to businesses in terms of both cost savings and employee satisfaction.

There are certain difficulties and benefits that organizations will face in the application of digitalization in HRM. The difficulties in implementation are in the form of choosing the right technological tools, overcoming the current organizational culture and managing the expectations of different generations of employees. The benefits that emerge in organizations that provide digital transformation in HRM can be listed, attracting the attention of new generation talents, developing and protecting them, effective and fast human resources operations and leaner human resources departments (Sivathanu & Pillai, 2018, p. 7).

The Concept of Digital HRM

Digital HRM is *sine qua non* for the successful implementation of an effective digital strategy. Thus, it is important to acknowledge that digital HRM should be conceptualized through the general digitalization of organizations (Strohmeier, 2020).

Considering this crucial importance, digital HRM is expected to have a crucial impact on company performance. Likewise, previous studies argued that HRM effectiveness is linked to the use of e-HRM solutions (Bondarouk et al., 2009). However, nowadays, the digital HRM definition has yet to be established and consented to among researchers (Zhou et al., 2020). First, Bondarouk and Ruël (2009, p. 507) have defined e-HRM as "an umbrella term covering all possible integration mechanisms and contents between HRM and Information Technologies aiming at creating value within and across organizations for targeted employees and management". From a strategic perspective, Mondore et al. (2011) emphasize HRM analytics by explaining the direct effect of employees on important business outcomes.

Attempting to improve the link between HR processes and decisions and organizational performance, Marler and Boudreau (2017, p. 15) defined digital HRM as "A HR practice activated by information technology that uses descriptive, visual, and statistical analyses of data related to HR processes, human capital, organizational performance, and external economic benchmarks to establish a business impact and enable data-driven decision-making". Now, the digital transformation has completely reached and changed the entire firm's activities and models, including those in HRM functions, to take full advantage of both opportunities and changes of digital technologies (Demirkan et al., 2016). According to Bharadwaj et al. (2013), the definition of digital business strategy must go beyond the traditional view, thinking of IT strategy as a function within firms. Based on this definition, a digital HRM strategy could be formulated and executed by leveraging digital assets to generate differential business value to firms. From this conceptual clarification perspective, we can suggest that developing and sustaining a digital talent management strategy is required to achieve a sustainable competitive advantage and to capture the full potential of digital transformation, including transforming HRM and other functions.

Benefits and Disadvantages of Digital HRM

Beyond dealing with challenges associated with e-HRM, firms need to capitalize on the benefits of digital HRM. It is stated that technological advancements will continue to alter the nature of those occupations (Levy & Murnane, 2013). Regarding the advantages and disadvantages of the intersection between IT and HRM, Bondarouk and Brewster (2016) argued that the advantages of e-HRM are not restricted to improving employment outcomes. E-HRM must be enacted by human actors in the management of HRM activities and processes. Based on previous overview analyses, they claimed that the adoption of e-HRM is linked to cost-cutting, efficiency, flexible services and employee involvement. On the other hand, Rotman (2013) stated that automation and digital technology are partially to blame for the current labor shortage. Since automation is frequently employed to make human labor more productive, it's difficult to identify the net impact on jobs (Rotman, 2013); the impact of digital transformation on job creation and job destruction mechanisms have yet to be investigated. Thereby, e-HRM eliminates the "HR middleman" (Bondarouk et al., 2009). Recent literature emphasized that the introduction of automation threatens more than 47 percent of the US workforce, including middle- and lower-skilled jobs (Pluess, 2015). Opportunely, technology will allow workers greater opportunities to be more efficient and productive by organizing their work and through flexible working hours. Besides the complexity of HR phenomena, using digital HR tools, employees can conduct real-time assessments of their colleagues' performance (Tambe et al., 2019). The managers' responsibility is to make data sharing a culture inside the organization and between team members by fostering employees' involvement in such practices. It contributes also to making many jobs safer, easier and more productive (Rotman, 2013). Nowadays, HRM practices in the digital age play a crucial role in the transformation process of companies (Nicolás-Agustín et al., 2021). Nevertheless, sustainable e-HRM systems are positively associated with firm performance (Bag et al., 2021). Given the complexity of HR phenomena and the fact that digital practices differ across organizations and departments, it is crucial to specify which HR questions to investigate to fully support the organization's digital transformation and to leverage new opportunities to create from information resources. Previous systematic reviews within the area of HRM reveal the importance of digital technologies in identifying and managing talent and predicting work-related issues (e.g., Margherita, 2022; McDonnell et al., 2017; Vrontis et al., 2021). These advanced technologies may ultimately improve HR activities and talent profiling, which may concern different talent management decisions that imply talent acquisition, talent development and talent retention. From this perspective, a company could gain a sustainable competitive advantage by efficiently managing employees with digital intelligence and digital technologies, that must support employees to grow up digital-related human resources capabilities. In the same vein, the positive impact of digital HRM can be observed through the diffusion of advanced recruitment platforms providing digital intelligence resources and talent experience management platforms (Margherita, 2022). Moreover, information technology facilitates team cooperation and coordination in complex and dynamic task environments. Vrontis et al. (2021) highlighted in their systematic review the effects of AI (artificial intelligence), robotics and advanced technologies on HRM strategies and activities at the organizational level and at the employee level. Their results show that we are still years away from wide-ranging consequences on HRM and levels of employment. However, the same technologies produce many types of human workers. Similarly, Chuang and Graham (2018) conclude that essential attributes of human behavior (human skills) cannot be substituted by automation technology, preventing the loss of some jobs. Thus, digital HRM improves the tracking and control of HR actions by speeding up transaction processing and reducing information errors (Bondarouk et al., 2009).

According to Sivathanu and Pillai (2018), the age of Smart HR 4.0 adoption will have the following benefits:

1 Attract, develop and retain new-age talent;
2 Efficient and faster HR operations; and
3 Leaner HR departments.

Benefits associated with digital HRM can be summarized as follows:

- Cost savings and expediting the HR processes
- Efficiency and organizational effectiveness
- Harmonization and integration of HR activities
- Promote high levels of employee involvement and participation
- Support and enable better decision-making in HR

To recapitulate the benefits due to this transformation, Ruël et al. (2004) suggest that a company should anticipate to achieve specific goals if it follows the digital HRM path, which covers an improvement in HR's strategic orientation, an improvement in client attention and satisfaction and a cost or efficiency reduction.

Digital HRM Functions

HR practices in the modern era should support the evolving employee–organization relationship (Bissola & Imperatori, 2020). Thus, Ruël et al. (2004) stated that the introduction of e-HRM is accompanied by the decentralization of HR tasks. Accordingly, in terms of the consequences of e-HRM for the HR department, the devolution of the HR department results in fewer administrative tasks for the HR department and a greater emphasis on the organization's strategic goals. Line managers as stakeholders in HRM, divided into middle-level and front-line managers (Bos-Nehles, 2010), may play an important strategic role in the design and dissemination of information and the implementation of HRM practices (Bondarouk & Brewster, 2016). Van Kruining (2017) suggested that the increased time spent in "personnel administration" can be caused by activities dealing with the implementation of digital HRM systems. In this context, the term "implementing" consists of making something work, putting something into practice or having something realized (Ruël et al., 2004). Currently, HRM managers use automation, chatbots, machine learning, blockchain, simulation, optimization, big data analytics, intelligent learning platforms and other emerging technologies while carrying out their human resources functions and considering in the artificial manner their intelligent resources. This may concern different hierarchical levels, HR activities and HRM policies. HR activities involve HR functions as well as recruiting, training and job performance (Vrontis et al., 2021). For instance, it's highlighted that big data can be applied to every stage of the hiring process as well as the entire workforce planning and management cycle (Isson & Harriott, 2016). Regarding the use of these Smart HR 4.0 tools that emerged from the Industry 4.0 technology, the results of a qualitative study conducted by Pillai et al. (2021) revealed that AI and chatbots are extensively used for recruitment and selection. Additionally, they revealed the use of augmented reality, virtual reality and mobile learning applications to ensure ubiquitous training of employees. Meanwhile, the study highlighted the use of big data analytics to better understand various HR performance metrics and to create predictive models for attrition and getting quality talent. Thereby, automation in HR functions is used in improving recruitment processes (Gupta et al., 2018). While smart factory requires the complementary nature of human–automation collaboration to increase productivity and quality, utilizing, mutually, the capabilities of humans and industrial automation devices (Evjemo et al., 2020), the HR departments across different organizations require Smart HR 4.0 implementation by changing both organization structure as well as leadership style (Sivathanu & Pillai, 2018). Vrontis et al. (2021) reported the facilitating role of AI algorithms in the management of HR processes.

In today's digital world, business leaders shift their recruiting investment priorities since Smart HR 4.0 paints a vivid canvas for digital transformation in the HR functions (Sivathanu & Pillai, 2018). Consequently, organizations would be able to manage their human resources effectively and to promote leadership characteristics and skills among employees that foster the capabilities of effective leaders in the workplace, which are ultimately required for their performance and sustainable advantage. Given this, the HR function could generate or comparative advantage through digital technologies when leveraging digital resources by attracting, hiring, developing, profilin, and retaining talented employees. One of the major purposes of recent technologies is to establish human–machine interaction and to connect the world to the future of business. Accordingly, companies need to develop a digital culture supported by various stakeholders to increase the commitment of the current employees toward the digital transformation of the workplace since digital business strategy cannot be conceived independently of the business ecosystem, alliances, partnerships and competitors (Bharadwaj et al., 2013). To deal with complexity and uncertainty, HRM professionals need more quantitative approaches based on "people science". They are also called to change the employees' mindset by creating an analytical mindset for HR professionals. Beyond the purely technical aspects of digital implications, digital HRM effectiveness is virtually equivalent to achieving effective human capital management by taking into account the digitalization, automatio, and robotization of production processes associated with the era of Industry 4.0. Furthermore, some activities are managed in the cloud, different platforms are used to manage talents teamwork, and digital agents, called also personal virtual assistants or AI helpers that are used purposefully to act on behalf of customers as well as for carrying out a range of HRM tasks, the digital HRM has to be considered now as a major source of competitive advantage and lever to identify and promote competitively superior human resources while achieving HR and organizational performance.

Conclusion and Recommendations

Digitization in HR is still a puzzle similar to the difficult challenge of establishing a suitable balance between humans and automation. The outcomes of this chapter provide recommendations for HRM professionals and policymakers and point out the necessity of taking both the challenges and benefits of digital HRM into account when developing digital business strategies. It will be essential to consider multiple stakeholders of the intersection between HRM and technology, HRM professionals, line managers and employees, external people and agencies (Bondarouk & Brewster, 2016). Particularly, HRM professionals should rethink their social responsibility in light of technological influence on workers (Chuang & Graham, 2018). Nevertheless, advanced technologies and AI technologies in HRM might consider possible challenges and risks (Vrontis et al., 2021). Consequently, digital HRM requires strategic orientation and a broader construct. Nowadays, firms should be able to employ new technological solutions to perform their HRM departments in the era of Industry 4.0. However, many questions need to be answered when transforming the HRM functions. Companies are invited to reflect how, when and where these technologies must be adopted. How are companies preparing themselves for intelligent automation? How are companies balancing problems with human–robot collaboration? And would the implementation of digital HRM bring resilient employees to prevent or overcome crisis during the COVID-19 pandemic and beyond? We still have yet to fulfill the answers related to the digital puzzle. Many important questions about human capital management and empirical studies on the development of leadership in Industry 4.0 are still required.

References

Bag, S., Dhamija, P., Pretorius, J. H. C., Chowdhury, A. H., & Giannakis, M. (2022). Sustainable electronic human resource management systems and firm performance: An empirical study. *International Journal of Manpower*, *43*(1), 32–51. https://doi.org/10.1108/IJM-02-2021-0099

Bass, B. M. (1994). Continuity and change in the evolution of work and human resource management. *Human Resource Management*, *33*(1), 3–31. https://doi.org/10.1002/hrm.3930330103

Baysal, A. C. (1993). *Çalışma Yaşamında İnsan*. İşletme Fakültesi Yayınları.

Beirne, M., & Ramsay, H. (1992). Manna or monstrous regiment? Technology, control, and Domocracy in the workplace. In M. Beirne & H. Ramsay (Eds.), *Information technology and workplace democracy*. Routledge.

Bharadwaj, A., El Sawy, O. A., Pavlou, P. A., & Venkatraman, N. (2013). Digital business strategy: Toward a next generation of insights. *MIS Quarterly*, *37*(2), 471–482. https://doi.org/10.25300/MISQ/2013/37:2.3

Bissola, R., & Imperatori, B. (2020). *Hrm 4.0 for human-centered organizations*. Emerald Publishing.

Bondarouk, T. V., & Brewster, C. (2016). Conceptualising the future of Hrm and technology research. *International Journal of Human Resource Management*, *27*(21), 2652–2671. https://doi.org/10.1080/09585192.2016.1232296

Bondarouk, T. V., & Ruël, H. J. M. (2009). Electronic human resource management: Challenges in the digital era. *International Journal of Human Resource Management*, *20*(3), 505–514. https://doi.org/10.1080/09585190802707235

Bondarouk, T. V., Ruël, H. J. M., & van der Heijden, B. (2009). E-Hrm effectiveness in a public sector organization: A multi-stakeholder perspective. *International Journal of Human Resource Management*, *20*(3), 578–590. https://doi.org/10.1080/09585190802707359

Bos-Nehles, A. (2010). *The line makes the difference: Line managers as effective Hr partners* [Doctoral thesis, University of Twente].

Brown, T. M. (1952). Habit persistence and lags in consumer behaviour. *Econometrica: Journal of the Econometric Society, 20*(3), 355–371.

Brynjolfsson, E., & McAfee, A. (2014). *The second machine age: Work, progress, and prosperity in a time of brilliant technologies.* WW Norton & Company.

Chuang, S., & Graham, C. M. (2018). Embracing the sobering reality of technological influences on jobs, employment and human resource development: A systematic literature review. *European Journal of Training and Development, 42*(7/8), 400–416. https://doi.org/10.1108/EJTD-03-2018-0030Cingöz, A. (2011). *SİKY ve SİKY'nin Örgütsel Performans ve İç Girişimcilik Üzerine Etkileri"* [Doktora Tezi, E.Ü., İşletme Anabilim Dalı].

Colbert, A., Yee, N., & George, G. (2016). The digital workforce and the workplace of the future. *Academy of Management Journal, 59*(3), 731–739.

Demirkan, H., Spohrer, J. C., & Welser, J. J. (2016). Digital innovation and strategic transformation. *IT Professional, 18*(6), 14–18. https://doi.org/10.1109/MITP.2016.115

El-Dirani, A., Hussein, M. M., & Hejase, H. J. (2019). The role of human resources in change management: An exploratory study in Lebanon. *Journal of Middle East and North Africa, 5*(6), 1–13.

Evjemo, L. D., Gjerstad, T., Grøtli, E. I., & Sziebig, G. (2020). Trends in smart manufacturing: Role of humans and industrial robots in smart factories. *Current Robotics Reports, 1*(2), 35–41. https://doi.org/10.1007/s43154-020-00006-5

Fenech, R., Baguant, P., & Ivanov, D. (2019). The changing role of human resource management in an era of digital transformation. *International Journal of Entrepreneurship, 22*(2), 166–175.

Fırat, O. Z., & Fırat, S. Ü. (2017). Endüstri 4.0 yolculuğunda trendler ve robotlar. *İstanbul Üniversitesi İşletme Fakültesi Dergisi, 46*(2), 211–223.

Gupta, P., Fernandes, S. F., & Jain, M. (2018). Automation in recruitment: A new frontier. *Journal of Information Technology Teaching Cases, 8*(2), 118–125. https://doi.org/10.1057/s41266-018-0042-x

Gush, K., Cambridge, G., & Smith, R. (2006). *CSIR, the digital doorway – Minimally invasive education in Africa.* Conference papers. Retrieved January 2, 2022, from http://citeseerx.ist.psu.edu/viewdoc/download? Doi=10.1.1.465.4485&rep=rep1&type=pdf.

Harrell, T. W. (1953). Industrial psychology. *Annual Review of Psychology, 4*(1), 215–238.

Hopkins, B., & Markham, J. (2003). *E-Hr: Using intranets to improve the effectiveness of your people.* Gower Publishing Publishing Limited.

Isson, J. P., & Harriott, J. S. (2016). People analytics in the era of big data: Changing the way you attract, acquire. In *Develop, and retain talent.* John Wiley & Sons.

Jackson, J. H., & Mathis, R. L. (1997). *Human resource management.* West Publishing Company.

Kane, G. C., & Ransbotham, S. (2016). Content as community regulator: The recursive relationship between consumption and contribution in open collaboration communities. *Organization Science, 27*(5), 1258–1274.

Lepak, D. P., & Snell, S. A. (1998). Virtual HR: Strategic human resource management in the 21st century. *Human Resource Management Review, 8*(3), 215–234. https://doi.org/10.1016/S1053-4822(98)90003-1

Levy, F., & Murnane, R. J. (2013). *Dancing with robots: Human skills for computerized work.* Third Way NEXT.

Margherita, A. (2022). Human resources analytics: A systematization of research topics and directions for future research. *Human Resource Management Review, 32*(2). https://doi.org/10.1016/j.hrmr.2020.100795

Markus, M. L., & Loebbecke, C. (2013). Commiditized digital processes and business community platforms: New opportunities and challenges for digital business strategies. *MIS Quarterly, 37*(2), 649–652.

Marler, J. H., & Boudreau, J. W. (2017). An evidence-based review of Hr analytics. *International Journal of Human Resource Management, 28*(1), 3–26. https://doi.org/10.1080/095 85192.2016.1244699

McDonnell, A., Collings, D. G., Mellahi, K., & Schuler, R. (2017). Talent management: A systematic review and future prospects. *European Journal of International Management, 11*(1), 86–128. https://doi.org/10.1504/EJIM.2017.081253

Mert, G. (2020). Kurumların stratejik yönetim Süreçlerinde Dijitalleşmenin rolü. *Journal OD Social, Humanities and Aministrative Sciences, 6*(22), 41–58.

Mitra, S., & Dangwal, R. (2010). Self organizing systems of learning. *British Journal of Educational Technology, 41*(5), 672–688.

Mohiuddin, M., Azad, M. S. A., Ahmed, S., Ed-Dafali, S., & Reza, M. N. H. (2022). Evolution of industry 4.0 and its implications for international business. In M. Mohiuddin, J. Wang, M. S. A. Azad, & S. Ahmed (Eds.), *Global trade in the emerging business environment.* IntechOpen. https://doi.org/10.5772/intechopen.101764

Mondore, S., Douthitt, S., & Carson, M. (2011). Maximizing the impact and effectiveness of Hr analytics to drive business outcomes. *People and Strategy, 34*(2), 21–27.

Nicolás-Agustín, Á., Jiménez-Jiménez, D., & Maeso-Fernandez, F. (2022). The role of human resource practices in the implementation of digital transformation. *International Journal of Manpower* [Ahead-of-print]. https://doi.org/10.1108/IJM-03-2021-0176

Pillai, R., Yadav, S., Sivathanu, B., Kaushik, N., & Goel, P. (2021). Use of 4.0 (I4.0) technology in Hrm: A pathway toward Shrm 4.0 and Hr performance. *Foresight* [Ahead-of-print]. https://doi.org/10.1108/FS-06-2021-0128

Pluess, J. D. (2015). Good jobs in the age of automation: Challenges and opportunities for the private sector. *Business for Social Responsibility, BSR, 33.*

Rotman, D. (2013). How technology is destroying jobs. *Technology Review, 16*(4), 28–35.

Ruël, H., Bondarouk, T., & Looise, J. K. (2004). E-Hrm: Innovation or irritation. An explorative empirical study in five large companies on web-based Hrm. *Management Revu, 15*(3), 364–380. https://doi.org/10.5771/0935-9915-2004-3-364

Schallmo, A., & Daniel, R. (2018). *Digital transformation now! Guiding the successful digitalization of your business model.* Springer Science+Business Media, LLC.

Shartle, C. L. (1950). Leadership aspects of administrative behavior. *Advanced Management Journal, 15*(11), 12–15.

Sivathanu, B., & Pillai, R. (2018). Smart HR 4.0 – How industry 4.0 is disrupting HR. *Human Resource Management International Digest, 26*(4), 7–11. https://doi.org/10.1108/HRMID-04-2018-0059

Smith, C. (1987). *Technical workers class, labour and unionism.* Macmillan.

Stenmark, D. (2001). Leveraging tacit organizational knowledge. *Journal of Management Information Systems, 17*(3), 9–24.

Stone, D. L., Deadrick, D. L., Lukaszewski, K. M., & Johnson, R. (2015). The influence of technology on the future of human resource management. *Human Resource Management Review, 25*(2), 216–231. https://doi.org/10.1016/j.hrmr.2015.01.002

Stone, D. L., & Dulebohn, J. H. (2013). Emerging issues in theory and research on electronic human resource management (eHRM). *Human Resource Management Review, 23*(1), 1–5. https://doi.org/10.1016/j.hrmr.2012.06.001

Strohmeier, S. (2020). Digital human resource management: A conceptual clarification. *German Journal of Human Resource Management: Zeitschrift für Personalforschung, 34*(3), 345–365. https://doi.org/10.1177/2397002220921131

Tambe, P., Cappelli, P., & Yakubovich, V. (2019). Artificial intelligence in human resources management: Challenges and a path forward. *California Management Review, 61*(4), 15–42. https://doi.org/10.1177/0008125619867910

Van Kruining, I. (2017). The dis-app-earance of Hrm: Impact of digitization on the Hrm profession. In *Electronic HRM in the smart era*. Emerald Publishing Limited.

Vrontis, D., Christofi, M., Pereira, V., Tarba, S., Makrides, A., & Trichina, E. (2021). Artificial intelligence, robotics, advanced technologies and human resource management: A systematic review. *International Journal of Human Resource Management*, 1–30. https://doi.org/10.1080/09585192.2020.1871398

Wayne, F. C. (1995). *Managing human resources management*. McGraw Hill.

Zhou, Y., Liu, G., Chang, X., & Wang, L. (2020). The impact of Hrm digitalization on firm performance: Investigating three-way interactions. *Asia Pacific Journal of Human Resources*, *59*(1), 20–43. https://doi.org/10.1111/1744-7941.12258

7

DIGITAL PROJECT MANAGEMENT

Muhammad Usman Tariq and Lukman Raimi

Introduction

Digital project management is a new practice driven by AI (artificial intelligence), robotics, and other disruptive technologies in contemporary business environments. Due to this, there are various methods recognized by professionals and scholars for digital project management in workplaces. Some scholars associate project management with a digital ability. Some do not understand the association of project management with a digital aptitude. Other researchers utilize it correspondently with information technology project management. Therefore, it is essential to understand the actual concept of digital management. It is about getting the tasks done digitally. Perhaps that seems too basic. Digital project management has a modest objective, but its functionality can be extended to implement multiple complicated tools to accomplish the tasks (Whyte, 2019). Conceptually, digital project management is the procedure of organizing and implementing these digital projects. This means bringing together developers, firms, stakeholders, content writers, marketers, and other employees engaged in the task together. Moreover, they team up to conclude a job within an assigned timeline and financial budget by utilizing software solutions (Moreira et al., 2018).

In view of the importance of digital project management in the newly emerging workplace, there is a need for a more conceptual discourse of the subject from multidisciplinary perspectives. This chapter responds to this call by discussing the concept of digital project management in the workplace and related matters. Apart from the introduction, there are five sections in this chapter. The next section discusses the people behind digital management and the rise of digital project management. Then, the following section reviews the literature to gain richer insights into the differences between digital project management and traditional project management. Next, innovative digital project management is explained.

DOI: 10.4324/9781003283386-9

The following section provides guidance on how to develop enhanced relationships by leading digital project management. Finally, the last section concludes with a discussion of the roles of digital project managers and digital tools required for effective and efficient project management.

People Behind Digital Management

Digital project management needs diversified skills and strategies. For example, the content available on YouTube, the blogger or influencer, or the financial application that maintains the financial records did not develop instantly. The individuals behind these tools and videos are required to explore the concept behind the project, its benefits, audience or which people may use these tools, expenses, and the research about the necessary technology. The diversified segments involve digital strategy, technological progress, user experience, content writing, business analysis, and design. Digital project management takes many strategies and unifies all the segments required to complete a digital project (Sepasgozar et al., 2019).

Rise of Digital Project Management

Over the previous decade, digital project management has developed into a more organized and known domain. Before recent years, the designation of a digital project manager was not available. Individuals performed their tasks under different designations, for example, developers, agency founders, account managers, and digital marketers. As the requirement for high-quality content across businesses rose, the title digital project manager was introduced. As technology evolves and progresses, there may be an essential requirement for advanced digital project management. The concept of digital project management is a relatively new and swiftly emerging field. Perhaps one search brings up thousands of job openings from digital project managers. As this concept advances, tracking its progress in a continuously evolving digital environment may be vital (Snow et al., 2017).

There is a variation between traditional project management and digital project management. Digital projects include website design, app development, execution, and planning of the whole marketing campaign. These projects are not much more accessible than traditional ones; the persistent operational parts and their fluidity can make them challenging to strategize and manage. This is why project management procedures are not always efficient (Demirkesen & Ozorhon, 2017).

Digital Project Management vs. Traditional Project Management

There are various comparisons between digital and traditional projects – both need groups to function together, and both require services and products provided promptly according to the budget and the scope. Both project management types include guidance meetings, arranging resources, carrying out collateral, and regular monitoring of specific tasks. The significant difference is that digital project management is mainly carried out online. It includes merging various technologies and needs a comprehensive understanding of the online platforms. In addition, things modify so quickly in the digital world that digital project management mostly understands balancing project requirements with evolving trends (Cooper & Sommer, 2018).

Stages of a Digital Project

The following are some four prime phases of the digital project:

- **Initiation**: It includes commencing the project and bringing the clients onboard in the proper manner to confirm the project makes a success.
- **Planning**: It includes plotting the scope, timelines, and handing over the tasks to related experts.
- **Execution**: This is the stage where the prime assets are developed.
- **Wrap Up**: It includes delivering outcomes and cross-examining all partners included.

To a great extent, it is not diverse to a conventional project management impression. However, it becomes much more complicated when there is an addition of technologies and tools into the combination and complement in the forwards and backwards reviews and edits (Mikalsen et al., 2018).

Vital Task Management Software

It helps in planning, tracking, and monitoring all the features of the tasks in every project or disintegrating them further with subprograms (Biazzo et al., 2020).

Lead Tasks With Coordination

Digital project management is vital; however, research depicts that firms that invest in verified management practices misspend twenty-eight times less money than those that do not consider demonstrated project management (Shivakumar, 2018).

Project Management Methods

There are three primary project management methods:

- **Waterfall**: A conventional project management type that includes disintegrating a project into consecutive stages, where every step commences only once the former stage is complete.

- **Agile**: This disintegrates projects in various steps and supports continuous association and persistent repetition at every phase.
- **Lean**: Created in the 1950s, this kind of project management increases the value and decreases wastage.

More advanced management technologies involve kanban, scrum, and the mixture of two known as scrumban (Raith et al., 2017).

Management of Each Stage of the Digital Project

An efficient digital project requires competent management. With so many switching segments, it is obvious to lose track of what has been done and who performs which tasks. Therefore, it makes sense to disintegrate the digital project into easy-to-understand stages instead of considering the project altogether (Damström, 2020).

Level 0: Initiation

Initiation commences before the actual start of the digital project. It includes getting the documents ready and accumulating the resources required to finish the project reasonably. This level can also have analysis calls, recruiting contractors, and getting new clients on board (Marder et al., 2021).

Preparation of Resources and Documenting Them

Most of the time, the preparation levels of a digital project are just as vital as the execution levels. Ultimately, things can go from bad to worse if there is an omission of a significant feature or if the client does not get all the required information to ensure that the project commences well.

When considering documentation and making required essential resources ready before a project is commenced, the following points are considered:

- A potent contract
- Developing new digital files and folders
- Developing a new project in the project management device
- A client offer that summarizes what must be done and indicates its completion time (Mitrofanova et al., 2021)

Onboarding

Efficacious onboarding is vital for an uninterrupted digital project. It is the segment where management provides clients with all the data they may require for the project period, involving the tools it may use, how the firm functions, the primary communication methods, and the foremost representative. Management may also require bringing new contractors on board who know the tools and procedures necessary for the project (Ershadi et al., 2021).

Constructing a Team

The concluding segment of the initiation stage is gathering people as a team for the project. It includes assuring the efficient skills and talent employed on a project and allowing each opting team member to know what the firm expects from them (Kerzner, 2019).

Level 1: Planning

Once the management completes onboarding and all documents are signed and sent, it moves to the next level of digital project management, i.e., planning; the firms function out all the twists and strategize to ensure that all the assets can be developed on time (Georgieva, 2018).

Make a Task List

The project is done with many tasks, and managers can swiftly face difficulties if they do not know what they are or what order they should be done in. Managers can start by making a task list, including small and large tasks, that can be combined to develop the whole project. Managers should include client calls and reviews; regardless of a tangible outcome, they create a vital procedure segment (Morcov et al., 2021).

Make a Budget

While the budget can undoubtedly emerge at the initiation level, when the manager begins to outline tasks included, they can get particular with it. Making a budget involves creating asset costs and includes budgeting for contractors, materials, and any add-ons (Baltasar & Breton, 2020).

Develop a Project Timetable

This is where the planning level connects. Managers take their task list and rank them dependent on what should be done first to complete other tasks. There is mainly an organic plan to the manners projects evolve, but it primarily assists in splitting the project into levels and then making task building blocks for all of those stages (Faub, 2020).

Allocating Tasks

When managers get a list of tasks and a schedule, they can allot each section to the relevant group member. However, first, managers must ascertain that the team is informed about who is working on what and has possible deadlines to finish their tasks (Ershadi et al., 2021).

Level 2: Execution

The execution stage of project management is the most comprehensive. It is when things move ahead and the project commences to unfold (Morcov et al., 2021).

Handle Tasks

Managers must observe the tasks being completed and what level team members are at with the project. It assists in having an efficient task management tool that summarizes the project and the projected deadlines for asset delivery. Mainly on lengthy projects, managers must regularly check the completed tasks. Therefore, it can assure them to move forward smoothly (Ershadi et al., 2021).

Collaboration

There can be numerous stakeholders that managers must associate with during a digital project. It might be clients, team members, contractors, or other involved parties, and collaboration must be managed properly for the smooth run of the project. It includes selecting suitable mediums to collaborate on, offering smooth communication, and holding periodic check-ins to check the collaborators' satisfaction levels (Morcov et al., 2021).

Managing Time

During a digital project, problems mainly occur. For example, it might take more time to identify a reliable contractor, or it might be that the first round of improvisations was not as correctly received as the manager expected. It is where the role of managing time is essential. Additionally, deciding time frames for even the most minor tasks supports additional time for failing tasks (Ershadi et al., 2021).

Reporting

Frequent reporting on task progress and delivered assets ensures that all included parties can observe the completed tasks and what is still in progress. It takes all the parties in the loop and supports the solidification of the subsequent steps (Morcov et al., 2021).

Level 3: Wrap Up

The wrapping and finishing of the project are as significant as the initial levels, so managers should not get laid back at this point (Ershadi et al., 2021).

Develop and Deliver the Output

Managers must keep a check and hand over the assets developed during the digital project. If managers keep things organized during this process, it can help to omit any mishaps while collaborating with other team members (Baltasar & Breton, 2020).

Evaluation and Editing

There is a possible chance that stakeholders may desire to make some modifications to the final outputs. Therefore, when the evaluation and editing procedure occurs, it should be handled as a mini project distinct from the actual one. Managers may also consider the previous levels for this segment of the procedure (Shivakumar, 2018).

Probing

Managers have to engage everyone to complete the project. Motivate collaborators, stakeholders, and contractors to recognize the best part of the project and which segment had issues and will require improvement next time. Managing a digital project is a learning procedure, and if managers examine and debrief it closely, it can be easier for future projects (Baltasar & Breton, 2020).

Digital Project Management Tools and Software

Management of a digital project becomes significantly easy when there is an incorporation of beneficial software and tools. It can help collaborate by providing everyone with accessibility to the deadlines and task lists. In addition, digital software for project management enhances performance.

The tools managers consider for digital management involve the following:

- **Collaboration tools:** These tools make it easier for several participants to obtain accessibility to modify assets.
- **Communication tools:** These tools boost communication levels between participants and offer a space where feedback and questions are entertained.
- **Timetable tools:** Managers set time scales for every task and provide an outline of the ongoing tasks and the tasks that still require completion.
- **Listing tools:** Managers should review completed tasks digitally and offer team participants the accessibility to finish tasks.
- **Asset administration tools:** Managers should make a secure place for assets to be accessed and stored for all stakeholders and team participants.
- **Datebook tools:** Managers should tangibly fix tasks that all people can review and access (Baltasar & Breton, 2020).

Innovative Digital Project Management

Learning digital project management is a procedure, and one cannot master it overnight. Instead, it is a consistent modification, measurement, experiment, and tracking task to observe what is working and what is not (Whyte, 2019).

Make an Efficient Workflow

Once managers complete various digital projects, they can understand what is best and what is not. After every project, managers can edit their workflows to modify tracking and complete the tasks. They should take suggestions from all the team participants and make the procedure collaborative (Shivakumar, 2018).

Enhance Team and Project Productivity

It is significant to make every person as productive as possible to make a project move forward. This means that managers should always keep collaborators informed, offer consistent feedback, and provide team participants with the necessary tools to complete the project successfully (Mitrofanova et al., 2021).

Developing Enhanced Relationships by Leading Digital Project Management

Efficient digital project management requires all team members and stakeholders to participate and take an active role in the procedure. As a result, managers skillfully make plans, carry out executions, and complete projects until the deadlines use the set budget, and they can quickly develop enhanced relationships with team participants, contractors, stakeholders, and clients (Whyte, 2019).

Project managers have to learn the art of merging to diversified environments. Sometimes they have to handle enraged developers about server problems and use the best techniques to solve the issue; sometimes, they have to discuss the financial reporting with the director. Digital project management is more easily trackable than a conventional project, as most required tasks are completed using technologies. Digital tasks can be tracked automatically and reported with different tools, offering an enhanced base for unfailing time reports and assessment. These assessments are essential for predicting budgets and deadlines and are necessary for the business's progress. An efficient digital project manager should have the ability to communicate with the company and technical teams. They should have the ability to comprehend the terms of both parts and be the channel that shifts essential information between the two. Obtaining the outline is vital, and deep excavation is necessary (Faub, 2020).

> **Software development:** Project managers should regularly update software and keep the alignment of the software with the current business strategy. They should confirm that every team member has equal knowledge (Shivakumar, 2018).

User experience/user design: Project managers should work with user design and experience teams to provide the best-quality output based on prioritization and existing business strategy. User experience ultimately helps make the customer happy and capture loyal customers (Sepasgozar et al., 2019).

Quality control: Quality control works best with user experience. Project managers should keep the teams aligned and confirm consistent progressive, quality-based, and proactive progress. They should emphasize the quality value for the customer.

Business research: Project managers should ensure that the firm progresses toward a profitable stage and attains enough profits. They should assess the project portfolio and emphasize the most treasured clients and projects. Value is the prime factor for a prosperous business (Mitrofanova et al., 2021).

Strategy: Managers should create and adjust the strategies regularly, as strategy is the principal basis for the rest of the business. It is essential to ensure that it is flexible and robust

Management of accounts: Project managers should ensure that all the associations and clients are involved. A prominent segment of a streaming business is to develop relationships between people (Shivakumar, 2018).

Teamwork: A cooperative environment across teams is possibly the essential element of a robust and successful business. Project managers should ensure the involvement and satisfaction of every team member. These people create the value that clients want. The culture of the firm is transparent to the clients. The utilization of project management tools can be beneficial, as it offers the project manager a focal point that links the entire team and becomes the final space for all the files and data. If a task requires transferring to another individual, it only needs a button click, and that specific team participant has everything he requires, all the estimations, files, or comments. Alternatively, if the project manager needs an additional person to work on the task, they can easily select someone who is available and get things completed in less time. There are various efficient tools with multiple combinations of user experiences and features; forecasting utilizes machine learning to predict future estimations at the task level. It uses existing data accumulated on the business and organizations, the project type, people engaged, and the titles assigned to all the tasks. These are segments of the algorithm that support the time and budget prediction in all projects. Consequently, it provides the most actionable and reliable visions about the business and delivers project managers to offer productive projects promptly within the assigned budget (Whyte, 2019).

Digital Project Manager

The digital project manager brings all the project segments together and delivers the outcome (Shivakumar, 2018).

The Role of a Digital Manager

The digital manager plays an essential role in creating digital projects. A digital project manager is an individual who has to take on different responsibilities. He carries out the responsibility of a project manager, quality analyst, sales manager, business specialist, digital policymaker, and SEO counselor. Most know about fine photography and can discuss HTML code with developers. They have to communicate with team participants, clients, and stakeholders about the project. similarly, various project managers in the digital environment define themselves as those who bring discipline to the disorder of the project.

Project managers work as leaders, policymakers, correspondents, predictors, implementors, and planners. On a regular day, firms can expect them to:

- Handle schedules, tools, budgets, and people
- Monitoring all the details
- Manage all the departments with flexibility and empathy
- Involving the entire team and taking responsibility for the completion of the project (Mitrofanova et al., 2021)

Due to the flexibility of the role, specialists in this position come from diversified backgrounds. Digital project managers arrange, communicate, and direct a team to complete the project.

The task list of a digital project manager can involve the following:

- Developing project plans, timetables, and financial budgets
- Forwarding those plans with all the participants included
- Allocating tasks to team participants
- Fixing deadlines
- Purposefully handling unforeseen challenges and changes
- Assuring the provision of the best product quality
- Providing updated reports to stakeholders and executives
- Utilizing data to track project accomplishment

Manually executing all of these tasks would be difficult, so digital project managers utilize technology to assist them through each project stage. Ninety percent of the project timetable is devoted to communication. It appears to be many meetings, calls, and emails. However, project managers must recognize which communication type is better for the requirements and personality of every team participant (Mitrofanova et al., 2021).

The following are some tips for digital project managers to achieve success:

> A digital project manager supervises the innovative ideas and technological development of email marketing, social media platforms, online banner, mobile applications, and e-commerce. In the digital world, digital project management is a rapidly progressing domain. Therefore, the project manager should have a diversified variety of skills and relevant knowledge.
>
> *(Raith et al., 2017)*

The digital project manager should:

Maintain flexibility: The digital project manager should be flexible, as the job demands so much. Briefly, digital project managers are continuously pulled in various diversified directions simultaneously. The objective of the digital project manager is to place different puzzle fragments together. Furthermore, they have to stay updated about the advanced technologies. Therefore, they have to work and study more than regular working time. Digital project managers must perform multiple tasks, and they must remember what each instruction requires. Project managers should have ample information capacity, as they have to absorb an exceptional amount of technical information. The information may come from different team members of the project. Fundamentally, project managers should be efficient at assigning jobs to the relevant people (Damström, 2020).

Sustain focus: With the systemized chaos in any digital project, it is essential to focus on each task. The problems digital project managers have to deal with can be highly complicated. There is a term known as single rapid-tasking. This means that project managers should have the ability to conclude all the single tasks with enhanced focus level and efficiency. Another method of explaining might be sequential multitasking. The team members of the development team and other experts can use the time to discuss solving one aspect of the project. Project managers do not have this opportunity. They have to switch between tasks impeccably while giving attention to each deserving task (Raith et al., 2017).

Try to prioritize: Project managers must understand who is the best option for every task to attain accessible milestones. There are extra demands and work from the commencement and end of each project. Any team members, various clients, or other departments can make this appeal. The work is not completed until the client is satisfied. As the tasks start piling up, project managers must explore methods to keep and organize the jobs according to the timetable. It is essential to have extreme emphasis so that project managers do not become easily unfocused (Faub, 2020).

Skills of people management: The project managers should have the necessary skills to manage people if they wish to be inspirational and motivational leaders. Frequently, project managers have to deal with intelligent developers and experts who seem to be lost in their technological world. As a project manager, it is necessary to learn all the team members' skills, competencies, and personalities. If digital project managers have working knowledge about the skills and capabilities of each team member, they can be better at making decisions relevant to their work expertise. The segment of the digital project managers' responsibilities is to develop and handle work instructions for the team of creative managers, search and web traffic experts, digital art directors, and other technical staff. If the digital project manager can efficiently organize the team, he can ensure that every project's aspects are concluded on time. Project managers should also match product quality and data integrity according to clients' expectations (Raith et al., 2017).

Learning to satisfy clients: Arranging meetings with clients is the essential step for the success of the digital project management domain. The digital project manager is the mediator between team performance and clients' demands. In many situations, the digital project manager is the part of the marketing group that has to go to the market to attract the client. In the beginning, it is advantageous to attain some marketing skills. The initial stage in marketing is to sell oneself. The subsequent step is active listening. However, the project manager would not be the focal salesperson. He would act more as the sales engineer, attend client meetings, and describe how the project management is being done. Therefore, present and potential clients may assume that the project manager must explain how all the tasks are completed (Shivakumar, 2018).

In contrast, it can be supposed that clients are more than just customers. The client list can also involve other resources or departments that can support the project promptly. The project manager must make people understand why they want to do the tasks precisely until the specific deadline. Therefore, the project manager must function appropriately with other team members. For example, if the project manager is employed in a small company, he may connect with other firms to support working ahead. If he has effective selling and communication skills, there can be significant benefits during communication with others (Sepasgozar et al., 2019).

Obtain the relevant qualification: Firms expect digital managers to have a bachelor's degree in a domain relevant to the project for which they are hired. It can differ, as several ways lead to this rank. Applicable bachelor's degrees emerge from business, such as communications, business administration, and marketing (Sepasgozar et al., 2019).

Working in collaborative domains: In many situations, the route to becoming a digital project manager can include working in various diversified positions. Hence, it can differ depending on the firms' expectations. Nevertheless, various fields are beneficial in getting a person chosen for a rank ahead of other applicants (Shivakumar, 2018).

Becoming a dynamic learner: If a person becomes a digital project manager, he must exhibit that he can effortlessly comprehend new systems and information. This means that the applicant for the project manager position can swiftly understand and utilize all the technology tools. It allows the digital project manager to start with projects and remain ahead of client demands and expectations. Every team participant may appreciate a project manager more if he depicts good knowledge of the tasks that are being performed by the team (Baltasar & Breton, 2020).

The field of project management is advantageous and exciting. Therefore, many firms are hunting for people who have relevant knowledge about this field (Shivakumar, 2018).

Tools used by project managers: Contemporary software solutions are the best support for a digital manager. SaaS solutions allow project managers to organize their teams, enhance communications with teams and clients, allocate tasks, and share files. Some available tools involve project management software, collaboration mediums, planning software, agility tools, and data analytics solutions. Project management software helps in completing the lifting of digital project management. The software assists in the planning, execution, initiation, and wrapping projects. Some best project management software in the present day is becoming famous award winners. Each has a verified record from final users (Baltasar & Breton, 2020).

Collaboration mediums have become more essential than ever. These platforms permit the benefit of experience outside of the working space. Some employees may prefer to work remotely. These famous tools allow digital project managers to support that the staff feels and works like they are sitting next to them. Just as significantly, team members in digital project management can also benefit from their remote skills. Some other digital project management tools that digital project managers can take benefits from may be involved in:

G Suite: This is a fine commencement point for any team that requires making various document types, forms, spreadsheets, and websites. Calendars and files can be edited and viewed by team participants. It helps in making collaboration smooth.

ClickUp: The top-rated project management solution developed to be linked and function with particular firm requirements. It is suitable for all project types.

MeisterTask: This is an agile project management system for digital project management teams to manage and organize their products in a personalized medium. It supports the enhancement of the workflow and managing time.

Slack: It was developed to boost collaboration between the team members. It consists of file sharing, messaging options, and collaboration with Dropbox and Google Drive (Faub, 2020).

Conclusion

Including digital technology into the basics of firms' business models is necessary for the prosperity of firms across present-day industries. Technological transformation has become a significant issue and requires the latest methods of administrative thinking. Project managers in the present era are shifting their procedures and teams online to keep them ahead of the competition and deliver at a more accelerated level than ever before. Web-based project management, cloud file-storage technology, and collaboration software are used productively and with enhanced outcomes. Digital project managers are new facets of present-day project management, and if a person wants to join the field, he has to attain the requisite knowledge about advanced technology. Digital project management is an efficient procedure for handling web-based projects from the idea to the outcome, remaining within the set budget, and utilizing specific resources. It includes planning, allocating, tracking, analyzing, and estimating results, mostly done using project management software.

Every project has a different objective, but the principal goal is to progress the business and observe valuable returns on investment from the project. Project types can vary from events to digital material projects. The responsibility of a digital project manager is to guarantee that all the required deliverables for a project are accomplished and delivered promptly using the fixed budget. Once again, project managers ensure that the projects follow the business objectives. In addition, for specific responsibilities, recognizing how project managers are managed. The job description for the position of a digital manager can vary depending on the project type and the toll used by the firm to handle those projects. Some firms may need the applicant to be experienced in using a particular tool. Some companies provide training sessions on the tools for project managers. Various digital project manager skills are attained through collaboration and regular work experience. Skills including time management, project communication management, resource management, organizing, delegating, and planning can be attained in almost any work position. There are various digital project management subjects, certifications, and books that people can get using online platforms, which can help them stand ahead of the competition. The expertise of every digital manager is different and is dependent on their background and work experience. All project managers need to make sure they continue learning how they can enhance their project management skills. According to the project, team, and firm, every project manager implements a different digital project management procedure (Damström, 2020).

There is a possibility that the two projects will not be the same, and they may need exclusive methods or procedures. Providently, there are various options for choosing. Some of the well-known project management methods appear in agile or waterfall. Waterfall methods are a more conventional project management method for creating scopes, handling resources, and working in stages. The procedure is sequential and straightforward. It functions specifically well for construction projects where one task must be finished before another task can be commenced. Agile is a much-modified method developed with the support of flexibility and collaboration. Whereas waterfall has to follow a stern plan, agile methods allow teams to remain responsive to change efficiently and swiftly. It allows the stakeholder or client to arrive at various stages and endure the tasks being performed according to their expectations before moving ahead to the following tasks. Collaboration tools and cloud-based project management tools allow project managers to benefit from digital project management's full potential. These tools serve as a single truth source, and they depict the actual status of the project in real time. These tools allow the project manager to communicate with up-to-date and accurate data with team participants, stakeholders, exclusive collaborators, and others. This means that digital project managers can omit status update meetings, saving time for the team to perform their tasks better. Digital project managers keep all the information, documents, and images in a cloud-based project management tool so that people can obtain the files and download them whenever there is a requirement without disturbing the manager. Everything is central, so the project team can proceed without waiting for a response and keep doing tasks on time. Feedback and tasks are all saved in the exact location, so the project manager can refer when needed. There is no need for discussion or arguments about who is responsible for what, as everything is documented in one location where every team participant can have access. If any team participant takes leave for some days, it causes a considerable delay in the timeline (Sepasgozar et al., 2019).

The use of digital project management tools with Gantt chart provides easy solutions for this issue. The project manager can review the Gantt chart to check if there is a chance to wait for the team member to return. If there is a chance to wait, the project manager can reorder the tasks on the Gantt chart to show the latest dates for deliverables and let the team know about the updated timetable. If there is an issue in waiting, the tasks can be reallocated. The appointee has been monitoring their work in the web-based management tool, and the new allottee can quickly obtain all the required information. When the project managers organize the project and relevant tasks using a digital project management tool shared with the team members, stakeholders can quickly check the project's progress. All the members in a project get access to check who is allotted what tasks, the due date of the tasks, the work level, responsible persons for detaining the project, and what is coming in the next stage. It helps the digital project manager motivate the team and encourage them by providing the requisite information and knowledge to be productive (Raith et al., 2017).

References

Baltasar, L. B. S., & Breton, S. J. (2020). Communication for cultural project teams: How to use digital tools. In *Advances in logistics, operations, and management science* (pp. 411–427). IGI Global. https://doi.org/10.4018/978-1-7998-1934-9.ch018

Biazzo, S., Fabris, A., & Panizzolo, R. (2020). Virtual visual planning: A methodology to assess digital project management tools. *International Journal of Applied Research in Management and Economics*, 3(4), 1–10. https://doi.org/10.33422/ijarme.v3i4.505

Cooper, R. G., & Sommer, A. F. (2018). Agile – Stage-Gate for manufacturers: Changing the way new products are developed integrating agile project management methods into a Stage-Gate system offers both opportunities and challenges. *Research-Technology Management*, 61(2), 17–26. https://doi.org/10.1080/08956308.2018.1421380

Damström, M. (2020). Digitalization and construction project management: What consequences the use of ICT-tools has had on the project manager role in the construction industry. Master of Science Project, 30 Credits, Second Level Stockholm, Sweden. https://www.diva-portal.org/smash/record.jsf?pid=diva2%3A1446043&dswid=-586

Demirkesen, S., & Ozorhon, B. (2017). Impact of integration management on construction project management performance. *International Journal of Project Management*, 35(8), 1639–1654. https://doi.org/10.1016/j.ijproman.2017.09.008

Ershadi, M., Jefferies, M., Davis, P., & Mojtahedi, M. (2021, January). Effective application of information technology tools for real-time project management. In *International *conference on digital technologies and applications* (pp. 719–729). Springer. https://doi. org/10.1007/978-3-030-73882-2_65

Faub, H. (2020). *Project management tools to support agile methods in the workplace* [Doctoral dissertation, North Carolina State University].

Georgieva, M. (2018). *Achieving efficiency in large-scale digitization project management with free IT tools.* Presentation at ALA Annual Conference & Exhibition, New Orleans, LA. https://digitalscholarship.unlv.edu/libfacpresentation/158/

Kerzner, H. (2019). *Innovation project management: Methods, case studies, and tools for managing innovation projects.* John Wiley & Sons.

Marder, B., Ferguson, P., Marchant, C., Brennan, M., Hedler, C., Rossi, M., Black, S., & Doig, R. (2021). 'Going agile': Exploring the use of project management tools in fostering psychological safety in group work within management discipline courses. *International Journal of Management Education, 19*(3), 100519. https://doi.org/10.1016/j.ijme.2021.100519

Mikalsen, M., Moe, N. B., Stray, V., & Nyrud, H. (2018). Agile digital transformation: A case study of interdependencies. In *Proceedings of the 39th International Conference on Information Systems (ICIS).* Association for Information Systems (AIS). Thirty Ninth International Conference on Information Systems, San Francisco. https://sintef.brage.unit.no/sintef-xmlui/handle/11250/2994288

Mitrofanova, Y. S., Chehri, A., Tukshumskaya, A. V., Vereshchak, S. B., & Popova, T. N. (2021). Project management of smart university development: Models and tools. In *Smart education and e-Learning 2021* (pp. 339–350). Springer. https://doi.org/10.1007/978-981-16-2834-4_29

Morcov, S., Pintelon, L., & Kusters, R. J. (2021). A practical assessment of modern it project complexity management tools: Taming positive, appropriate, negative complexity. *International Journal of Information Technology Project Management, 12*(3), 90–108. https://doi.org/10.4018/IJITPM.2021070106

Moreira, F., Ferreira, M. J., & Seruca, I. (2018). Enterprise 4.0 – The emerging digital transformed enterprise? *Procedia Computer Science, 138*, 525–532. https://doi.org/10.1016/j.procs.2018.10.072

Raith, F., Richter, I., & Lindermeier, R. (2017, July). How project-management-tools are used in agile practice: Benefits, drawbacks and potentials. In *Proceedings of the 21st international database engineering and applications symposium* (pp. 30–39). ACM Digital Library.

Sepasgozar, S. M. E., Karimi, R., Shirowzhan, S., Mojtahedi, M., Ebrahimzadeh, S., & McCarthy, D. (2019). Delay causes and emerging digital tools: A novel model of delay analysis, including integrated project delivery and PMBOK. *Buildings, 9*(9), 191. https://doi.org/10.3390/buildings9090191

Shivakumar, S. K. (2018). Models, tools, and templates used in digital project management. In *Complete guide to digital project management* (pp. 123–154). Apress.

Snow, C. C., Fjeldstad, Ø. D., & Langer, A. M. (2017). Designing the digital organization. *Journal of Organization Design, 6*(1), 1–13.

Whyte, J. (2019). How digital information transforms project delivery models. *Project Management Journal, 50*(2), 177–194. https://doi.org/10.1177/8756972818823304

8
DIGITAL CONFLICT MANAGEMENT IN THE WORKPLACE

Joanna Paliszkiewicz and Esra Sipahi Döngül

Introduction

The global information and communication environment has expanded dramatically over the past decade. Digital media differs from traditional media in terms of the production of content (including misinformation and disinformation). As it is widespread by a wide variety of media users, often non-institutional actors contribute to a wide range of information; digital communication often reflects and/or creates a variety of information sets.

This is why the use of digital technology is important as globalized digital technologies and platforms evolve, including increasing socially based polarization based on religion and political and other interests or ideologies, because the context of conflict-prone or affected societies is encountered. With the democratization of the media shifting into high gear, natural conflicts that increasingly transcend borders and geography have also varied. The geographical characteristics of corporate and traditional media in digital communication and their effects on the media should be understood from a behavioral point of view in the conflict. Controlling the media and its contents often leads to a violation of freedom of speech, which is the antidote to conflict (Kahl & Larrauri, 2013, p. 1).

Conflict-affected communications interventions should not only align their resources and programs, but should act with local technological realities and avoid over-emphasis on hypothetical digital technologies (Morozov, 2011).

Given that conflict is as old as the existence of humanity, and that each person has his own character, characteristics and reactions, not everyone can be expected to think the same thing and behave in the same way. Although conflicts sprout from disagreements, it is not the differences of opinion that grow it, but the way people approach each other.

DOI: 10.4324/9781003283386-10

Literature

What Is Conflict?

Conflicts cannot cease to exist, as they are intrinsic to human beings, forming an integral part of their moral and emotional growth (Valente et al., 2020).

According to Thomas, conflict arises when one party perceives that its interests are being hindered by the other. Here the word interest, need, want, official purposes can include standards of behavior. When the causes of conflict are examined, many kinds of interests are encountered. For example, role interests arise in interpersonal and interdepartmental conflicts, and autonomy interests arise in subordinate-superior and interdepartmental conflicts. Other interests that may cause conflict may include promotion, limited economic resources, norms of behavior, expectations, compliance with rules, agreements, values and various interpersonal needs (Thomas, 1976).

Conflict, in its most general definition, means all kinds of resistance and negative relations. Conflicts often arise as a result of differences in the perspectives or approaches of the parties. In bringing together people from different structures and cultures, misunderstandings, disagreements and "personality conflicts" occur, and this is inevitable for an organization.

Today, the conflict between employees in many workplaces is seen as part of corporate life. According to an article published by Forbes, 60–80% of problems in institutions are caused by conflicts between employees.

According to a study of remote workers by MyPerfectResume (2021), 81% of employees have experienced a conflict with their workplaces in the last year; 65% of these conflicts were with colleagues, 19% with direct managers, 11% with other managers and 5% with people working in another company (Kücükcan, 2021).

Thirty-six percent of respondents cited bosses' aggressive attitude as the cause of the conflict, while 25% said a lack of teamwork and 25% said work stress was the cause. Eighteen percent stated that these conflicts were caused by not being transparent and honest enough about important issues. Nine percent cited the reason for this as a conflict of values.

One of the striking facts revealed by the survey was that 39% of remote workers who had a conflict with a colleague or boss wanted to quit or had already left.

We can say that these statistics indicate that employee loyalty cannot be mentioned in workplaces that are inadequate in conflict management and that it is inevitable that employee circulation will increase.

According to the new management approach, a "reasonable level of conflict" increases organizational efficiency. However, for the conflict to have positive effects, it needs to be well managed. For conflict management to be successful, the factors affecting the conflict and the behavior of individuals in conflict situations should be analyzed well and objectively.

Conflict, when well-managed, achieves a positive output. However, in the management of a bad crisis, i.e., failure to end the conflict, dire consequences can arise.

Therefore, the most important step in resolving the conflict is to first acknowledge that the conflict exists and to define the conflict.

What Triggers Digital Conflict?

Different personalities: Digital conflicts caused by different personalities can occur not only in the workplace but wherever social life exists. Digital environments that can be talked about and encourage empathy within the framework of respect can help in this regard.

Poor communication: Correspondence in a misunderstood digital environment caused by a lack of communication and deviating from its purpose can sometimes lead to tension.

Incomplete information sharing: Failure to properly share information, reports, or requests that need to be shared among employees, when necessary, can create conflicts for the workflow to proceed healthily.

Stress factor: The stress caused by many factors, such as the struggle against the distracting conditions of the digital work environment, the process of adjusting to working remotely, uncertainties about the future of the company or a person within the company, can negatively affect the way people communicate.

Feeling of exclusion: In cases where remote work is a necessity, not a choice, an employee who feels alone and excluded by his team or company can change his or her approach toward other employees.

Failure to meet the common denominator in the form of work: Each person can have their own way of working. For example, some people like to plan and act quickly, while others may take it slower or want to move in different ways. Such disputes can arise between the employee and the leader, or among the leaders themselves.

Inability to agree: Failure to agree on important decisions about work or a product can lead to conflict.

Rude or discriminatory attitudes: No one wants to communicate with someone who is constantly acting angry and being rude. However, workplaces are places where it is imperative to communicate with everyone to a certain extent. It is also inevitable that conflicts will arise in a digital environment where constant psychological harassment and discrimination occurs.

What Prevents Digital Conflict?

In general, conflict means all kinds of resistance and mutual negative relations, based on a lack of power, resources or social position and changing value judgments (Robbins, 1978).

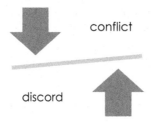

FIGURE 8.1   Balance in Conflict

Note: The figure was created by the authors.

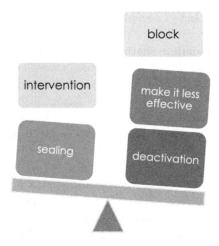

FIGURE 8.2   Balance Board in Conflict

Note: The figure was created by the authors.

Similarly, Deutsch, who viewed conflict as incompatible behavior and actions, described the conflict as "a process of interfering, clogging or otherwise preventing or making someone else's behavior less effective" (Tjosvold, 1989).

Luthans (1992) states that the conflict is an emergency that disrupts the organization's cohesion and therefore must be destroyed and is related to the resolution of the conflict. However, resolving and managing conflict are two different concepts (Wilson & Rosenfeld, 1990).

The most common interpersonal conflicts are caused by subordinate-upper conflicts and personal disputes between staff and command managers. In addition, conflicts are encountered due to individual differences at the same organizational level. Disagreements between workers, opinions and differences of interest between the manager, chief and officer are entered into the types of interpersonal conflicts. The conflict between sales personnel and production personnel within the same organization is a good example of intergroup conflict. Since disputes

Conflict within people

interpersonal conflict

Conflicts between individuals and groups

Conflicts within and between groups

Inter-organizational conflicts

FIGURE 8.3   Types of Conflict

Note: The figure was created by the authors.

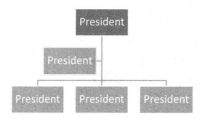

FIGURE 8.4   Uncertainty About the Management Area

Note: The figure was created by the authors.

between employees are inevitable, if not resolved, they can disrupt the productivity of the organization, reduce motivation and even cause some good staff to quit. Since it is the responsibility of an administrator to solve problems in the organization, employees must resolve it among themselves, unless a problem involves behavior or performance that needs to be addressed. When managers intervene and exercise authority, employees miss the opportunity to develop their own conflict-management skills.

Managing such conflicts is more difficult for the manager since sometimes the manager can also be part of the conflicting group as a member of a group.

The average number of hours spent per week to resolve workplace conflict varies between 0.9 and 3.3 hours for organization employees from nine countries. In the U.S.A., this averages to be 2.8 hours. If you think about it on a year-by-year basis, in 2008, in the context of calculated expenses based on average hourly earnings, the lost time was $359 billion. This is due to organizations where conflict is mismanaged. Depending on the way inter-business inter-inter-interdependence is managed, there may be a low or high potential for conflict. Sometimes conflict can arise when groups that are mutually dependent on work are given a lot of work or tasks to do (Thrive Global Human Captial Report CPP, 2008).

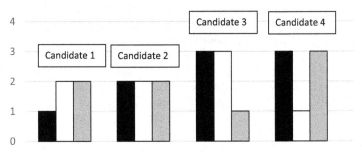

FIGURE 8.5   Uncertainty About the Management Area

Note: The figure was created by the authors.

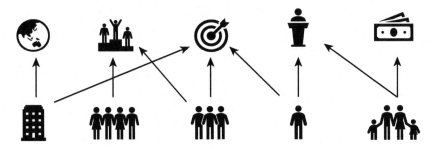

FIGURE 8.6   Differences in Interest

Note: The figure was created by the authors.

The benefits of improved conflict management have also been proven when case studies are taken into account. It has shown that teaching effective communication skills to a group results in a 10% improvement in their habit of facing difficult problems. In this context of change, customer and employee satisfaction, efficiency and quality also increased automatically. An information technology (IT) group found that their improved applications resulted in a 30% increase in productivity, nearly a 40% increase in productivity and a nearly 50% decrease in costs (Patterson et al., 2005).

In organizations, the problems created by perceptions of awards, assignments, adjustment conditions and status symbols create status conflicts.

Every manager has his own management style. In addition, the use of different forms of management in various departments and the way each manager looks at and evaluates problems in their own way of perceiving may result in some agreements.

The fact that the interests and values of individuals, groups or units in a system are incompatible with each other or the system occurs as a cause of conflict. When

FIGURE 8.7 Polarizations in Employee–Employer Relations

Note: The figure was created by the authors.

the norms and standards set by the self-emergence non-formal groups within formal organizations do not match the rules and standards of the formal organization, conflicts arise. Unions' demands for wage increases and management's low-cost desires is an example of conflicts arising from differences in value.

It is typical of individuals in a social system to come from different social and cultural environments and to try to maintain the habits of the environments they come from in the new system.

The ability of the members of the organization to expand their power space for various reasons can put them in a state of conflict with others. What matters here is that others perceive this event. Therefore, it is more important that a manager's behavior is perceived by others as power-building behavior, rather than what the truth is. It's the perception that determines behavior.

In order to resolve the conflicts and manage them for organizational purposes, the first thing to do is to investigate the causes of conflict.

Here Are Some Things Managers – and Even Individual Colleagues – Can Do to Address the Tension or Conflict With Distant Teammates

1   Email should be taken out of the equation. When there's a digital conflict, it's appropriate to make a phone call. Or better yet, use Skype or video conferencing. Making eye contact, monitoring nonverbal communication and hearing each other's tones can suppress negative assumptions.
2   A mutually acceptable time should be set, when each person can focus on speech.
3   Take notes outlining the points that are important so they don't get lost.
4   The problems or differences of digital conflict must be articulated before they become larger monsters. We shouldn't sweep them under the carpet thinking they're going to leave. They are likely to feed and breed in the dark.

Do not allow bad feelings to inflame to the point that you cause real and lasting damage to your team or project.

Effective Digital Conflict Management

Conflicts that progress in the form of conflicts of individuals or subordinates and superiors of the same level are the most common forms of conflict in organizations.

In terms of effective digital conflict management, these conflicts need to be well identified and their causes analyzed correctly.

The main causes of conflict are structural factors arising from the nature of the organization and work and conflicts consisting of personal factors arising from differences between individuals.

Results

For effective conflict management, managers who will ensure cooperation between the parties need to properly understand the situation of the conflict and ensure that the parties are confident and free of prejudices. Only in this way can conflict management in institutions be effectively initiated. Regardless of the method, the importance of reaching consensus should be taken into account for the success of the institution, that conflict is a part of business life, as it is at every moment of life, and that conflict management can be maintained effectively.

Positive Results of Conflict Resolution in Digital Work Environments

With modern understanding, digital conflict management has taken on a new dimension. Digital conflict management is not limited to conflict resolution; it has a wider meaning. Today, the positive effects of conflicts have been accepted as the necessity of a certain amount of conflict in terms of organizational performance. According to the generally accepted judiciary for today, digital conflicts in enterprises are inevitable, and some conflicts have functional consequences.

Instead of eradicating digital conflict, administrators should encourage conflict to a certain point. Since conflicts are inevitable in the organization, the beneficial effects of the conflicts should be uncovered, and the non-functional effects should be prevented. Managers should direct digital conflict for organizational purposes. For this purpose, conflicts and their causes should be analyzed well, and the way they handle conflict should be adopted according to the situation.

If the level of digital conflict in the organization is more than the optimum level of conflict and harms the organization due to its negative consequences, the solution techniques of the conflict should be applied. In organizations where the level of conflict is below the optimum level, some conflict is required to promote participation and creativity. In order to improve performance throughout the organization, it is necessary to take advantage of the positive consequences of the conflict. In organizations where constructive and functional conflicts are at low levels, employees do not strive to develop newer and more effective ways of doing business, are irrelevant and passively accept the current situation. In order to keep up with the changes and developments in the business world, the organization needs to renew itself by mobilizing creativity.

Suggestions

Advice for the President

- **Digitally, you should listen carefully to your staff and be allowed to tell the employee's story.** You should try to be as objective as possible, and all prejudices should be put aside.
- **Related issues must be correctly identified.** Many employees may not tend to overcome problems caused by conflicts in the digital environment in which they live and may avoid directly stating their problems.

Advice for Teams

- **All parties concerned should be allowed to describe digital issues.** If this is a group problem, the problem should be resolved as a group. In addition, all members of the team should be allowed to explain whether they are directly involved in the situation.
- **Identify gaps in areas of information or uncertainty.** Since digital conflict often occurs around uncertainty, it can go a long way to investigate information gaps and resolve digital conflict.
- **Brainstorming solutions should be made as a group.** Digital problems can be solved by leveraging the team's creativity. As a result, the organization will be stronger and more resilient in the long run.

References

Barlow, D. H. (2000). Unraveling the mysteries of anxiety and its disorders from the perspective of emotion theory. *American Psychologist, 55*(11), 1247–1263. https://doi.org/10.1037//0003-066x.55.11.1247

Kahl, A., & Puig Larrauri, H. (2013). Technology for peacebuilding. *Stability: International Journal of Security and Development, 2*(3), 1–15. http://doi.org/10.5334/sta.cv

Kücükcan, G. (2021). *Uzaktan Çalışmada Çatışma Yönetimi.* https://kolayik.com/blog/uzaktan-calismada-catisma-yonetimi/

Luthans, F. (1992). *Organizational behaviour* (7th ed.). McGraw-Hill. https://bdpad.files.wordpress.com/2015/05/fred-luthans-organizational-behavior-_-an-evidence-based-approach-twelfth-edition-mcgraw-hill_irwin-2010.pdf.

Morozov, E. (2011). *The net delusion.* Public Affairs.

Patterson, K., Grenny, J., McMillan, R., & Switzler, A. (2005). *Crucial confrontations: Tools for resolving broken promises, violated expectations, and bad behavior* (Vol. xviii, p. 284). McGraw-Hill.

Robbins, S. P. (1978). "Conflict management" and "conflict resolution" are not synonymous terms. *California Management Review, 21*(2), 67–75. https://doi.org/10.2307/41164809

Thomas, K. W. (1976). Conflict and conflict management. Handbook in industrial and organizational psychology. In M. D. Dunnette (Ed.). Rand McNally. ss. 889–935.

Tjosvold, D. (1989). Interdependence and power between managers and employees: A study of the leader relationship. *Journal of Management, 15*(1), 49–62. https://doi.org/10.1177/014920638901500105

Valente, S., Lourenço, A. A., & Németh, Z. (2020). *School conflicts: Causes and management strategies in classroom relationships* [Online first]. IntechOpen. https://doi.org/10.5772/intechopen.95395; http://www.intechopen.com/online-first/74550.

Wilson, D. C., & Rosenfeld, R. H. (1990). *Organizational behavior management.* McGraw-Hill. http://www.worldcat.org/title/managing-organizations-text-readings-and-cases/oclc/40483340.

Workplace conflict and how businesses can harness it to thrive global human capital report. (2008). http://www.cpp.com/pdfs/CPP_Global_Human_Capital_Report_Workplace_Conflict.pdf; https://lp.servicemax.com/Zinc-WP-Communication-Trends-Across-Deskless-Workforces-in-the-US.html (accepted on December 12, 2021); http://www.myperfectresume.com/career-center/careers/basics/remote-work-conflict (accepted on December 12, 2022).

9

THE EFFECTS OF DIGITAL ORGANIZATIONAL FUNCTIONS ON THE WORKPLACE

Arturo Luque González and
Cristina Raluca Gh. Popescu

Digital solutions to the COVID-19 pandemic have multiplied in the face of the new needs arising from social isolation, although these tools are not equally available to everyone, nor do they develop in a linear fashion. The practices of day-to-day working and life in society are continually restructured by the progress of time and by the incidence of the transmission of the virus. The consequences of social isolation as a response to the pandemic have imposed a one-size-fits-all paradigm of working from home, that is, one that is mandated by law without taking into account the means, capacity and resources of much of the public and without considering the impact such measures may have on the present and future quality of work. The imposed social isolation and remote working conditions have often left workers without guidance on where to obtain resources, information and support, which in turn produces delays and alterations in the normal development of their work; this phenomenon has been seen around the globe (Bick et al., 2020). The documented effects of lockdown include insomnia, post-traumatic stress disorder, irritation and depression, as well as a general experience of feeling exhausted and overwhelmed with work (Brooks et al., 2020; Kolakowski, 2020).

It is clearly necessary to monitor remote working conditions with the same vigor as is standard for work activity carried out on-site, and thereby promote interactivity and employee protection as an identity (ILO, 2020b). Problems of connectivity and other technological shortcomings have manifested themselves as stark and virulent elements of inequality. As an example, the increase in domestic connected devices during lockdowns for the purpose of remote working, studying and leisure activities created bottlenecks in Wi-Fi routers (Assia, 2020). In Italy, the first European country to enforce a lockdown, data traffic in homes through broadband and mobile networks increased by 75 percent in that period.[1] In Latin America and the Caribbean, which is considered at an intermediate level of digital development, the technological limitations have further hampered solutions that

DOI: 10.4324/9781003283386-11

seek the effective digitalization of labor (Luque & Galora, 2020). In fact, the UN Economic Commission for the region was motivated to observe that

> digital technologies are changing production, business and consumption models, they are increasingly important in production processes. Therefore, reducing the digital divide is now essential to move towards new patterns of development. The risk is that the gap in access to digital technologies will become the new face of inequality.
>
> *(ECLAC, 2020a)*

Table 9.1 sets out the growth of internet use in the 5-year period between 2018 and 2023. The region with the highest rate of adoption of digital technology will be North America (followed by Western Europe), with the fastest growth projected to occur in the Middle East and Africa (10 percent CAGR expected from 2018 to 2023). Regarding internet use, nearly two-thirds of the global population will have access by 2023. There will be 5.3 billion internet users (66 percent of the world's population) by 2023, compared to 3.9 billion in 2018; the number of devices connected to IP networks will be more than 3 times the global population by 2023 (29.3 billion), with 3.6 networked devices per capita (there were 2.4 networked devices per capita in 2018). Additionally, the total number of global mobile subscribers will grow from 5.1 billion (66 percent of the population) in 2018 to 5.7 billion (71 percent of the population) by 2023 (Cisco, 2021).

Hatayama et al. (2020) and the International Labour Organization (ILO) (2020a) have carried out contrastive analyses of the feasibility of working remotely in places with different economic and developmental capacities, reaching the conclusion that it is necessary to 1) establish internet access with sufficient quality to perform tasks effectively, 2) promote computer ownership and 3) effectively analyze the economic possibilities of individuals as differentiating and exclusive elements that may impede the ability to work remotely. However, despite the significant advances of the last 15 years in the development of the digital ecosystem, Latin America and the Caribbean still lags significantly behind Western Europe (with an index of

TABLE 9.1 Internet users as a percentage of population by global region

Region	Year	
	2018	2023
Global	51%	66%
Asia Pacific	52%	72%
Central and Eastern Europe	65%	78%
Latin America	60%	70%
Middle East and Africa	24%	35%
North America	90%	92%
Western Europe	82%	87%

71.06), North America (80.85), Eastern Europe (52.90) and the Arab states within the MENA region (55.54) (ECLAC, 2020b). Aspects such as data analysis or the implementation of processes carried out by robots, drones, rescue platforms, 5G technologies, apps, information systems, remote work, education and health have now become normalized and indispensable for both the public and the companies that create them (although it should be borne in mind that not everything that is technically possible is also economically viable). These circumstances have, to a greater or lesser extent, had to be modified through public policies in response to the tsunami of imposed needs.

In view of this, and through a retrospective of the new digitalized working environment, it is necessary to analyze 1) the complexity and origins of the elements that affect, both by act and omission, the processes of labor digitalization; 2) examine the rate of change of the phenomenon, bearing in mind the direct impact of the COVID-19 pandemic and the derivations of the processes of globalization, and 3) establish a taxonomy of inconsistencies through a descriptive and analytical inductive approach.

Addressing the problem

The origins of the term "digital workplace" are diffuse. Technology that is inherent to working practices drove relentless changes deriving from intrinsic knowledge management processes and, in parallel to this process, the first publications with the term "digital workplace" emerged in order to describe the phenomenon of the intrusion of technology in everyday work and its impact on profits (Paul & Grantham, 1995; Sotto, 1996; Briken et al., 2017). Needs and capacities change over time, and added value is no longer exclusively derived from the workforce. Technology imposes itself by conditioning the fortunes of both the worker and the organization itself (Voogt & Roblin, 2012). The leap forward that was witnessed in the early stages of global industrialization was based on inventions and historical discoveries, such as handlooms to make textile garments, the steam engine, the railways, electricity and telephone communication (Schwab, 2017). Now, the current economic processes represent an unprecedented paradigm shift, with the time-honored mantra of land, labor and capital replaced by the more complex formula of land, speculation and capital. This has made labor more volatile and has changed the rules of the game to a situation of uncertainty and deregulation. All of these multidimensional processes are subject to a common denominator: the maximization of capital (Passet, 2012). The processes derived from the prevailing asymmetry of globalization lead to high volatility, uncertainty, complexity, ambiguity and insecurity while generating increased profits for those who control them (Bennett & Lemoine, 2014; Sassen, 2017). The circumstances that demand greater sacrifice, effort and, in many cases, exclusion – that is, the preponderant economic system – lead to a restructuring of working practices (Baylos, 2017; Martínez-Climent et al., 2019; Trost, 2019).

Growth policies and technological tyranny

Many of the measures adopted to counteract the effects of COVID-19 have contributed to the establishment of policies that weaken the welfare state and, indeed, have provided cover for the growing wave of job insecurity and ephemeral labor relations that has long been spreading from east to west[2] (Standing, 2014; Luque et al., 2016; Luque & Casado, 2020). This comes within a scenario in which the market dominates, no company is willing to reduce profits, and limitless growth is scientifically evidenced and endorsed by any available means despite the knowledge that Earth's resources are manifestly finite. According to the International Monetary Fund (IMF) (2021), the global growth projection for 2021 was revised down only marginally to 5.9 percent and is unchanged for 2022 at 4.9 percent. At the same time, the deployment and promotion of disruptive economic processes, alien to normal labor regulation, commodifies social rights. Processes emerge, apparently beyond the reach of traditional morality, that directly benefit transnational corporations while exempting them from any liability, hence the imperative need for global regulation.[3] Technological practicality is imposed as a rule and not as an exception, while the regulations[4] governing transnational technological companies are ephemeral, leaving much of society with no means or tools of redress[5] and at the mercy of the current technological tyranny (Luque, 2021). Not only does leisure and the way it is accessed change, but also the day-to-day experience at work is altered. Shopping, for example, has been transformed, but is an experience not available to everyone. In fact, technology has undoubtedly improved the quality of life of people and society in general, but it has also generated asymmetries and sequelae that are difficult to counteract in the face of inexorable progress. By way of example, according to the philosopher Byung-Chul Han (2021):

> The smartphone is today a digital workplace or a digital confessional. Every device, every technique of domination generates cult items that are employed for subjugation. This is how domination takes hold. The smartphone is the cult item of digital domination. As an apparatus of subjugation, it acts as a rosary and its beads; this is how we keep the mobile constantly in hand. It is the digital amen. We continue to confess. We strip naked by choice. But we do not ask for forgiveness, but for attention to be paid to us.

Some of these circumstances were explained decades ago by Polanyi and MacIver (1944), who warned of the shock caused by the emergence of a national market leading to the dismantlement of the mechanisms of collective reciprocity (that is, the disarming of the common to empower the particular). Many of the prevailing technological platforms such as Uber, Glovo, Rappi, Airbnb, Indriver and Amazon cater to these same private interests. This breakdown of values leads to processes of inequality and systemic crises. Meanwhile, the predominant business model imposes *de facto* the self-organization of the worker, which brings with it a degree of (pseudo)freedom, but is also impregnated with uncertainty (Mainemelis et al., 2002; Hughes et al., 2018; Islam et al., 2020a, 2020b). Salaries are increasingly based on the competition of labor within the global supply chain, generating a precarious and poorly paid model that is currently aggravated by the obligation to cover critical services in lockdown, such as cleaning or the provision of basic services (Benner et al., 2020). In other words, the poor are doubly punished by their circumstances. The current labor force is pushed toward a system of limitless flexibility and obscurantism, at least with their existing lack of tools for redress accompanied by little political will for regulation. According to Aranguiz (2021):

> Digital platforms will have to make an algorithm available to trade unions, or any artificial intelligence of sorts, which may have an impact on such conditions – including individual access to, and maintenance of, employment and their profiling. This right to information is granted to everyone working through a platform – not only "riders" – and thus the transparency requirement applies to all digital platforms equally.

To this end, nation-states themselves try to find a way to establish mechanisms of protection and redistribution, that is, to convey the general interest. This is where the market clearly establishes a differentiation between those inside and those outside. A *de facto* social pyramid is formed, conditioned by the spending power of each individual, and the elite in this system puts on a friendly face that promotes artificial needs (Luque, 2017).

Remote working has been imposed as a necessary autonomy and not as an intentional autonomous element in itself, meaning that it has often been carried out *ad hoc* and with insufficient resources. Consequently, the economic impact of working from home is not the only element to be weighed. There is a clear need to move the consensus on public policies away from private interests: no private enterprise has a greater need than the state itself for employees, vehicles, supplies (e.g., uniforms for doctors, police, printing paper) or the maintenance of basic services (electricity, water, internet). In light of this, it is necessary to restructure many of the existing processes in order to adapt them to today's somewhat rudderless society.

Method

The effects of digital organizational functions on the workplace are becoming more complex (Stephens & Davis, 2009; Attaran et al., 2019; Popescu, 2021a). While fatigue sets in to many of the processes and the legislation becomes out of date, there arises an imperative need to invest in the development of tools developed by research and innovation processes in order to retain competitiveness in the market. Companies are only too aware that the processes of globalization dominate all working practices (Luque, 2019) and the way in which workers interact with their employers has been modified as a result of physical distancing. Almost 4 out of 10 workers in Europe have experienced working from home (Eurofound, 2020), and a common experience has been to work more hours than in the office; according to Microsoft China, 90 more minutes are added to the working week by remote working in certain jobs (McCulley, 2020; Spataro, 2020; Popescu, 2021b). New working modalities have emerged together with well-established outsourcing processes, conspiring not only to reduce costs but to erase any type of legal and employment responsibility toward the parent company (Luque & Guamán, 2021).

Due to this complexity and due also to the fact that digitization and its associated processes are not all regulated at present, the methodology of this study moved away from established canons. There was a need for a corresponding complexity in the different research methods to be brought together in order to obtain direct, indirect and non-regulated information. A qualitative methodology of a synthetic analytical nature was selected, based on the need to deconstruct the problem and in order to identify its constituent parts (historical, predictive, normative and inductive). Validity in the achievement of the objectives was guaranteed through the following steps (Echavarría et al., 2010).

1   An extensive and exhaustive analysis of academic sources was carried out, from which the object of study was defined (Rodríguez & Valldeoriola, 2007). Priority was given to academic documents indexed in Scopus, Web of Science and Latindex databases related to the object of study. To this end, a Boolean search was implemented between January 9, 2021, and January 3, 2022, establishing all the possible combinations of search chains, such as "digital organizational functions in the workplace", "remote working", "future of work", "technology", "technological globalization", "COVID-19 and technology", "technological practicality", "technological tyranny" and "effects of technology", among others.

2   A descriptive journey was traced from the declaration of the COVID-19 pandemic by the World Health Organization on March 11, 2020, through January 1, 2022. This compiled the changes in legislation and/or behavior of both companies and workers who have modified the development of their work functions since the declaration of the pandemic.

3   A theoretical understanding of the social phenomenon was put forward and then its possible interpretations were discussed, based on the taxonomy of inconsistencies present both in the existing legislation, in the public policies implemented, as well as in the informed opinions of the participants. A synthesis of these interpretations was then formed.

4   Various solutions were proposed, aimed at facing the challenges posed by the processes of digital transformation, mostly based on the principles of globalization, digital literacy and worker empowerment.

Discussion and analysis

Technology and the digitalization of processes have played a key role in mitigating and easing the effects of the COVID-19 pandemic. There is no doubt that the complex, global productive system must work in unison with all of its stakeholders, but the lack of mechanisms for redistribution and collaboration between governments, supranational organizations, industry, academia and civil society creates undesirable asymmetries with uncertain results. Remote working and its intrinsic elements have been imposed, not only by the effects of the pandemic but also by the imperative of cost reduction. Consequently, it has been seen how the considerable waste of time resulting from the need to commute to the workplace can be dispensed with. Neither companies nor workers need waste this time and their economic resources unless it is strictly necessary, as in the case of certain activities of absolute necessity, such as health, research or the operation of non-autonomous machinery. Results-based management has become standardized, based on consensual agreements of work conduct, that is, the establishment of formal commitments between the parties to evaluate, through objective and inclusive processes, the productivity of the worker on the agreed tasks, their completion ahead of or behind schedule, the achievement of goals and milestones and the use of existing resources (Sorensen, 2016). In fact, the tools of supervision and control that *a priori* might be considered most valid or simply established *de facto* by the rule of "whatever is best/fastest/most efficient" may contain ethical dilemmas (or even verge on the illicit) and certainly may diminish the trust between the parties by fomenting negative and unwanted attitudes that are counterproductive to the organization (McParland & Connolly, 2020). Any element related to work activity is capable of being measured, and hygiene-monitoring systems also fall within the remit of "key performance indicators" (KPIs) (Bittle, 2020). Seemingly, workers with higher-paid jobs are more frequently able to work from home and to do so with better tools and timetables; in contrast, the bulk of lower-paid workers go from one precarious situation to another without optimal means or training. Many of the tasks of such jobs cannot be performed remotely or are not feasible at certain times, while some workers have no alternative but to provide their own resources in order to avoid exclusion. This leads to marked differences in occupational roles, even within the same company (Bonacini et al., 2020; Cetrulo et al., 2020). It is evident that technological tools are often used to reconfigure relationships[6] between employers and workers within and between organizations (Kellogg et al., 2020) and a new paradigm coalesces from the interconnection of these relationships.

Conclusion

The tools of technology have a direct impact on the future of work. The current reality formed from Revolution 4.0 has, to date, squandered the productive system, establishing an unprecedented level of technification that impacts the distribution of income and that establishes *de facto* a labor force that is subordinate and quasi-dispensable. It also highlights the primacy of some functions over others. Historically, the increase in the use of technology has also led to increases in the employment rate, but today much of the quality of employment has been compromised by the standardization of precariousness. This model is difficult to exit once it has been entered despite the emergence of new well-paid professions[7] (e.g., in the field of artificial intelligence). Equally, there have never before been problems derived from increasing knowledge and the new tools it creates to facilitate greater production to the satisfaction of all stakeholders. At present, consumption is weakened and the most reliable option going forward is to improve wealth redistribution systems through measures such as the basic income while improving sustainability by embracing degrowth processes. Effective and ethical digital organization in the workplace requires the establishment of solid public policies relating to gender, the environment and social issues, together with the adoption of inclusive social economy processes.

Technology and its misuse have the ability to pervert any ethical and eco-social aspect. The quality of life of workers, as well as the sustainability of the planet, will depend on the people as well as on the creation of solid, active and vigilant public powers.

Notes

1 EU warns of broadband strain as millions work from home, www.ft.com/content/b4ab03db-de1f-4f98-bcc2-b09007427e1b
2 Organic Law on Humanitarian Support. 229 of 22-Jun.-2020, record n° an-sg-2020–0355-o, available at https://bit.ly/3evrsyz, which establishes labor flexibility as a rule and not as an exception.
3 In early April 2021, a draft EU Regulation on a European Approach to Artificial Intelligence was leaked to the press. https://bit.ly/3FhRt2V
4 Royal Decree-Law 9/2021, of 11 May, amending the revised text of the Workers' Statute Law, approved by Royal Legislative Decree 2/2015, of 23 October, to guarantee the labor rights of those involved in the distribution of digital platforms by which stakeholders will be considered employees on 12 August, according to the new law. www.boe.es/boe/dias/2021/05/12/pdfs/BOE-A-2021-7840.pdf
5 "Facebook gutted in the U.S. Senate: 'Nobody knows what's going on inside'"; "The company hides vital information from the public, the U.S. government, its shareholders and governments around the world", informed Frances Haugen, author of the leak about Facebook's toxic impact on society and its attempts to hide it. Retrieved from Eldiario.es 5 October 2021, at https://bit.ly/3pZZPI7

 • "Facebook Whistleblower Frances Haugen Opening Statement" retrieved from C-SPAN at www.youtube.com/watch?v=Lq32sECQ9g8

6 Identity document validation technology in the right to work and right to rent schemes, and DBS pre-employment checking (accessible version). 27 December 2021, gov.uk, https://bit.ly/3ne9pFO
7 These are the digital skills companies need in order to succeed in a changing economy. Retrieved from World Economic Forum January 6, 2022, at https://bit.ly/3fgwnHG. "No job is exempt from digitalization, says the Industry Skills report from online learning platform Coursera. Companies with 'cutting edge' skills proficiencies saw better

returns on their stock in 2020 than those with lagging skills proficiencies. Most desirable skills include cloud computing, cybersecurity, data analysis and software development. Every global region is facing a skills gap, making upskilling workers vital. Skills in the automotive sector are growing but not in the critical areas required. Professional services companies are investing in virtual processes to supplement human interactions".

References

Aranguiz, A. (2021). *Spain's platform workers win algorithm transparency.* https://socialeurope.eu/spains-platform-workers-win-algorithm-transparency

Assia. (2020). *Deliver better wi-fi to residential subscriber.* ASSIA. http://www.assia-inc.com/products/cloudcheck/

Attaran, M., Attaran, S., & Kirkland, D. (2019). The need for digital workplace: Increasing workforce productivity in the information age. *International Journal of Enterprise Information Systems, 15*(1), 1–23. https://doi.org/10.4018/IJEIS.2019010101

Baylos, A. (2017). El Futuro de las normas del trabajo que queremos. *Cuaderno Jurídico y Político, 3*(10), 52–68. https://doi.org/10.5377/cuadernojurypol.v3i10.11082

Benner, C., Mason, S., Carré, F., & Chris, T. (2020, February 24). *Delivering insecurity: E-commerce and the future of work in food retail.* U.C. Berkeley Labor Center. Working Partnerships USA.

Bennett, N., & Lemoine, G. J. (2014). What a difference a word makes: Understanding threats to performance in a VUCA world. *Business Horizons, 57*(3), 311–317. https://doi.org/10.1016/j.bushor.2014.01.001

Bick, R., Chang, M., Wei Wang, K., & Yu, T. (2020, marzo 23). *A blueprint for remote working: Lessons from China.* McKinsey & Company. http://www.mckinsey.com/business-functions/mckinsey-digital/our-insights/a-blueprint-for-remote-working-lessons-from-china

Bittle, J. (2020). Your boss wants to know whether you are washing your hands. *Slate* [Web site]. Retrieved October 5, 2021, from https://bit.ly/2Rl7aDy.

Bonacini, L., Gallo, G., & Scicchitano, S. (2020). Working from Home and income inequality: Risks of a "new normal" with COVID-19. *Journal of Population Economics, 34*(1), 1–58. https://doi.org/10.1007/s00148-020-00800-7

Briken, K., Chillas, S., & Krzywdzinski, M. (2017). *The new digital workplace: How new technologies revolutionise work.* Macmillan International Higher Education.

Brooks, S. K., Webster, R. K., Smith, L. E., Woodland, L., Wessely, S., Greenberg, N., & Rubin, G. J. (2020). The psychological impact of quarantine and how to reduce it: Rapid review of the evidence. *Lancet, 395*(10227), 912–920. https://doi.org/10.1016/S0140-6736(20)30460-8

Cetrulo, A., Guarascio, D., & Virgillito, M. E. (2020). The privilege of working from Home at the time of social distancing. *Inter Economics, 55*(3), 142–147. https://doi.org/10.1007/s10272-020-0891-3

Cisco. (2021). *Cisco annual Internet report (2018–2023).* Cisco. http://www.cisco.com/c/en/us/solutions/collateral/executive-perspectives/annual-internet-report/white-paper-c11-741490.pdf

Echavarría, J. D. L., Gómez, C. A. R., Aristazábal, M. U. Z., & Vanegas, J. O. (2010). El método analítico como método natural. Nómadas. *Critical Journal of Social and Juridical Sciences, 25*(1), 1–27.

ECLAC. (2020a). *Es urgente universalizar el acceso a las nuevas tecnologías para reconstruir mejor con igualdad y sostenibilidad.* Cepal. http://www.cepal.org/es/noticias/es-urgente-universalizar-acceso-nuevas-tecnologias-reconstruir-mejor-igualdad

ECLAC. (2020b). *Las oportunidades de la digitalización en América Latina frente al COVID-19.* Cepal. http://www.cepal.org/es/publicaciones/45360-oportunidades-la-digitalizacion-america-latina-frente-al-covid-199

EuroFound. (2020). *Vida, trabajo y COVID-19 Primeras conclusiones – Abril de 2020.* EuroFound. http://www.eurofound.europa.eu/es/publications/report/2020/living-working-and-covid-19-first-findings-april-2020.

Han, B. (2021, October 9). *Byung-Chul Han: "El móvil es un instrumento de dominación. Actúa como un rosario".* Retrieved from Elpaís.com: https://elpais.com/ideas/2021-10-10/byung-chul-han-el-movil-es-un-instrumento-de-dominacion-actua-como-un-rosario.html?outputType=amp&__twitter_impression=true

Hatayama, M., Viollaz, M., & Winkler, H. (2020). *Jobs' amenability to working from Home: Evidence from skills surveys for 53 countries.* Policy Research Working Paper no. 9241. World Bank.

Hughes, M., Rigtering, J. P. C., Covin, J. G., Bouncken, R. B., & Kraus, S. (2018). Innovative behaviour, trust and perceived workplace performance. *British Journal of Management, 29*(4), 750–768. https://doi.org/10.1111/1467-8551.12305

ILO. (2020a). *Working from home: Estimating the worldwide potential.* Nota de políticas de la OIT. http://www.ilo.org/wcmsp5/groups/public/–ed_protect/–protrav/–travail/documents/briefingnote/wcms_743447.pdf

ILO. (2020b). *Frente a la pandemia: Garantizar la Seguridad y Salud en el Trabajo.* Ginebra. http://www.ilo.org/wcmsp5/groups/public/–ed_protect/–protrav/–safework/documents/publication/wcms_742732.pdf

Islam, N., Gyoshev, S., & Amona, D. (2020a). External complexities in discontinuous innovation-based R&D projects: Analysis of inter-firm collaborative partnerships that lead to abundance. *Technological Forecasting and Social Change, 155*, 119303. https://doi.org/10.1016/j.techfore.2018.05.014

Islam, N., Marinakis, Y., Majadillas, M. A., Fink, M., & Walsh, S. T. (2020b). Here there be dragons, a pre-roadmap construct for IoT service infrastructure. *Technological Forecasting and Social Change, 155*, 119073. https://doi.org/10.1016/j.techfore.2017.09.016

Kellogg, K. C., Valentine, M. A., & Christin, A. (2020). Algorithms at work: The new contested terrain of control. *Academy of Management Annals, 14*(1), 366–410. https://doi.org/10.5465/annals.2018.0174

Kolakowski, N. (2020). *COVID-19 burnout growing among remote workers. 5 de mayo.* https://insights.dice.com/2020/05/05/covid-19-burnout-growing-remote-workers/

Luque, A. (2017). Promoción del hiperconsumo textil transnacional: la moda y el exceso como leit motiv. *Chasqui. Revista Latinoamericana de Comunicación, 134*, 83–104. https://doi.org/10.16921/chasqui.v0i134.3016

Luque, A. (2019). Gestión del conocimiento y su impacto en la economía mundial en el marco de una sociedad globalizada. *Veritas & Research, 1*(1), enero-junio, 54–63. ISSN 2697-3375.

Luque, A. (2021). Practicality, support or premeditated calculation in the digital age: The case of Ecuador. *Revista Venezolana de Gerencia, 26*(6 Edición Especial), 29–46. https://doi.org/10.52080/rvgluz.26.e6.3. https://bit.ly/3q2cdrm

Luque, A., & Casado, F. (2020). Procesos de Covid-19 en Ecuador: Cuando la distopía se convierte en realidad. *Revista Venezolana de Gerencia, 25*(92), 1271–1281. https://doi.org/10.37960/rvg.v25i92. ISSN 1315-9984.

Luque, A., & Galora, R. (2020). Impacto de la tecnología en la sociedad: el caso de Ecuador. *Revista Ciencias Pedagógicas e Innovación, 7*(2), enero-junio, 40–47. https://doi.org/10.26423/rcpi.v7i2.299

Luque, A., & Guamán, A. (2021). Transnational textile outsourcing: Exceptional or standard? *International Journal of Business and Globalisation*, 27(2), 143–170. https://doi.org/10.1504/IJBG.2021.10034942

Luque, A., Hernández Zubizarreta, J., & de Pablos, C. (2016). Weaknesses within the processes of globalization in the textile sector and their relation to CSR through a Delphi analysis: Ethical or aesthetic. *Revista Recerca*, 19, 35–71. https://doi.org/10.6035/Recerca.2016.19.3

Mainemelis, C., Boyatzis, R. E., & Kolb, D. A. (2002). Learning styles and adaptive flexibility: Testing experiential learning theory. *Management Learning*, 33(1), 5–33. https://doi.org/10.1177/1350507602331001

Martínez-Climent, C., Rodríguez-García, M., & Ribeiro-Soriano, D. (2019). Digital transformations and value creation in international markets. *International Journal of Entrepreneurial Behavior and Research*, 25(8), 1603–1604. https://doi.org/10.1108/IJEBR-11-2019-820

McCulley, L. (2020). Lockdown: Homeworkers putting in extra hours – Instant messaging up 1900%. *27 de abril*. http://www.thehrdirector.com/business-news/the-workplace/new-data-over-a-third-38-admit-to-working-longer-hours-when-working-from-home/

McParland, C., & Connolly, R. (2020). Dataveillance in the workplace: Managing the impact of innovation. *Business Systems Research Journal*, 11(1), 106–124. https://doi.org/10.2478/bsrj-2020-0008

Passet, R. (2012). *Las grandes representaciones del mundo y la economía a lo largo de la historia: del universo mágico al torbellino creador*. Clave Intelectual.

Paul, E. D., & Grantham, C. E. (1995). The 'greening' of organizational change: A case study. *Innovation: The European Journal of Social Science Research*, 8(2), 221–233.

Polanyi, K., & MacIver, R. M. (1944). *The great transformation*, 2 (p. 145). Beacon Press.

Popescu, C. R. G. (2021a). Sustainable and responsible entrepreneurship for value-based cultures, economies, and societies: Increasing performance through intellectual capital in challenging Times. In C. Popescu & R. Verma (Eds.), *Sustainable and responsible entrepreneurship and key drivers of performance* (pp. 33–58). IGI Global. https://doi.org/10.4018/978-1-7998-7951-0.ch002

Popescu, C. R. G. (2021b). Measuring progress towards the sustainable development goals: Creativity, intellectual capital, and innovation. In C. Popescu (Ed.), *Handbook of research on novel practices and current successes in achieving the sustainable development goals* (pp. 125–136). IGI Global. https://doi.org/10.4018/978-1-7998-8426-2.ch006.

Rodríguez, D., & Valldeoriola, J. (2007). *Metodología de la investigación*. Universitat Oberta de Catalunya.

Sassen, S. (2017). The state and globalization 1. In *The third way transformation of social democracy* (pp. 59–72). Routledge.

Schwab, K. (2017). *The fourth industrial revolution*. Crown Business.

Sorensen, H. (2016). *Best practices for managing telecommuting employees*. Capella University. http://www.provexam.com/en-us/aboutus/prov-pulse/articles/best-practices-for-telecommuting.

Sotto, R. (1996). Organizing in cyberspace: The virtual link. *Scandinavian Journal of Management*, 12(1), 25–40. https://doi.org/10.1016/0956-5221(95)00039-9

Spataro, J. (2020). *Key findings about remote work: Lessons from our colleagues in China*. Microsoft Website. http://www.microsoft.com/en-us/microsoft-365/blog/2020/04/17/key-findings-remote-work-lessons-colleagues-china/. Microsoft Press.

Standing, G. (2014). *A precariat charter: From denizens to citizens*. A&C Black.

Stephens, K. K., & Davis, J. (2009). The social influences on electronic multitasking in organizational meetings. *Management Communication Quarterly, 23*(1), 63–83. https://doi.org/10.1177/0893318909335417

The International Monetary Fund. (2021). *Outlook international monetary fund. Recovery during a pandemic. Health concerns, supply disruptions, and price pressures.* IMF. http://www.imf.org/en/Publications/WEO/Issues/2021/10/12/world-economic-outlook-october-2021.

Trost, A. (2019). *Human resources strategies: Balancing stability and agility in times of digitization.* Springer. https://doi.org/10.1007/978-3-030-30592-5.

Voogt, J., & Roblin, N. P. (2012). A comparative analysis of international frameworks for 21st century competences: Implications for national curriculum policies. *Journal of Curriculum Studies, 44*(3), 299–321. https://doi.org/10.1080/00220272.2012.668938

10
DIGITAL INNOVATION IN THE WORKPLACE

Lukman Raimi and Muhammad Usman Tariq

Introduction

In the era of Adams Smith (1723–1790) and Frederick Winslow Taylor (1856–1915), the desire to improve workplace performance, employee monitoring, and operational efficiency through the adoption of scientific methods has been the focus of measurement engineers, factory managers, and management thinkers (Jacobs et al., 2004; Kwok, 2014; Rosenblat et al., 2014). A scientific method in the workplace is desirable because it assists organisations in identifying, fragmenting, and regimenting workflows to reach production targets (Sewell, 2005; Rosenblat et al., 2014). The quest for continuous improvement of the workplace is unending. In contemporary times, the phenomenon of digital innovation through smart technologies is a renewed attempt to improve workplace surveillance, productivity improvement, operational efficiency, reduction of operational risk, and maximisation of profits and competitiveness (Ball, 2010; Rosenblat et al., 2014).

Beyond the theoretical benefits of digital innovation, several empirical findings explicate that the adoption of digital innovation in workplaces produces positive operational outcomes. For instance, Deloitte found that digital technologies in the workplace have improved financial performance and actualisation of business objectives by 22% (Malik, 2021). Almost two decades ago, Isa and Tsuru (2002) found that digital innovations introduced by leading electrical and electronic firms in Japan positively affected productivity, operating profit rates, and ordinary profit rates. Moreover, Palumbo (2021) found that workplace digitization positively contributes to enhancing employee–manager relationships, better employee involvement, and a positive impact on organisational performance. However, workplace digitization triggers a depersonalisation of workplaces and desensitises the social, organisational climate. In addition, digital innovation in the workplace instils fear and change resistance among segments of employees and leadership (Malik, 2021).

DOI: 10.4324/9781003283386-12

The drawbacks of digital innovation in the workplace, as previously enunciated, are surmountable. To redress these drawbacks, employers need to reassure, educate, and sensitise the workforce that digitalisation is not harmful to their occupational interest; it is rather the virtual, digital equivalent of the physical work that comes with new digital tools and technologies to stimulate improved organisational formation and effectiveness (Miller, 2016). Amid this euphoria, employees and other stakeholders in industrial society must fully understand digital innovation to maximise its inexhaustive benefits, including employees' centredness and people-centred human resource management practices (Palumbo, 2021).

Moreover, theories of digital innovation abound. Some digital innovation theories include diffusion of innovation theory, task-technology fit theory, technology acceptance model, and creative destruction theory. Digital innovation in the workplace as a new field of research and practice driven by artificial intelligence (AI), drones, telematics, robotics, and other disruptive technologies requires more extensive studies. At present, scholars and professionals have different perspectives about digital innovation in workplaces. Some scholars associate digital innovation strictly with digital ability, digital capability, and digital aptitude, which, when combined, positively influence firm performance (Nwankpa & Roumani, 2016) and enhance competitive advantage (Chae et al., 2014). Other researchers linked digital innovation to information technology infrastructure in the workplace. Therefore, it is essential to understand the actual concept of digital innovation. It is about getting the tasks done digitally.

In view of the mixed reactions to digital innovation in the workplace, there is a need for more conceptual, policy-focused, and empirical studies on the subject from multidisciplinary perspectives. This chapter responds to this call by discussing the concept of digital innovation in the workplace and related matters. Apart from the introduction, there are six sections in this chapter. The first discusses methods and approaches. The next section reviews the literature to gain richer insights. The following section explains the multidimensional benefits of digital innovation for future workplaces, including the implementation challenges, and provides frameworks for digital workplace innovation (DWI) to aid and support digital innovation management. Finally, the last section concludes with a contextualisation of emerging insights, practical implications, limitations, and policy recommendations.

Methods and analysis

In developing this chapter, we purposely adopted qualitative research (an interpretivist paradigm) to provide deeper insight into the discussion on digital innovation in the workplace. We sourced relevant information from scholarly articles, texts, policy documents, working papers, and online resources to achieve the chapter deliverables. After that, a content analysis was used to review, integrate, and synthesise the extracted textual information. The methodology literature explains that content analysis is a logical procedure for quantifying the contents of texts, writings, interviews, picture speeches, books, correspondences, and other verbal data

(Denscombe, 2017). We found content analysis useful because it allows the texts, words, and other visual and verbal data to be compressed, classified, summarised, and tabulated into fewer content categories for meaningful and useful interpretation in research (Saunders et al., 2016). For more clarity, we follow a four-stage process:

1 **Stage 1: Data sourcing** – At this stage, we sourced the required numeric secondary data on digital innovation in workplace to address our chapter objectives. For data sourcing, we previewed eScience Direct and Google Scholar, from which more than 65 articles were downloaded, from which 47 were selected based on the purposive sampling technique. The two selection criteria used are explained here:

   • Selected articles that discuss digital innovation in the workplace from diverse perspectives and contexts.
   • The selected articles that provide insights into the theories, prospects, and challenges of digital innovation in the workplace.

2 **Stage 2: Data development and conversion** – At this stage, we compiled insightful pieces of information based on relevance, recency, and suitability in readiness for analysis data.
3 **Stage 3: Data analysis** – In this stage, the insightful pieces of information were critically reviewed, appraised, synthesised, and contextualised using content analysis.
4 **Stage 4: Contextualisation using tables and figures** – At this final stage, the insightful pieces of information were contextualised using tables for easy comprehension by readers. This methodological approach is supported by Jepson (2009) and Williams and Shepherd (2017).

Conceptual clarifications

Defining the concept of digital

The term "digital" is linked to technological capabilities that provide embeddedness to organisational processes, which allow businesses and people to become more agile, better, and faster in making decisions (McKinsey Insights, 2015). From a broader perspective, digital technology involves all things linked to the internet that utilise pixels, data, and screens. There are many platforms for digital connectivity and communication, for example, email, social media, online games, websites, apps, and e-commerce websites. The actual point is that a person may understand "digital" when he sees it or utilises it. It is the services, apps, and content that people use online. It leads to getting tasks done digitally during digital project management (Soybir & Schmidt, 2021). As a generic term, digital conceptualisation has received diverse applications in multidisciplinary fields, such as digital sustainability (Bradley, 2007), digital literacy (Buckingham, 2010), digital humanities (Vanhoutte, 2013), and digital medicine (Elenko et al., 2015).

Defining digital innovation

Digital innovation has become an enabler for contemporary companies to improve their products, and digital innovation is viewed as the use of digital technology in a wide range of innovations (Nambisan et al., 2017). Additionally, digital innovation in the workplace refers to innovations in information processing and communication technologies that address the agelong challenges of determining the structures and technologies that can ensure efficiency and integrity in the management of business and employees (Zureik, 2003; Rosenblat et al., 2014). Hinings et al. (2018) describe digital innovation as the concerted deployment of technologies for the orchestration of new products, processes, services, platforms, and business models with an organisational context. All the definitions of digital innovation alluded to digital technology because it is both the input (the basis for digital innovations) and output (the result of digital innovation adoption). In a changing world characterised by the adoption of disruptive technologies, organisations must be proactive in adopting new technologies. Several years ago, Blockbuster, Circuit City, and Kodak became obsolete, forgotten, and ceased to exist because they failed to adopt digital innovation (Gans, 2016; Albanese & Manning 2015).

Digital innovation management

Digital innovation in the workplace is practically a project that requires meticulous implementation following four phases (Mikalsen et al., 2018; Biazzo et al., 2020). The following are four prime phases of the digital project:

- **Initiation**: It includes commencing the project and bringing the clients on board in the proper manner to confirm the project makes a success.
- **Planning**: It includes plotting the scope, timelines, and handing over the tasks to related experts.
- **Execution**: It is the stage where the prime assets are developed.
- **Wrap up**: It includes delivering outcomes and cross-examining all partners included.

The initiation phase commences before the actual start of the digital innovation project. It includes getting the documents ready and accumulating the resources required to finish the project reasonably. This level can also have analysis calls, recruiting contractors, and getting new clients on board (Marder et al., 2021). The planning phase starts after the management completes onboarding and all documents get signed and sent; it moves to the next level of digital innovation project management, i.e., planning; the firms function out all the twists and strategise to assure that all the assets can be developed in a timely manner (Georgieva, 2018). The execution phase of digital innovation projects is the most comprehensive because it is the point when digital innovation things move ahead and the various aspects of the innovation project are unfolded in the workplace (Morcov et al., 2021). Finally, the wrap-up phase relates to the wrapping and finishing stage of the digital innovation project, which is as significant as the initial levels (Ershadi et al., 2021).

Relevant theories underpinning digital innovation

The current discourse of digital innovation in the workplace requires theory building and theory adoption. This is premised on the paucity of theories in this area. According to Oeij and Dhondt (2017), a theoretical underpinning of workplace innovation (WPI) is highly required and expedient because, at present, there are scattered theoretical approaches that draw largely from human relations, systems theory, work organisation, change management processes, and strategic business choice thinking. After a review of the extant literature, this chapter found that several innovation theories support the thematic issue of digital innovation in the workplace. The most important theories that provide grounding for this chapter are the diffusion of innovation theory, task-technology fit theory, technology acceptance model, and creative destruction theory. A brief insight into the four preferred theories is provided hereunder.

Diffusion of innovation theory (DIT), also called the technology adoption lifecycle, was postulated by E.M. Rogers, with insights from communication. Rogers synthesised research from more than 508 diffusion studies and postulated the DIT. The theory explicates "the process by which an innovation is communicated through certain channels over time among the members of a social system" (p. 9). DIT explained that innovation and adoption happened after going through several stages: (a) understanding, (b) persuasion, (c) decision, (d) implementation, and (e) confirmation. In addition, the DIT identified five types of people based on their readiness and preference for innovation in society. Geoffrey Moore, the world's leading high-tech and communications researcher/expert made useful contributions to developing the technology adoption lifecycle in his treatise "Crossing the chasm" (Moreor, 1991; Moore & McKenna, 1999).

With specific application to innovative products in the high-tech industry, people based on their level of adoption and acceptance of innovation during the early startup period can be categorised chronologically as innovators, early adopters, early majority, late majority, and laggards based on the timing of adoption behaviour (Moore, 1999; Roger, 2003).

1   Innovators/Techies (2.5%) – These are the first set of individuals to try the new innovation because they are very much willing to take risks.
2   Early Adopters/Progressives (13.5%) – People who represent opinion leaders who enjoy leadership roles and embrace change opportunities. They are already aware of the need to change and so are very comfortable adopting new ideas.

3　Early Majority/Pragmatists (34%) – People are rarely leaders, but they adopt new ideas before the average person has seen evidence of the innovation's effectiveness.
4　Late Majority/Conservatives (34%) – People are sceptical of change and will only adopt an innovation after the majority has tried it.
5　Laggards/Sceptics (16%) – People are bound by tradition and very conservative. They are very sceptical of change and are the hardest group to bring on board.

The task-technology fit (TTF) theory is associated with Goodhue and Thompson (1995) and examines how task-technology fit impacts performance. TTF theory measures individual impact in terms of improved efficiency, effectiveness, and/or higher quality. TTF is hinged on the premise that a good fit between task and technology tends to increase the likelihood of utilisation, adoption, and diffusion of smart experimentation products because they boost the performance impact. In other words, technology is adopted because it meets users' task needs and wants more closely. TTF is very suitable for investigating the actual usage of the technology, especially the testing of new technology, to obtain feedback. TTF is also good for measuring the technology applications already released in the marketplace.

The technology acceptance model has three parts (TAM 1, 2, and 3). TAM 1 was introduced by Fred Davis (1986). TAM 1 is specifically tailored for modelling users' acceptance of information systems or technologies that emerged from experimentation. The goal of TAM is to explain the general determinants of technology acceptance in relation to users' behaviour in a given context. The basic TAM model included two specific beliefs: perceived usefulness (PU) and perceived ease of use (PEU). The term "perceived usefulness" refers to a potential user's subjective likelihood that the use of a particular technology will improve their action, while "perceived ease of use" refers to the degree to which the potential user expects the target system to be effortless.

TAM 2 was introduced by Davis et al. (1989), with some enhanced assumptions. The intent of TAM 2 is to explain the general determinants of technology acceptance in relation to users' behaviour and external factors. TAM 2 included three specific variables: PU, PEU, and external variables. External variables refer to extraneous factors that influence the PU and PEU in TAM (Davis et al., 1989). TAM 3 was introduced by Venkatesh and Davis (1996), with further enhanced assumptions by eliminating the attitude construct and replacing it with behaviour intention. TAM 3 included three specific variables: PU, PEU, and external variables (Venkatesh and Davis, 1996).

The creative destruction theory (CDT) of Joseph Schumpeter (1934) stated that entrepreneurship is simply a process of introducing new combinations, new products, production methods, markets, sources of supply, or industrial combinations to move the economy from its equilibrium to a better stage than enhances economic growth. The CDT presumes that knowledge, innovation, and creativity are forces

TABLE 10.1 Digital innovation workplace and new lifestyles

Lifestyle mode	Back-to-normal people	Wireless materialists	Gregarious simplifiers	Click rebels
Digital innovation workplace and new lifestyles	Those who favour partial and conditional adoption of telework because it provides convenience, status signalling, and profit	Those who fully adopt telework, work from home (WFH), and other digital technologies in order to maximise their professional potential in workplaces	Those who resist telework and new norms; are relatively more comfortable with shortened work weeks	Those who welcome telework and touchless workspace because it enables self-realisation, freelancing ethos, and open collaboration

Source: Adapted from Echegaray (2021, p. 572).

that propel and stimulate new products, processes, technology, and markets. At the end of innovation adoption in organisations, new products, services, and technologies create far-reaching changes in the economy.

From the preceding digital innovation theories, the takeaway is that employers of labour must launch a talent strategy that would develop three competencies of their employees in readiness for digital innovation in future workplaces, namely, (a) critical digital and cognitive capabilities, (b) social and emotional skills, and (c) adaptability and resilience (Dixit et al., 2020). In the future digitalized workplace, the workplace lifestyle behaviours are explained in Table 10.1.

Multidimensional benefits and frameworks for DWI

From the plethora of viewpoints explored thus far, it is obvious that digital innovation in the workplace has multidimensional benefits for all players in industrial society. Isa and Tsuru (2002) reported that the benefits of digital innovation include decentralisation of workshops, better customer relations and fast delivery, effective coordination and production decisions, enhanced inventory and cost-control systems, and more performance-based personnel practices. Rosenblat et al. (2014) posited that the most important benefits of digital innovation are effective workplace surveillance (employee monitoring and performance tracking), improved social networks, expansion of organisational reach by large businesses, and competitiveness in a growing market.

This chapter produced a framework for digital workplace innovation (DWI) from foregoing. DWI is a process-oriented transformation with unlimited opportunities and benefits for all stakeholders. The operational implementation of DWI is divided into three functional stages: input, process, and output. The input stage of the digital workplace explicates the management of the workplace leveraging digital technologies by deploying the right people at the right time in the right quantity for the right operation. The process stage of a digital workplace represents a running workflow or series of interlinked tasks, responsibilities, activities, and/ or steps for which resources are appropriated to meet a predefined goal or output (Garvin, 1998; Florac & Carleton, 1999). Finally, the output stage of the digital workplace produces operational outcomes/results measured in terms of increased task flexibility, improved work efficiency, organisational performance, improved sustainability, lower business risk, improved decision-making, improved topline and bottom-line, better quality of working life, and growth of market shares, among others.

Table 10.2 provides a detailed explanation of the transition from the input stage (introduction of digital technologies) to the process stage (types of digital technologies) to the output stage (beneficial outcomes of digital technologies).

TABLE 10.2 Frameworks for digital workplace innovation (DWI)

Digital innovation in workplace	Components of digital innovation in workplace	Benefits of digital innovation in workplace
Input stage	**Process stage**	**Output stage**
• Information	• Work from home (WFH)	• Increased tasks flexibility
• Technology	• Telecommuting	• Improved work efficiency
• Management	• Global positioning system (GPS)	• Organisational performance
	• Robots/robotics	• Improved sustainability
	• Enterprise resource planning (ERP)	• Improved workplace surveillance
	• Data analytics	• Lower business risk
	• Cybersecurity	• Competitive advantage
	• Machine-to-machine relationship	• Improved decision-making
	• Monitoring control systems (MCS)	• Improved topline and bottom-line
	• Virtual reality app/video conferencing	• Better quality of working life
	• Unmanned aerial vehicles (UAVs)	• Reduced operational costs
	• Orders/request management systems	• Growth of the market share
	• Cloud-based collaboration tools	• Real-time communication
	• Cloud computing	
	• Secure group messaging systems	
	• Employee-centred apps	
	• Smart virtual assistants	
	• Artificial intelligence (AI)	
	• Internet of Things (IoT)	
	• Telematics	

Source: Authors' configuration.

Conclusion and practical implications

This chapter discusses the concept of digital innovation in the workplace to strengthen research and practice. In developing the chapter, a content analysis was adopted. The authors reviewed, integrated, and synthesised the extracted textual information from scholarly articles, texts, and online resources. At the end of the content analysis, four insights emerged on digital innovation in the workplace. First, the understanding of digital innovation converges around the deployment of novel technologies and unique combinations of other organisational resources in the workplace for generating new products and better service offerings to meet production targets, competitiveness, and profitability. Second, the four relevant theories that provide a theoretical underpinning for this discourse are a diffusion of innovation theory, task-technology fit theory, technology acceptance model, and creative destruction theory. Third, digital innovation in the workplace stimulates four new lifestyles among employees and members of management based on their digital capability, attitude, and aptitude, namely, back-to-normal people, wireless materialists, gregarious simplifiers, and click rebels. Fourth, the multidimensional benefits of digital innovation in the workplace include increased task flexibility, improved work efficiency, enhanced organisational performance, improved sustainability, improved workplace surveillance, lower business risk, competitive advantage, improved decision-making, improved profitability (topline and bottom-line), a better quality of working life, reduced operational costs, growth of the market share, and better real-time communication, among others.

From the critical discourse, some practical implications have clearly emerged that may be of immense benefit to stakeholders in the transformation journey of digital innovation in the workplace. First, to forestall fear, phobia, sabotage, and resistance to the introduction of digital innovation in the workplace, there is a need for collaboration by tripartite stakeholders (governments, employers, and employees) in industrial society. Second, to improve digital literacy, capability, attitude, and aptitude, managers and policymakers in the workplace need to develop three competencies of their employees and members of management in readiness for digital innovation in workplaces. These competencies are critical digital and cognitive capabilities, social and emotional skills, and adaptability and resilience. Additionally, a change management programme is imperative before implementing the digital innovation workplace. This approach helps build motivation throughout the implementation process to entrench the culture of digital innovation in the workplace. Furthermore, managers need to institute digital innovation enforcement procedures, which should be accompanied by a periodic review where those with high levels of digital capabilities, attitudes, and aptitudes are recognised and rewarded.

References

Albanese, J., & Manning, B. (2015). *Revive: how to transform traditional businesses into digital leaders*. FT Press.

Ball, K. (2010). "Workplace surveillance: an overview." *Labour History 51*(1), 87–106.

Biazzo, S., Fabris, A., & Panizzolo, R. (2020). Virtual visual planning: A methodology to assess digital project management tools. *International Journal of Applied Research in Management and Economics*, *3*(4), 1–10. https://doi.org/10.33422/ijarme.v3i4.505

Bradley, K. (2007). Defining digital sustainability. *Library Trends*, *56*(1), 148–163. https://doi.org/10.1353/lib.2007.0044

Buckingham, D. (2010). Defining digital literacy. In *Medienbildung in neuen Kulturräumen* (pp. 59–71). VS Verlag für Sozialwissenschaften.

Chae, H. C., Koh, C. E., & Prybutok, V. R. (2014). Information technology capability and firm performance: Contradictory findings and their possible causes. *MIS Quarterly*, *38*(1), 305–326. https://doi.org/10.25300/MISQ/2014/38.1.14

Davis, F. D. (1986). *A technology acceptance model for empirically testing new end – user information systems: Theory and results* [PhD dissertation. MIT Sloan School of Management].

Davis, F. D., Bagozzi, R. P., & Warshaw, P. R. (1989). User acceptance of computer technology: A comparison of two theoretical models. *Management Science*, *35*(8), 982–1003.

Denscombe, M. (2017). *EBOOK: The good research guide: For small-scale social research projects*. McGraw-Hill Education (UK).

Dixit, J. K., Agrawal, V., Agarwal, S., Gerguri-Rashiti, S., & Said, D. S. (2020). Competencies development for women edupreneurs community – an integrated AHP-TOPSIS approach. *Journal of Enterprising Communities: People and Places in the Global Economy*, *15*(1), 5–25.

Echegaray, F. (2021). What POST-COVID-19 lifestyles may look like? Identifying scenarios and their implications for sustainability. *Sustainable Production and Consumption*, *27*, 567–574.

Elenko, E., Underwood, L., & Zohar, D. (2015). Defining digital medicine. *Nature Biotechnology*, *33*(5), 456–461. https://doi.org/10.1038/nbt.3222

Ershadi, M., Jefferies, M., Davis, P., & Mojtahedi, M. (2021, January). Effective application of information technology tools for real-time project management. In *International conference on digital technologies and applications* (pp. 719–729). Springer.

Florac, W. A., & Carleton, A. D. (1999). *Measuring the software process: Statistical process control for software process improvement*. Addison-Wesley Professional.

Gans, J. (2016). *The disruption dilemma*. MIT press.

Garvin, D. A. (1998). The processes of organization and management. *Sloan Management Review*, *39*(4), 33–51.

Georgieva, M. (2018). *Achieving efficiency in large-scale digitization project management with free IT tools*. https://digitalscholarship.unlv.edu/libfacpresentation/158

Goodhue, D. L., & Thompson, R. L. (1995). Task-technology fit and individual performance. *MIS Quarterly*, 213–236.

Hinings, B., Gegenhuber, T., & Greenwood, R. (2018). Digital innovation and transformation: An institutional perspective. *Information and Organization*, *28*(1), 52–61. https://doi.org/10.1016/j.infoandorg.2018.02.004

Isa, K., & Tsuru, T. (2002). Cell production and workplace innovation in Japan: Toward a new model for Japanese manufacturing? *Industrial Relations: A Journal of Economy and Society*, *41*(4), 548–578. https://doi.org/10.1111/1468-232X.00264

Jacobs, F. R., Chase, R. B., & Aquilano, N. J. (2004). *Operations management for competitive advantage* (pp. 64, 70). McGraw-Hill.

Jepson, D. (2009). Studying leadership at cross-country level: A critical analysis. *Leadership*, *5*(1), 61–80. https://doi.org/10.1177/1742715008098310

Kwok, A. C. (2014). The evolution of management theories: A literature review. *Nang Yan Business Journal*, *3*(1), 28–40.

Malik, P. (2021, September). *What is digital innovation? + Corporate benefits and examples*. https://whatfix.com/blog/digital-innovation/

Marder, B., Ferguson, P., Marchant, C., Brennan, M., Hedler, C., Rossi, M., Black, S., & Doig, R. (2021). 'Going agile': Exploring the use of project management tools in fostering psychological safety in group work within management discipline courses. *International Journal of Management Education*, *19*(3), 100519. https://doi. org/10.1016/j.ijme.2021.100519

McKinsey Insights. (2015, July). *What 'digital' really means.* McKinsey & Company. http://www.mckinsey.com/industries/technology-media-and-telecommunications/ our-insights/what-digital-really-means

Mikalsen, M., Moe, N. B., Stray, V., & Nyrud, H. (2018). Agile digital transformation: A case study of interdependencies. In *Proceedings of the 39th International Conference on Information Systems (ICIS). Association for Information Systems (AIS).* Thirty Ninth International Conference on Information Systems.

Miller, P. (2016, August). *4 essential ingredients for digital employee experience success.* https://digital-workplacegroup.com/4-essential-ingredients-for-digital-employee-experience-success/

Moore, G. A. (1991). *Crossing the chasm.* HarperBusiness.

Moore, G. A. (1999). *Crossing the chasm.* HarperBusiness.

Moore, G. A., & McKenna, R. (1999). *Crossing the chasm: Marketing and selling high-tech products to mainstream customers.* HarperBusiness.

Morcov, S., Pintelon, L., & Kusters, R. J. (2021). A practical assessment of modern it project complexity management tools: Taming positive, appropriate, negative complexity. *International Journal of Information Technology Project Management*, *12*(3), 90–108. https://doi. org/10.4018/IJITPM.2021070106

Nambisan, S., Lyytinen, K., Majchrzak, A., & Song, M. (2017). Digital Innovation Management: Reinventing innovation management research in a digital world. *MIS Quarterly*, *41*(1), 223–238. https://doi.org/10.25300/MISQ/2017/41:1.03

Nwankpa, J. K., & Roumani, Y. (2016). IT capability and digital transformation: A firm performance perspective. In *Thirty-seventh international conference on information systems.* https://core.ac.uk/download/pdf/301370499.pdf.

Oeij, P. R. A., & Dhondt, S. (2017). Theoretical approaches supporting workplace innovation. In P. Oeij, D. Rus & F. Pot (Eds.), *Workplace innovation. Aligning perspectives on health, safety and well-being.* https://doi.org/10.1007/978-3-319-56333-6_5. Springer.

Palumbo, R. (2021). Does digitizing involve desensitizing? Strategic Insights into the side effects of workplace digitization. *Public Management Review*, 1–26. https://doi.org/10.10 80/14719037.2021.1877796

Rogers, E. (2003). *Diffusion of innovations* (5th ed.). Free Press.

Rosenblat, A., Kneese, T., & Boyd, D. (2014). *Workplace surveillance* (pp. 1–19). Open Society Foundations' future of work commissioned research papers/data and society Research Institute. https://papers.ssrn.com/sol3/papers.cfm?abstract_id=2536605

Saunders, M., Lewis, P., & Thornhill, A. (2016). *Research methods for business students* (7th ed.). Pearson Education.

Sewell, G. (2005). Nice work? Rethinking managerial control in an era of knowledge work. *Organization, 12*(5), 685–704.

Schumpeter, J. A. (1934). *The Theory of Economic Development.* Harvard University Press.

Soybir, S., & Schmidt, C. (2021). Project management and RPA. In *The digital journey of banking and insurance, I* (pp. 289–305). Palgrave Macmillan.

Vanhoutte, E. (Ed.). (2013). *Defining digital humanities: A reader.* Ashgate Publishing, Ltd.

Venkatesh, V., & Davis, F. D. (1996). A model of the antecedents of perceived ease of use: Development and test. *Decision Sciences*, *27*(3), 451–481.

Williams, T. A., & Shepherd, D. A. (2017). Mixed method social network analysis: Combining inductive concept development, content analysis, and secondary data for quantitative analysis. *Organizational Research Methods*, *20*(2), 268–298. https://doi. org/10.1177/1094428115610807

Zureik, E. (2003). Theorizing surveillance: The case of the workplace. In D. Lyon (Ed.), *Surveillance as social sorting: Privacy, risk, and digital discrimination.* Routledge.

11

DIGITAL CORPORATE ENTREPRENEURSHIP IN THE WORKPLACE

Mahmoud El Samad, Hani El-Chaarani,
Sam El Nemar, and Lukman Raimi

Introduction

The COVID-19 pandemic and its global impact on socioeconomic conditions led to changes in managerial behavior in business affairs. Many fields and sectors (e.g., education, hospitality, health care, supply chains, communication, transportation) were negatively affected by this international health pandemic (El-Chaarani et al., 2021).

The advancement of technology was a cornerstone to bypass the economic and social crises caused by the new pandemic. Digital entrepreneurship and digitalization in corporate businesses increased during the pandemic as a key factor to develop the economic cycles and business activities in both developed and developing countries (Glinyanova et al., 2021).

Many entrepreneurs and firms employed innovative tools to ensure the continuity of their work (e.g., Zoom for online meetings, Google Classroom as a platform for education, and hundreds of new applications related to supply chains). The appearance of the COVID-19 virus also led governments, SMEs (small-to-medium enterprises), supply chain firms, and medical organizations to review their processing and operational systems based on the big flow of data generated by their activities. Currently, big data management appears as a basic tool to develop corporate entrepreneurship in the workplace and face the new economic and social challenges caused by the COVID-19 pandemic.

Several studies showed that big data and efficient data management can improve organizations' innovation competences in many ways (Capgemini, 2012; Zhan et al., 2017; El-Chaarani & El-Abiad, 2018). Capgemini (2012) revealed that big data analytics (BDA) can improve the average performance by 26% over the past three years. In the context of supply chain management (Trkman et al., 2012), big data management can help to take smart decisions that enhance the business

DOI: 10.4324/9781003283386-13

process innovation. On the other hand, this digital field is still facing many challenges at many levels before being implemented by all corporate entrepreneurs, such as data quality (Chen & Lin, 2014; Liu et al., 2016; Gudivada et al., 2017), data security and privacy (Jain et al., 2016; Yang, 2021), and data analytics (Steed et al., 2013).

Big data is a very promising field where digital corporations needs to invest to be adapted with the dynamic business environment (Doerr et al., 2021). Recently, information technology (IT) specialists have been working to combine big data with artificial intelligence (AI) to upgrade the added value of the new technology in workplaces. More precisely, AI algorithms can be applied at many levels in big data processing such as data analysis, data cleaning, and many more. For example, big data in combination with machine learning (ML, a branch of AI) can be employed in the banking sector (Doerr et al., 2021). Banks' interest in the domain of big data and ML has noticeably augmented over the last years, by around 80%. Many banks are leading new projects based on big data and ML to support their financial stability (El-Chaarani & El-Abiad, 2020).

Moreover, big data in combination with AI can be largely used by corporate entrepreneurs for the development of smart cities where data are collected from different sensors using the Internet of Things (IoT) (Allam & Dhunny, 2019). The objective of this combination is to increase urban livability while enhancing innovation and economic evolution. Smart cities are a great example for applying ML algorithms for real-time data generated continuously from IoT, which relies on data sensors. These data sensors can be installed at workplaces, hospitals, streets, and airports to collect huge amounts of data to be analyzed quickly and efficiently for smart decisions. It is a very challenging task in a big data environment since data is generated continuously at a very high rate where algorithms should be very effective and work under many different scenarios.

Nowadays, many countries are working to develop their public workplaces by implementing the e-governance system based on the application of AI algorithms in big data processing (Rajagopalan & Vellaipandiyan, 2013). The idea behind the combination of big data and AI is to capture real-time data coming from different sources (variety), store it (using new approaches like NoSQL), analyze it, and finally take the right decision at the right time (Chu et al., 2007).

The first objective of this chapter is to highlight the concepts of big data and AI and their applications in workplaces. The second objective in this chapter is to provide corporate entrepreneurs with new digital tools to enhance their innovation and improve decision-making processes in a very dynamic environment.

The rest of the chapter is organized as follows. The second section will discuss the big data concept and its importance in workplaces. The third section will propose a big data flow model that could be employed by corporate entrepreneurs. The fourth section presents the challenges of combining big data with AI for digital corporations. The fifth section shows how big data and AI can help for decision support systems. Finally, the last section concludes this chapter.

Big data for digital corporations

Data can lead to development in many fields, such as e-commerce, social media, health care, finance, and education. These data are processed first into information, then knowledge (Martín-Rojas et al., 2020). Raw data are not meaningful at all. The information is analyzed and turned into knowledge. Hence, we can benefit from the knowledge for decision-making systems (Giménez et al., 2018).

Today, digital corporations and entrepreneurs handle huge amounts of data, and thus they cannot use traditional approaches (e.g., relational data model) to store their data. In fact, classical approaches to store data cannot handle the nature of big data.

Big data are characterized by the four Vs (Labrinidis & Jagadish, 2012; Sagiroglu & Sinanc, 2013): Volume, Variety, Velocity, and Value. Other Vs exist, such as Veracity, Visibility, Variability, and Venue, but we will describe the first four Vs here:

- Volume means that we are handling a large amount of data (data can reach exabytes or even zettabytes). Big data means there is so much data that it cannot be processed via old-style approaches. The data is now generated massively from the Internet of Things (e.g., data sensors are now installed almost everywhere in smart cities), social media (e.g., Twitter, Facebook, YouTube), e-government data, health care record data, etc.
- Variety means that data are coming from different sources in different formats (e.g., structured, XML, NoSQL), such as social media, data sensors, social networks, log files, and IoT devices.
- Velocity means that data is generated in an intensive and massive way each minute, or even each second. As an example, 500 million tweets are posted on Twitter each day, and 3.5 billion searches per day were processed by Google in 2021.
- Value is of most importance since at this stage the digital corporation needs to extract useful decisions for the business. Put differently, value is how to extract business rules after all the effort put forth to handle big data. We can consider the term "value" as the end game in big data.

Given this complex nature of data, large digital corporations should consider adopting new tools to handle big data, especially for corporate entrepreneurship. All the stakeholders should benefit from the existence of big data. In fact, the main challenge in big data is not only in storing and integrating these data, but the most motivating and exciting part is in analyzing this big data to get meaningful value at the right time and targeting the right stakeholders. To handle big data in any digital corporation, we must use a big data framework. Hence, we will present in the next section a generic framework for big data that can be used in any digital corporation. The objective of this framework is to let the reader be familiar with such a framework and to show the main steps needed to adopt such a big data system.

A generic framework for digital corporations to handle big data

The main question related to big data implementation is the following: "how can the corporation and entrepreneur decide which framework must be adopted to handle big data?" After checking the literature review (Tekiner & Keane, 2013; Bahri et al., 2018; Mohamed et al., 2020; Wu et al., 2020), big data frameworks for digital corporation should include four main phases: (a) data collection, (b) data processing, (c) data analytics, and (d) data visualization. Our recommendation for digital corporate entrepreneurs is to implement the following four main steps.

Data collection

Data collection consists of collecting data from different sources. For example, data sources can be data generated from e-commerce websites, smartphones, data sensors installed in a car or a building, or the IoT). This process is very complex and needs highly qualified IT or computer scientists who can use or develop APIs (application programming interfaces) that can retrieve data from different data sources. It should be noted that data is generated in a very quick manner when dealing with big data (Munshi & Yasser, 2017).

When a digital corporation wants to move forward on integrating data from different sources, these sources should also be trusted and need to keep monitoring the data coming from these sources. Data might include erroneous information that should be filtered and monitored in the framework.

Data processing

Most digital corporations have one database management system (DBMS) to store and handle all the data for an organization, such as a hospital, and an online website that sells goods and services. Most of the traditional DBMSs are based on relational DBMSs (e.g., traditional Oracle, Microsoft SQL server, or DB2). These classical and traditional ways of storing data cannot tackle the diversity of big data, as stated previously. Big data come from different sources with different formats (e.g., relational model, NoSQL, XM files, text files). Obviously, large companies such as Oracle move forward toward big data and propose solutions to handle big data. Oracle provides a Hadoop-based data storage using data lakes; Spark for data processing; and the analysis is achieved via Oracle Cloud SQL where the user (e.g., the customer) can use a personalized analytical tool.

Data analytics

Data analytics is a very critical phase since data is analyzed in this phase to generate efficient and smart decisions for workforces. This phase is based on the usage of data-mining algorithms that can produce meaningful value, such as increase the discount for some items. Nowadays, data analytics in big data do not rely only on data-mining techniques but also use AI algorithms. AI proposes prediction algorithms and ML algorithms. These algorithms are responsible for predictions and can produce valuable decisions. The idea here is to use the most suitable algorithm to analyze the large amounts of data to study the correlation between data. As an example, making a quick and correct decision in health care corporations can dramatically reduce the number of persons who can be affected by a virus or even reduce the cost of treatment in a dramatic way (Pham et al., 2021). Later, we will provide more details about AI algorithms that can be used for big data.

Data visualization

Data visualization allows data scientists to visualize the results of the data analytics phase, and hence we can get some statistics and predictions. This phase is the fruitful output of all the previous steps. At this stage, data scientists can visualize the results based on some visualization tools and can take action based on these data. For example, a medical center must stop the treatment of anti–inflammatory for COVID-19 patients if they notice severe complications. In fact, data visualization should be monitored and decisions should be taken quickly in workplaces since data is generated massively each minute. At this stage, digital corporations should recruit professionals (e.g., salespeople) that can efficiently make quick decisions to enhance the performance of the overall business.

The mission of digital corporate entrepreneurs at this this level of big data management is to propose new business ideas based on the observed information. It is a very challenging task, but corporate entrepreneurs should recruit new staff that can understand better their business. The decision to integrate a big data framework within SME and large organizations can change the workflow and business design. Later, we will tackle the problem of decision support systems and its importance for corporate entrepreneurs.

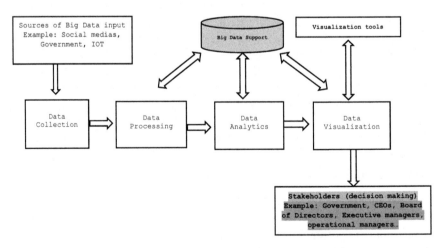

FIGURE 11.1   Framework for Big Data on Decision Making

Artificial intelligence and big data in service of corporate entrepreneurship development: opportunities and challenges

The research on AI and big data are evolving in many fields, such as management (Ransbotham et al., 2017), health care (Ahmed et al., 2021; Gou & Xu, 2021), economics (Acemoglu & Restrepo, 2018), and innovation (Giménez-Figueroa et al., 2018; Aghion et al., 2017). The combination of AI and big data greatly help the digital corporations to improve their structures and upgrade their competitive advantages (Martín-Rojas et al., 2020).

As an example, in the context of the health care field, the studies of Pham et al. (2021) and Bragazzi et al. (2020) showed that big data technology in combination with AI helped in avoiding the severe effects of the COVID-19 virus. The AI field includes ML algorithms and DL (deep learning) algorithms that greatly helped the medical sector to capture, store, manage, analyze, and predict the impact of new diseases, such as that of COVID-19 (Indumathi et al., 2020).

Hence, large digital corporations should include the concept of AI and big data to enhance their services (e.g., clinical services, financial services, e-commerce sales, social websites) and develop their competitive advantage (Agrawal et al., 2018, 2019).

However, the research papers on corporate entrepreneurship reveal that not all organizations are ready yet for the employment and development of AI and big data in their operational process due to their technical complexity and high costs (Zhou et al., 2017; Martín-Rojas et al., 2020).

One of the main challenges of big data employment within corporations is called data cleaning or data pre-processing. In fact, we need to clean data and remove the redundancies and noise before sending the data to the ML phase (Bengio et al., 2013). This is a very important preparatory phase before applying ML algorithms. This phase is complex since we are dealing with heterogenous data coming from different sources distributed geographically.

Another challenge that could limit the employment of big data and AI by corporations is the need for parallelization techniques for ML algorithms. The ML process needs to use scalable algorithms for large data sets (Zhang et al., 2021). For instance, the famous platform Hadoop (Apache Hadoop, 2021) for big data relies mainly on MapReduce that is used for ML on distributed and parallel computing platforms (Daghighi & Chen, 2022). MapReduce allows an algorithm to run in parallel in a big data environment. The complexity of MapReduce is that the user needs to rewrite some parts of an algorithm from a sequential mode to a parallel mode in order to be adapted in a big data environment.

In total, it is recommended that digital corporations should consult experts from the AI and ML fields to decide which tool (based on intelligent algorithms) they must apply based on their field and their technical and financial capacity. They should recruit an expert in ML algorithms that can choose the most appropriate algorithm if they are looking to enhance the innovation in their company.

Artificial intelligence and big data in service of decision support systems within workplaces

Corporate entrepreneurship relies heavily on creative decision-making; this includes turning data and information into usable knowledge so that decisions can be built on accurate and current facts. Decision support systems (DSSs) is a blend of computer output and human judgment during the decision process (Figure 11.2). In corporate work, in-house corporate entrepreneurs need to collect information such as feedback from stakeholders to assess the validity of their assumptions when trying to make decisions (Dellermann et al., 2019).

In addition, prepared software algorithms are becoming predominantly relied upon due to the improvement in technology in ML and machine intelligence, which is supporting the identification, extraction, and processing of various types of data from different sources when required to support decisions in the workplace (Dellermann et al., 2019; Yuan et al., 2016).

The new transformation in computer technology is machine intelligence, where machine intelligence is now equipped with advanced algorithms that can produce statistical suggestions based on configurations identified in previously observed situations and learning as the data input cultivates (Dellermann et al., 2019; Jordan & Mitchell, 2015).

Furthermore, DSSs, such as AI and big data, support managers in attempting corporate entrepreneurial responsibilities and attaining corporate goals (Obschonka & Audretsch, 2020). As DSSs are a supportive tool for corporate entrepreneurship, they benefits decision-makers by producing relevant reports that navigate, manage, and structure a corporation's analysis of the data available at a workplace. DSSs are multifaceted, dynamic, flexible, quick, and responsive, and integrate corporation departments that can produce interactive reports that change as the firm's data change (Giménez-Figueroa et al., 2018).

Special characteristics of DSSs in decision-making include providing support for decision-makers in semi-structured and unstructured situations, improving the effectiveness of decision-making, and supporting individuals or groups. Advanced

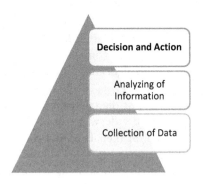

FIGURE 11.2   Decision Support Systems (DSSs)

DSSs are equipped with a knowledge component, can handle large amounts of data, and perform "what-if" and goal-seeking analyses (Asemi et al., 2011).

DSSs are treated as effective managerial tools that deliver updated reports in changing environments. The more accurate the reports are, the more correct decision-making becomes; however, corporate entrepreneurship does not only rely on data, information, and knowledge; decision-makers also need to be creative, imaginative, innovative, and original in their decisions, which cannot be delivered through DDSs.

Conclusion

Big data and AI offer great opportunities in many active areas, such as banking and finance, e-commerce, health care sectors, and much more (Obitade, 2019). One of the main challenges is the availability of IT infrastructure and human resources (Doerr et al., 2021). In fact, there is an urgent need to buy new hardware with high computing power and the necessary tools and software. Cloud computing offers great support for shared computing resources (e.g., CPU, memory, storage, network) and software tools in a big data environment (Das & Dash, 2021). The application of cloud computing as an infrastructure for big data can provide many advanced solutions (Yang et al., 2017).

In addition, corporate entrepreneurs must invest in the training of the staff as well as hiring new data scientists that can help them to better understand this new field. Moreover, they must protect their workplaces from cyberattacks, so they must be sure that their IT staff are aware of the latest technology (Bailey et al., 2014).

Another important challenge for corporate entrepreneurs is that some data are very private (e.g., data used in e-governance, medical data) and sensitive (Mehmood et al., 2016). These data cannot be broadcasted or shared in a big data framework. For example, an employee using a big data framework should not be able to read all the data for a patient. He or she should be able to access the patient's name, ID, and social security number, but should not be given access to all his or her medical information.

Data quality is another problem corporate entrepreneurs could face. Due to the nature of big data, it is crucial to control the quality of generated data. More precisely, data can include tons of errors, including bad, messy, and incomplete data. Hence, many recent studies tackle the problem of enhancing the quality of data (Ehsani et al., 2021; Cai & Zhu, 2015; Kandel, 2011). If we collect bad data, then the data analysis phase will give bad results since the data is not accurate. Poor data quality can have significant economic and social impacts. Cai and Zhu (2015) described the challenges of data quality for big data; the problem is that there are no unified and approved data quality standards for data quality. Hence, many efforts are still ongoing in this area of research. (El Samad et al.,2022)

References

Acemoglu, D., & Restrepo, P. (2018). *Artificial intelligence, automation and work* (no. w24196). National Bureau of Economic Research, NBER WORKING PAPER SERIES.
Acemoglu, D., & Restrepo, P. (2019). *Artificial intelligence, automation, and work* (pp. 197–236). University of Chicago Press. https://doi.org/10.2139/ssrn.3098384

Aghion, P., Jones, B. F., & Jones, C. I. (2017). *Artificial intelligence and economic growth* (no. w23928). National Bureau of Economic Research, NBER WORKING PAPER SERIES.

Aghion, P., Jones, B. F., & Jones, C. I. (2019). *Artificial intelligence and economic growth* (pp. 237–290). University of Chicago Press.

Agrawal, A., Gans, J., & Goldfarb, A. (2018). *Prediction machines: The simple economics of artificial intelligence.* Harvard Business Press.

Agrawal, A., Gans, J., & Goldfarb, A. (2019). Economic policy for artificial intelligence. *Innovation Policy and the Economy, 19*(1), 139–159. https://doi.org/10.1086/699935

Ahmed, I., Ahmad, M., Jeon, G., & Piccialli, F. (2021). A framework for pandemic prediction using big data analytics. *Big Data Research, 25,* 100–190. https://doi.org/10.1016/j.bdr.2021.100190

Allam, Z., & Dhunny, Z. A. (2019). On big data, artificial intelligence and smart cities. *Cities, 89,* 80–91. https://doi.org/10.1016/j.cities.2019.01.032

Apache Hadoop. (2021). Https://Hadoop.Apache.Org/. Retrieved 2021, from https://hadoop.apache.org.

Asemi, A., Safari, A., & Asemi Zavareh, A. A. (2011). The role of management information system (MIS) and Decision support system (DSS) for manager's decision making process. *International Journal of Business and Management, 6*(7), 164–173. https://doi.org/10.5539/ijbm.v6n7p164

Bahri, S., Zoghlami, N., Abed, M., & Tavares, J. M. R. S. (2018). Big data for healthcare: A survey. *IEEE Access, 7,* 7397–7408. https://doi.org/10.1109/ACCESS.2018.2889180

Bailey, T., Miglio, A. D., & Richter, W. (2014). The rising strategic risks of cyberattacks. *McKinsey Quarterly, 2,* 17–22.

Bengio, Y., Courville, A., & Vincent, P. (2013). Representation learning: A review and new perspectives. *IEEE Transactions on Pattern Analysis and Machine Intelligence, 35*(8), 1798–1828. https://doi.org/10.1109/TPAMI.2013.50

Bragazzi, N. L., Dai, H., Damiani, G., Behzadifar, M., Martini, M., & Wu, J. (2020). How big data and artificial intelligence can help better manage the COVID-19 pandemic. *International Journal of Environmental Research and Public Health, 17*(9), 3176. https://doi.org/10.3390/ijerph17093176

Cai, L., & Zhu, Y. (2015). The challenges of data quality and data quality assessment in the big data era. *Data Science Journal, 14*(2). https://doi.org/10.5334/dsj-2015-002

CapGemini. (2012). *Unlocking the power of data and analytics: Transforming insight into income.* Retrieved January 8, 2015, from http://www.uk.capgemini.com/resources/business-process-analyticsunlocking-the-power-of-data-and-analytics-transforming-insight.

Chen, X. W., & Lin, X. (2014). Big data deep learning: Challenges and perspectives. *IEEE Access, 2,* 514–525. https://doi.org/10.1109/ACCESS.2014.2325029

Chu, C., Kim, S. K., Lin, Y., Yu, Y., Bradski, G., Ng, A. Y., & Olukotun, K. (2007). Map-reduce for machine learning on multicore. *Advances in Neural Information Processing Systems, 19,* 281.

Daghighi, A., & Chen, J. Q. (2022). Robustness comparison of scheduling algorithms in MapReduce framework. In *Intelligent computing* (pp. 494–508). Springer.

Das, M., & Dash, R. (2021). Role of cloud computing for big data: A review. *Intelligent and Cloud Computing,* 171–179.

Dellermann, D., Lipusch, N., Ebel, P., & Leimeister, J. M. (2019). Design principles for a hybrid intelligence decision support system for business model validation. *Electronic Markets, 29*(3), 423–441. https://doi.org/10.1007/s12525-018-0309-2

Doerr, S., Gambacorta, L., & Garralda, J. M. S. (2021). *Big data and machine learning in central banking.* BIS Working Papers, 930.

Ehsani-Moghaddam, B., Martin, K., & Queenan, J. A. (2021). Data quality in healthcare: A report of practical experience with the Canadian Primary Care Sentinel

Surveillance Network data. *Health Information Management, 50*(1–2), 88–92. https://doi. org/10.1177/1833358319887743

El-Chaarani, H., & El-Abiad, Z. (2018). The impact of technological innovation on bank performance. *Journal of Internet Banking and Commerce, 23*(3).

El-Chaarani, H., & El-Abiad, Z. (2020). Knowledge management and job performance: The case of Lebanese banking sector. *International Review of Management and Marketing, 10*(1), 91–98. https://doi.org/10.32479/irmm.9225

El-Chaarani, H., Vrontis, P. D., El Nemar, S., & El Abiad, Z. (2022). The impact of strategic competitive innovation on the financial performance of SMEs during COVID-19 pandemic period. *Competitiveness Review, 32*(3), 282–301. https://doi.org/10.1108/CR-02-2021-0024

Giménez-Figueroa, R., Martín-Rojas, R., & García-Morales, V. J. (2018). *Business intelligence: An innovative technological way to influence corporate entrepreneurship. Entrepreneurship-development tendencies and empirical approach* (pp. 113–132). INTECH.

Glinyanova, M., Bouncken, R. B., Tiberius, V., & Cuenca Ballester, A. C. C. (2021). Five decades of corporate entrepreneurship research: Measuring and mapping the field. *International Entrepreneurship and Management Journal, 17*(4), 1731–1757. https://doi.org/10.1007/s11365-020-00711-9

Gou, X., & Xu, Z. (2021). An overview of Big Data in Healthcare: Multiple angle analyses. *Journal of Smart Environments and Green Computing, 1*(3), 131–145. https://doi.org/10.20517/jsegc.2021.07

Gudivada, V., Apon, A., & Ding, J. (2017). Data quality considerations for big data and machine learning: Going beyond data cleaning and transformations. *International Journal on Advances in Software, 10*(1), 1–20.

Indumathi, N., Shanmuga Eswari, M., Salau, A. O., Ramalakshmi, R., & Revathy, R. (2022). Prediction of COVID-19 outbreak with current substantiation using machine learning algorithms. In *Intelligent interactive multimedia systems for e-healthcare applications* (pp. 171–190). Springer.

Jain, P., Gyanchandani, M., & Khare, N. (2016). Big data privacy: A technological perspective and review. *Journal of Big Data, 3*(1), 1–25.

Jordan, M. I., & Mitchell, T. M. (2015). Machine learning: Trends, perspectives, and prospects. *Science, 349*(6245), 255–260. https://doi.org/10.1126/science.aaa8415

Kandel, S., Paepcke, A., Hellerstein, J., & Heer, J. (2011, May). Interactive visual specification of data transformation scripts. In *Wrangler. Proceedings of the SIGCHI conference on human factors in computing systems* (pp. 3363–3372), ACM, Digital Library.

Labrinidis, A., & Jagadish, H. V. (2012). Challenges and opportunities with big data. *Proceedings of the VLDB Endowment, 5*(12), 2032–2033. https://doi.org/10.14778/2367502.2367572

Liu, J., Li, J., Li, W., & Wu, J. (2016). Rethinking big data: A review on the data quality and usage issues. *ISPRS Journal of Photogrammetry and Remote Sensing, 115*, 134–142. https://doi.org/10.1016/j.isprsjprs.2015.11.006

Martín-Rojas, R., García-Morales, V. J., Garrido-Moreno, A., & García-Sánchez, E. (2020). Can business intelligence enhance organizational performance through corporate entrepreneurship? In *Handbook of research on approaches to alternative entrepreneurship opportunities* (pp. 198–221). IGI Global.

Mehmood, A., Natgunanathan, I., Xiang, Y., Hua, G., & Guo, S. (2016). Protection of big data privacy. *IEEE Access, 4*, 1821–1834. https://doi.org/10.1109/ACCESS.2016.2558446

Mohamed, A., Najafabadi, M. K., Wah, Y. B., Zaman, E. A. K., & Maskat, R. (2020). The state of the art and taxonomy of big data analytics: View from new big data framework. *Artificial Intelligence Review, 53*(2), 989–1037. https://doi.org/10.1007/s10462-019-09685-9

Munshi, A. A., & Yasser, A. R. M. (2017). Big data framework for analytics in smart grids. *Electric Power Systems Research*, *151*, 369–380. https://doi.org/10.1016/j.epsr.2017.06.006

Obitade, P. O. (2019). Big data analytics: A link between knowledge management capabilities and superior cyber protection. *Journal of Big Data*, *6*(1), 1–28.

Obschonka, M., & Audretsch, D. B. (2020). Artificial intelligence and big data in entrepreneurship: A new era has begun. *Small Business Economics*, *55*(3), 529–539. https://doi.org/10.1007/s11187-019-00202-4

Pham, Q. V., Nguyen, D. C., Huynh-The, T., Hwang, W. J., & Pathirana, P. N. (2021). Artificial intelligence (AI) and big data for coronavirus (COVID-19) pandemic: A survey on the state-of-the-arts. *IEEE Access*, *8*, 130820–130839. https://doi.org/10.1109/ACCESS.2020.3009328

Rajagopalan, M. R., & Vellaipandiyan, S. (2013, November). Big data framework for national e-governance plan. In *Eleventh international conference on ICT and knowledge engineering, 2013* (pp. 1–5). IEEE.

Ransbotham, S., Kiron, D., Gerbert, P., & Reeves, M. (2017). Reshaping business with artificial intelligence: Closing the gap between ambition and action. *MIT Sloan Management Review*, *59*(1).

Sagiroglu, S., & Sinanc, D. (2013, May). Big data: A review. In *2013 international conference on collaboration technologies and systems (CTS)* (pp. 42–47). IEEE.

Steed, C. A., Ricciuto, D. M., Shipman, G., Smith, B., Thornton, P. E., Wang, D., Shi, X., & Williams, D. N. (2013). Big data visual analytics for exploratory earth system simulation analysis. *Computers and Geosciences*, *61*, 71–82. https://doi.org/10.1016/j.cageo.2013.07.025

Tekiner, F., & Keane, J. A. (2013, October). Big data framework. In *2013 IEEE international conference on systems, man, and cybernetics* (pp. 1494–1499). IEEE.

Trkman, P., Bronzo Ladeira, M., De Oliveira, M. P. V., & McCormack, K. (2012). Business analytics, process maturity and supply chain performance. In F. Daniel, K. Barkaoui, & S. Dustdar (Eds.), *Business process management workshops. BPM 2011. Lecture notes in business information processing* (Vol. 99). Springer. https://doi.org/10.1007/978-3-642-28108-2_10

Wu, J., Wang, J., Nicholas, S., Maitland, E., & Fan, Q. (2020). Application of big data technology for COVID-19 prevention and control in China: Lessons and recommendations. *Journal of Medical Internet Research*, *22*(10), e21980. https://doi.org/10.2196/21980

Yang, C., Huang, Q., Li, Z., Liu, K., & Hu, F. (2017). Big data and cloud computing: Innovation opportunities and challenges. *International Journal of Digital Earth*, *10*(1), 13–53. https://doi.org/10.1080/17538947.2016.1239771

Yang, J. (2021). Big data privacy protection technology. *Journal of Physics: Conference Series*. IOP Publishing, *2037*(1), 21–36. https://doi.org/10.1088/1742-6596/2037/1/012136

Yuan, H., Lau, R. Y. K., & Xu, W. (2016). The determinants of crowdfunding success: A semantic text analytics approach. *Decision Support Systems*, *91*, 67–76. https://doi.org/10.1016/j.dss.2016.08.001

Zhan, Y., Tan, K. H., Ji, G., Chung, L., & Tseng, M. (2017). A big data framework for facilitating product innovation processes. *Business Process Management Journal*, *23*(3), 518–536. https://doi.org/10.1108/BPMJ-11-2015-0157

Zhang, F., Chen, Z., Zhang, C., Zhou, A. C., Zhai, J., & Du, X. (2021). An efficient parallel secure machine learning framework on GPUs. *IEEE Transactions on Parallel and Distributed Systems*, *32*(9), 2262–2276. https://doi.org/10.1109/TPDS.2021.3059108

Zhou, L., Pan, S., Wang, J., & Vasilakos, A. V. (2017). Machine learning on big data: Opportunities and challenges. *Neurocomputing*, *237*, 350–361. https://doi.org/10.1016/j.neucom.2017.01.026

12
DIGITAL SOCIAL RESPONSIBILITY IN THE WORKPLACE

Gözde Baycur and Amin Shoari Nejad

Introduction

The strongest trends that shape the business world in the recent decade are digitalization and sustainability. The rapid development of technology has enabled businesses to increase their production, sales, and profitability thanks to digital transformation. Although digital transformation has brought unique opportunities for businesses, it also created a cost for society and the planet. The environmental and societal consequence of business practices is not a newly discovered phenomenon. Numerous scientists, activists, and organizations have been warning governments and companies about the harm they create since the post–Industrial Revolution era began. As production technologies advance and consumption culture dominates the world, sustainability concerns have mounted. However, the real threat has become visible when the internet revolution altered the modus operandi of the business world. Digitalization contributed to overproduction and overconsumption as well as plenty of ethical problems; thus, it dampened sustainability.

Digitalization is not a fad. A slowdown in digitalization is not expected; on the contrary, the speed of digitalization will get even faster. The COVID-19 pandemic has served as a digital transformation steroid (Wade & Shan, 2020). Due to lockdowns, most people have found digital alternatives for their daily routines, such as working, socializing, or shopping. Many people had been already become accustomed to online commerce, virtual meetings, or social networking long before the pandemic; however, after the pandemic, these things have become the only option, as offline lives are seriously constrained. Moreover, many activities that are assumed to be offline in nature, such as doctor visits, theatregoing, concerts, or yoga classes have shifted to virtual platforms. While the daily lives of consumers were affected by such a major transformation, businesses could not isolate themselves from the digital transformation. Technology-savvy businesses have managed

DOI: 10.4324/9781003283386-14

this shift smoothly and safely; however, for traditional businesses and brick-and-mortar stores, the transition period has been shaky and painful. Millions of small and traditional enterprises all over the world have tried to provide their services or products online for the first time. Companies that have already adopted digital technologies before the pandemic have increased their investment in digital technologies and their infrastructure to serve customers better in the digital era. As the pandemic era has already shown, digital technologies are integral parts of the lives of consumers and business practices. Rather than opposing digitalization due to its potential harms, governments, businesses, and civil organizations should collaborate to find ways to harmonize sustainability and digitalization. If digitalization is here to stay, all stakeholders have to focus on how to survive digital transformation while minimizing its harm on society and the environment.

From corporate social responsibility to digital social responsibility

The relationship between society and businesses have been thoroughly discussed in management academia for decades (Carroll, 1979). Socioeconomic actors demand businesses to act responsibly and minimize the damage their business practices create. Moreover, in the contemporary world, expectations exceed preventing harm; today's customers demand businesses to create value for the whole society. On the contrary to the neoclassical approach, a business is a part of society and cannot be thought of in isolation; therefore, ethical and responsible practices are not solely adopted to delight customers but also to sustain the business.

The responsibilities of businesses to their stakeholders, and society in general, has led to a new concept called corporate social responsibility (CSR). CSR is defined as "the notion that corporations have an obligation to constituent groups in society other than stockholders and beyond that prescribed by law or union contract" (Jones, 1980, p. 59). This definition highlights two important aspects of CSR. First, companies should consider society in broader terms, not only shareholders or key stakeholders. Second, businesses should act responsibly even if no legal obligations exist. CSR should be voluntary-based and should not ignore any groups within the society.

As digital transformation has completely altered business practices, the relationship of businesses with society and the environment has evolved into a more complex one. New concerns about the consequences of digitalization for society have emerged, leading companies to revisit the CSR concept. In order to emphasize the use of digital technologies by businesses, digital social responsibility (DSR), or corporate digital responsibility, emerged as a subset of CSR. According to Frick (2021), DSR "addresses how your organization uses digital products, services, programs, or practices to benefit society". Wade (2020) defines corporate digital responsibility (CDR) as "a set of practices and behaviors that help an organization use data and digital technologies in a way that is socially, economically, technologically, and environmentally responsible". This definition emphasizes four sub-categories of CDR: Social CDR, economic CDR, environmental CDR, and technological CDR. Social CDR concerns societal consequences of digital practices and focuses on bridging the digital divide and protecting data privacy. Economic CDR involves managing the economic effect of digitalization, such as the replacement of jobs due to automatization and the shift of the workforce to gig economics. Technological CDR is linked to the ethical usage of artificial intelligence (AI) and unbiased algorithms and not using technologies that are harmful to society. Environmental CDR involves the impact of digital business practices on the physical environment and involves energy saving, disposal, and recycling policies.

Key components of digital social responsibility

In this section, we discuss six key components of DSR. The aim of this section is to introduce main topics that are of high importance and briefly state current problems related to these areas and prescribe potential solutions. These topics that will be discussed in these sections are so broad and deep that they cannot all be discussed in an entire chapter or even a book. Therefore, due to the limits of the chapter, only the main issues will be summarized.

Responsibility for data privacy and protection

What is the most important input for all businesses regardless of the industry? If this question was asked a few decades ago, most respondents would say "energy". Businesses still need the energy to sustain their activities; yet the answer is "data". The famous phrase "Data is the new oil" was coined by Clive Humby (British mathematician and mastermind of Tesco's marketing department) in 2006, long before most businesses understand the real value of customer data (Young Entrepreneur Council, 2021). In the 20th century, conflicts to obtain petroleum resources used to cause oil wars. After the digital revolution, battles have been fought for data. While consumers have gotten used to the ease and comfort that new digital technologies brought, digital technologies get access to the most intimate information about them. When consumers purchase something using their credit card, make an online reservation, or stalk a friend on social media, they create digital footprints that can be traced by many companies. Digital devices and applications may know our friends and family better than us. Research has shown that Facebook likes can be used to predict sensitive personal traits, such as sexual orientation, religious and political views, personality traits, use of addictive substances, and parental separation (Kosinski et al., 2013). Furthermore, technology giants know our health risks, vacation plans, financial statements, or even if our partner is cheating or not to the point that in 2022 Amazon aired a comic ad called "Amazon's Big Game Commercial: Mind Reader" showing how Alexa, an AI virtual assistant developed by the company, is good at reading people (Shakir, 2022). Sometimes customers take advantage of sharing their data, for example, when a recommendation engine finds the most suitable product or when an e-commerce platform keeps credit card information and enables them to check out in two minutes. However, most of the time, loss of privacy and being watched 24/7 is creepy rather than comforting. Besides, misuse of information can have bigger impacts, such as disrupting elections and threatening democracy by knowing how to target and manipulate voters using their private data. In 2018, Mark Zuckerberg, Facebook's CEO at the time, testified before the US Congress about the misuse of Americans' private data by Cambridge Analytica, a data company accused of creating psychological profiles of Facebook users and using them to swing votes in favor of Brexit in the UK and Donald Trump getting elected in the United States (*New York Times*, 2018).

The use of customer data by businesses did not start after the invention of the internet. A good barman knows the favorite cocktail of loyal customers and remembers if the customer is allergic to peppermint. Salespeople in a boutique remember recent purchases of frequent shoppers and cross-sell a jumper to combine with the skirt purchased last month. Data is not always kept in the company's database. However, in today's world, it is impossible for marketers to keep in mind all details about customers; hence, the help of digital technologies is a must. The digital revolution has led to a sharp increase in the richness and variety of data. Before the invention of mobile devices, customer databases used to include only previous purchases, addresses, and phone numbers. Yet today, businesses have access to limitless data from consumers' hobbies to their fears, and unfortunately, the availability of data makes consumers vulnerable and open to manipulation. Moreover, customers who share their data and those who prefer not to share can face discrimination that obliges them to devote their privacy to be served equally. For example, wearable technologies and health apps record very detailed and intimate information that can be demanded by insurance companies to calculate premiums, and customers who do not use those apps or are reluctant to share the data might face the risk of higher premiums or rejection by insurance companies (Lobschat et al., 2021).

As concerns for data privacy and security mount, businesses should reassess their data policies beyond legal obligations. Data-driven marketing is a double-edged sword. In a privacy-first world, customers should be ensured that their data is safe and will be used to create better value, not solely to serve the interest of the company. The ability of businesses to collect data does not mean that they should collect it. Managers should ask the following questions before planning to collect data: "Why do we need that piece of information?" "If we have this information, will it help us to serve this customer better?" "Does this information include private details about the customer that may exceed ethical boundaries?" If collecting and using the data exceed ethical boundaries, if it does not create a better value offer for the customer, or if the company does not know how and why to use the data, data-collection decisions should be reconsidered (Baycur et al., 2022). Data-privacy concerns are expected to rise more in the near future. The winners of this transition will be the companies who use customer data to create better value for customers and those that act proactively for data security without waiting for harsher legal regulations. As well as data privacy and security, transparency of data utilization is among the responsibilities of businesses toward society. Companies should openly communicate with customers why and how they use the data they collect. Businesses should also offer easy opt-out choices for customers who do not want to grant permission to collect and keep data. Finally, data security is the responsibility of everyone in an organization, not only a particular department. Therefore, all employees and other stakeholders that have access to customer data should be trained about data security, and ethical values about data privacy should be communicated throughout the whole organization.

Algorithm unbiasedness

As a result of the availability of massive data and powerful analysis tools, AI-based decision-making has been a crucial part of our daily lives. Algorithmic decision-making is used from ordinary daily tasks, such as online shopping, to highly critical decisions, such as justice, health care services, or recruitment. Although AI has the power to analyze complex data sets and potentially on many occasions make better decisions than humans, various cases provided evidence that algorithmic decisions can be unfair and biased (Kaur et al., 2020). AI algorithms such as deep learning are frequently referred to as "black boxes" because of their complex and uninterpretable structure, which makes it difficult to detect when they are biased. To prevent dangerous consequences of biased algorithm decisions, both producers and users of algorithmic decision-making systems are responsible for ensuring that the algorithm is trustworthy and accountable. This needs careful evaluation and development of protocols for bias diagnostics before releasing AI-based products.

Most biasedness problems of AI are linked to training with biased data. Microsoft's AI-based chatbot Tay started racist tweets after a few hours of its launch because people had tweeted racist remarks, thus feeding inappropriate data to the bot which then made the bot start mimicking them like a digital parrot (Hunt, 2016). Like racist Tay, Amazon's algorithmic recruitment software was blamed for being sexist since it favored male applicants (BBC, 2018). These examples show how dangerous AI can be if ethical requirements are overlooked. AI cannot be sexist, ageist, or racist and has no intention to favor young, white, heterosexual men if we do not train it on biased data (Baycur et al., 2022). To ensure the algorithm is unbiased and to build trust in AI, algorithm transparency is required (Manyika et al., 2019).

As more decisions are delegated to algorithms, there will be an urgent need to clarify who is responsible for AI's decisions and actions. When a self-driving Uber car killed a pedestrian in Arizona, the liability was unclear (Wakabayashi, 2018). This tragic incident demonstrated that companies who make use of an AI system are responsible for its consequences as much as the developer of the system. Therefore, businesses should stress how ethical, unbiased, and trustworthy the algorithms they use are and have a control system in place to constantly monitor the validity of their whole AI operations (aka MLOps).

Future of work in the digital era

As digitalization has altered all business practices, a revolutionary change in employment structure is inevitable. The invention of robots, Industry 4.0, and Internet of Things (IoT) decrease the need for labor and could potentially disrupt the workforce environment. Many employees feel threatened about the unemployment risk due to the shift of automated tasks to AI. More and more companies invest in chatbots rather than hiring customer representatives. Banks prefer ATMs over branches to minimize personnel expenses. Retailers replace their personnel with self-checkout platforms. Taxi drivers will probably be replaced by autonomous cars in the near future. However, delegating mundane tasks to technology does not necessarily decrease employment rates. A survey conducted by Pew Research Center stated that more than half of the respondents (52%) think that technology will create more jobs than it displaced (Smith & Anderson, 2014). As some jobs are completely digitalized, there will be new employment opportunities that technology brings. The employment structure has never been static since the Industrial Revolution, which caused many craftsmen to quit their jobs due to automation and turned to different business lines. Nevertheless, machines have not left people unemployed; only employment shifted to different areas. Rather than resisting change, we should get prepared for it. Businesses, not only the government, have the responsibility to enable employees and students to build new skill sets to adapt to in the new job market by offering training and mentorship (Baycur et al., 2022).

Besides the employment shift due to automation, another change the digital revolution has brought to work is the rise of the gig economy (Petriglieri et al., 2018). Gig economy is defined as "labor market that comprises short-term contracts or freelance work as opposed to permanent jobs" (Illuzzi & Tang, 2021). Temporary, contract-based works are older than the invention of the internet; however, the internet made it very convenient to find someone to hire and enabled workers and employers from all over the world to connect rapidly thanks to applications such as Uber, Lyft, TaskRabbit, or Upwork. Research conducted by Mastercard (2019) estimated that gig economy generated $204 billion in gross volume globally and is expected to grow 17% by 2023. After the pandemic, demand for gig jobs has increased because of shutdowns and temporary or permanent unemployment in some industries, such as entertainment or hospitality. Pew Research Center (2021) stated that 16% of American adults have earned money from a gig platform. Although the gig economy is growing exponentially and more employees are shifting from traditional jobs to the gig economy, the safety and other rights of these workers are mostly neglected. Gig economy brings valuable opportunities, such as creating new jobs suitable to a large variety of skill sets and flexibility; on the other hand, if not regulated carefully, it can cause threats, such as a lack of regulations, social security, or benefits. Governments, online platforms, and companies that outsource some tasks to gig workers are responsible for protecting gig workers and offering them equal working conditions.

Digital inclusion and bridging the digital gap

Digitalization has brought unique opportunities for people to improve their skills, careers, and social lives; however, different groups benefit from digital technologies unequally, and the gap between different social groups has widened even more. IGI Global (n.d.) defines the digital gap as "New forms of social inequality derived from the unequal access to the new information communications technologies, by gender, territory, social class, and so forth". The digital gap (or digital divide) is evident between urban and rural, high income and low income, educated and undereducated populations. Living in low-bandwidth areas, using low-performance devices, having disabilities, and limited access to subscription-based content widens the gap.

Digital Divide Council (2019) describes three subcategories of the digital divide: gender divide, social divide, and universal access divide. Women, especially in underdeveloped countries, are disadvantaged when it comes to digital inclusion. Eighty-four million women do not own mobile devices. Even though they have mobile devices, 1.2 billion women in underdeveloped countries have no internet access (Digital Divide Council, 2019). Social divide stems from differences in internet access and non-connected groups' exclusion from connected social groups. A universal access divide can be the result of physical disabilities or geographical disadvantages stemming from inadequate broadband infrastructure.

The digital divide creates severe inequalities. Digitally excluded students suffer from a poor education due to limited access to resources. When schools shifted classes to online platforms, the digital divide had more severe harm on digitally excluded students. Digital exclusion leads to economic disadvantages due to numerous reasons. First, digitally excluded people cannot improve their financial literacy and cannot make use of fintech solutions that will enable them to better handle their financial situation. They cannot benefit from online job opportunities. Moreover, they cannot compare online and offline prices and benefit from online exclusive price promotions.

To overcome the negative consequences of the digital divide and digital exclusion, governments, companies, and nongovernmental organizations have responsibilities. Bridging the digital gap and increasing widening digital inclusion are vital objectives in the digital social responsibility agendas of businesses. Companies that produce digital products, either software or hardware, should focus on increasing the availability of the products. A digital product that will bridge the digital divide should work with a wide range of devices, including old technologies; should not ignore disabled users; and its pricing needs to be fair. Businesses out of the tech industry can still contribute to digital inclusion by introducing digital literacy programs, providing free internet connection spots for students, educating children to make them tech-savvy users, and providing training programs such as coding or content creation. While new digital technologies are reshaping our daily lives and bringing new opportunities, all economic actors are responsible to ensure everyone in our society has access to those opportunities. Big-scale projects to expand the coverage of the internet globally can lead to promising results in terms of shortening the digital divide. Although some projects, such as Google Balloon Internet, failed to fulfill this goal, the efforts have not stopped. SpaceX's Starlink project is an example of ongoing projects, and a world in which everyone can access the internet is not beyond reach.

Responsibility for environmentally-friendly digital technologies

Polonsky, in his seminal paper on green marketing (1994, p. 388), suggested that "As society becomes more concerned with the natural environment, businesses have begun to modify their behavior in an attempt to address society's 'new' concerns". In the 21st century, the concern of society is not new anymore, and green marketing has become the mainstream. Society has become more concerned about the consequences of business practices and pushes companies to act more responsibly toward the environment and to diminish the harm their business causes. Hence, environmental responsibility has become an integral part of CSR.

As businesses shift some core business activities to digital, such as sales, marketing, or archiving, it is assumed that the impact on the environment will be less negative. However, digital business activities can still threaten the environment, in some cases, the harm of digital businesses can be even more hazardous. A few decades ago, offices used to have much more paper waste since all documents were paper based. When workplaces shifted from paper to digital documents, invoices, and emails, it was a promising step to save trees. However, the cost of the internet and electricity for the environment is neglected. Footprinting methodologies are necessary to have a sustainable digital future (Obringer et al., 2021). A recent Wired report declared that most data centers' energy source is fossil fuels (Oberhaus, 2019). When we store bigger data on clouds, increased carbon emissions make our green clouds gray. The carbon footprint of an email is smaller than mail sent via a post office, but still, it causes four grams of CO_2, and it can be as much as 50 grams if the attachment is big (Griffiths, 2020). Berners-Lee and Clarke (2010) estimated that in a typical workplace, the carbon footprint is around 135 kilograms per person. Organizations should be aware that unnecessary use of mail, cloud, or online documentation will be a part of environmental problems in the near future.

Numerous companies plan to invest in blockchain technologies, yet only a few of them are aware of its burden on the planet. Bitcoin mining and trading use electricity equivalent to that of 4.3 million American households annually (Lobschat et al., 2021). Bitcoin's energy consumption trend is increasing, yet the real danger is not the level of energy consumed but the source of energy, since most Bitcoin-mining facilities use fossil fuels, such as coal (Digiconomist.net, 2022).

One of the most serious environmental problems digitalization brought is digital marketing and its strong impact on overconsumption and overproduction. The internet is not the inception of consumption culture, yet it has become a huge accelerator and scapegoat. Traditionally, shopping was limited by time and space in the offline context. However, online shopping can be done 24/7 from anywhere that you are connected to the internet. A polyester blouse that is added to the cart in five minutes and worn only three times biodegrades in the soil in 200 years. Producing one pair of jeans uses 7,600 liters of water while water scarcity is the most urgent global environmental problem (Preuss, 2019). Besides the production process, the distribution of products harms the environment, as carbon footprints are higher for online purchases. Shahmohammadi et al. (2020) suggested that buying online is worse for the environment than driving to the store because consumers tend to buy online frequently but they buy few items per purchase. On the other hand, most shoppers aggregate purchases in a single bulk purchase when they go to physical stores. Even if online shoppers make bulk purchases, most items are delivered from different distribution centers. Moreover, packaging waste due to online deliveries deepens the harm of online shopping. Decreasing the carbon footprint of their production, using biodegradable packaging material, and encouraging bulk purchases can make digitalization more sustainable.

Protection from fake news

The rapid spread of fake news has become a more popular discussion topic during the pandemic as never before since, in times of crisis, the urgent need for information blocks perceptual filtering of information and raises the desire to share this unfiltered, unchecked information (Aral, 2020; Vosoughi et al., 2018). During the pandemic, the misinformation about the COVID-19 vaccine was a fatal problem that policymakers dealt with. Conspiracy theories caused millions of people to resist vaccination, which left them unprotected against the disease that threatened their lives. Obviously, fake news can lead to numerous negative consequences besides anti-vaccination. Fake news can change the results of an election, hurt a company's image and cause it to lose millions of dollars, contribute to racist actions, and fuel hate toward vulnerable groups such as immigrants or LGBTIQ people.

In the age of misinformation, disinformation, and fake news, businesses and governments have responsibilities to protect people from fake news. Since digital channels are the main medium for the dissemination of fake news deeply and widely, digital literacy is a must to be protected from fake news. When people know how to fact check and know which sources are reliable, they can distinguish misinformation from the truth. Fighting with fake news is the ultimate responsibility for social networking sites, message applications, and media channels, but it is not limited to them since it is a serious societal problem and businesses out of the tech industry can also be a part of the solution by offering media literacy training or supporting fact-checking platforms.

Conclusion

The digital revolution has radically changed the relationship between businesses and society. As a subset of corporate social responsibility, organizations need to rethink the consequences of their digital activities for society and the environment.

As businesses digitalize, they have new responsibilities, such as protecting data privacy, ensuring AI unbiasedness, ensuring that workers are prepared for the future labor market, minimizing environmental harm of digital activities, fighting fake news, and contributing to digital inclusion to bridge the digital gap.

References

Aral, S. (2020). *The hype machine*. Currency.

Baycur, G., Delen, E., & Kayışkan, D. (2022). Digital conflicts in marketing and sales. In F. Özsungur (Ed.), *Conflict management in digital business: New strategy and approach* (In Production). Emerald Publishing.

BBC. (2018). *Amazon scrapped "sexist AI" tool*. http://www.bbc.com/news/technology-45809919

Berners-Lee, M., & Clarke, D. (2010). *What's the carbon footprint of . . . email*. http://www.theguardian.com/environment/green-living-blog/2010/oct/21/carbon-footprint-email

Carroll, A. B. (1979). A three-dimensional conceptual model of corporate social performance. *Academy of Management Review*, 4(4), 497–505. https://doi.org/10.5465/amr.1979.4498296

Digiconomics. (2022). *Bitcoin energy consumption*. https://digiconomist.net/bitcoin-energy-consumption

Digital Divide Council. (2019). *What is digital divide?* http://www.digitaldividecouncil.com/what-is-the-digital-divide/

Frick, T. (2021). *Understanding digital social responsibility*. http://www.mightybytes.com/blog/social-digital-responsibility/

Griffiths, S. (2020). *Why your internet habits are not as clean as you think*. http://www.bbc.com/future/article/20200305-why-your-internet-habits-are-not-as-clean-as-you-think

Hunt, E. (2016). *Tay, Microsoft's AI chatbot, gets a crash course in racism from Twitter*. http://www.theguardian.com/technology/2016/mar/24/tay-microsofts-ai-chatbot-gets-a-crash-course-in-racism-from-twitter?CMP=twt_a-technology_b-gdntech

IGI Global. (n.d.). *What is digital gap?* http://www.igi-global.com/dictionary/digital-divide-education-knowledge-society/7630

Illuzzi, K., & Tang, P. (2021). *Gig economy trends and impact on small and medium practices*. http://www.ifac.org/knowledge-gateway/contributing-global-economy/discussion/gig-economy-trends-and-impact-small-and-medium-practices

Jones, T. M. (1980). Corporate social responsibility revisited, redefined. *California Management Review*, 22(3), 59–67. https://doi.org/10.2307/41164877

Kaur, D., Uslu, S., & Durresi, A. (2020). Requirements for trustworthy artificial intelligence – A review. In *International conference on network-based information systems* (pp. 105–115). Springer.

Kosinski, M., Stillwell, D., & Graepel, T. (2013). Private traits and attributes are predictable from digital records of human behavior. *Proceedings of the National Academy of Sciences of the United States of America*, 110(15), 5802–5805. https://doi.org/10.1073/pnas.1218772110

Lobschat, L., Mueller, B., Eggers, F., Brandimarte, L., Diefenbach, S., Kroschke, M., & Wirtz, J. (2021). Corporate digital responsibility. *Journal of Business Research*, 122, 875–888. https://doi.org/10.1016/j.jbusres.2019.10.006

Manyika, J., Silberg, J., & Presten, B. (2019). *What do we do about the biases in AI?* https://hbr.org/2019/10/what-do-we-do-about-the-biases-in-ai

Mastercard. (2019). *Mastercard gig economy industry outlook and needs assessment*. https://newsroom.mastercard.com/wp-content/uploads/2019/05/Gig-Economy-White-Paper-May-2019.pdf

New York Times (2018). Cambridge Analytica and Facebook: The scandal and the fallout so far. http://www.nytimes.com/2018/04/04/us/politics/cambridge-analytica-scandal-fallout.html

Oberhaus, D. (2019). *Amazon, Google, Microsoft: Here's who has the greenest cloud?* http://www.wired.com/story/amazon-google-microsoft-green-clouds-and-hyperscale-data-centers/

Obringer, R., Rachunok, B., Maia-Silva, D., Arbabzadeh, M., Nateghi, R., & Madani, K. (2021). The overlooked environmental footprint of increasing Internet use. *Resources, Conservation and Recycling, 167*, 105389. https://doi.org/10.1016/j.resconrec.2020.105389

Petriglieri, G., Ashford, S., & Wrzesniewski, A. (2018, March–April). Thriving in the gig economy. *Harvard Business Review*, 140–143.

Pew Research Center. (2021). *The state of gig work in 2021.* Retrieved from https://www.pewresearch.org/internet/2021/12/08/the-state-of-gig-work-in-2021/

Polonsky, M. J. (1994). An introduction to green marketing. *Electronic Green Journal, 1*(2), 388–412. https://doi.org/10.5070/G31210177

Preuss, S. (2019). *15 Sustainability efforts of the denim industry in 2019.* https://fashionunited.com/news/business/15-sustainability-efforts-of-the-denim-industry-in-2019/2019123031453

Shahmohammadi, S., Steinmann, Z. J. N., Tambjerg, L., van Loon, P., King, J. M. H., & Huijbregts, M. A. J. (2020). Comparative greenhouse gas footprinting of online versus traditional shopping for fast-moving consumer goods: A stochastic approach. *Environmental Science and Technology, 54*(6), 3499–3509. https://doi.org/10.1021/acs.est.9b06252

Shakir, U. (2022). *Amazon's new Super Bowl ad features a creepy mind-reading Alexa.* http://www.theverge.com/2022/2/7/22922002/amazon-alexa-super-bowl-ad-2022-mind-reading-scarlett-johansson-colin-jost

Smith, A., & Anderson, J. (2014). *AI, robotics, and the future of jobs.* Pew Research Center.

Vosoughi, S., Roy, D., & Aral, S. (2018). The spread of true and false news online. *Science, 359*(6380), 1146–1151. https://doi.org/10.1126/science.aap9559

Wade, M. (2020). Corporate responsibility in the digital era. *MIT Sloan Management Review.* https://sloanreview.mit.edu/article/corporate-responsibility-in-the-digital-era/.

Wade, M., & Shan, J. (2020). COVID-19 has accelerated digital transformation, but may have made it harder not easier. *MIS Quarterly Executive, 19*(3), 213–220. https://doi.org/10.17705/2msqe.00034

Wakabayashi, D. (2018). *Self-driving uber car kills pedestrian in Arizona, where robots roam.* http://www.nytimes.com/2018/03/19/technology/uber-driverless-fatality.html

Young Entrepreneur Council. (2021). *Data isn't the new oil – Time is.* http://www.forbes.com/sites/theyec/2021/07/15/data-isnt-the-new-oil – time-is/?sh=2cb37e7635bb

13

DIGITAL WORKPLACE ENTREPRENEURSHIP

Duygu Hıdıroğlu and Rustamov Parviz Hajı oğlu

Introduction

In digital workplaces, it is possible to ensure that these digital tools are used with full efficiency by employees, only by making them believe that these tools will make their lives easier. Digital workplaces with employees who believe that they can do their work in a more practical way by digital tools and who believe that digital tools in the digital workplace will save employees time and effort could achieve sustainability in business success. Otherwise, no employee would desire to use any digital tools that require too much time and effort. This is one of the most critical barriers to efficiency in digital workplaces. Despite the barriers, digital workplace transformation is no longer a necessity but an obligation in this age.

Digital workplaces offer significant opportunities for entrepreneurs and small businesses. Digital workplaces do not have a very deep past. But especially after the COVID-19 pandemic, people are generally convinced that digital workplaces and digital technologies should exist in the business world. For example, early-stage entrepreneurs and small businesses leverage digital workplaces to sell goods and services directly to customers through e-commerce and have the opportunity to do business worldwide as a link in the supply chains of large companies. Without digital technologies, these entrepreneurs entering the new sector do not have the opportunity to have these big customers, or even to have a share in the market in a short time. Digital workplaces will continue to evolve in the near future as the technological infrastructure strengthens and advanced technological tools evolve. These developments will ensure that technological infrastructure and cybersecurity problems will be resolved quickly in the near future.

Entrepreneurship, E-Commerce and Digitalization

After the mid-1990s and the improvement of information and digital technologies, entrepreneurs have the opportunity to both open up to new markets and carry

DOI: 10.4324/9781003283386-15

out activities with more appropriate financing opportunities. Therefore, a lot of developments in information and digital technologies have positive effects on the entrepreneurship facilities (Maier & Nair-Reichert, 2007). Regarding knowledge-based economies, information sharing and information technologies have a crucial role on the actors in economies, and information technology support businesses easily gain a competitive advantage over their rivals. The competitive advantage supports new entrepreneurs to start their unique enterprises in all sectors (Schallmo et al., 2020). Today, entrepreneurs should make the Internet, e-commerce and information technologies a part of their businesses and may even put these current technologies at the center of their businesses.

Today, every development relevant to Internet technologies allows entrepreneurs to bring new brilliant entrepreneurial ideas. In other words, the most successful and sustainable entrepreneurial idea comes through the Internet. Where people send their goods via the Internet and where and how the buyers can reach these products determines the scope of the e-commerce, international trade and almost all entrepreneurial activities. After the spread of the Internet, the scope has expanded and especially geographic borders have disappeared. Via the Internet, it is possible to reach consumers from all over the world, and selling products and services to them is easier (Ghosh et al., 2021). Every place the cargo can reach can be a target market where sellers aim to sell their products.

Having websites where businesses can promote their products and services and perform marketing facilities is sufficient to start e-commerce. Many people trade billions of dollars in a day through e-commerce sites such as Amazon, eBay, auction sites or thematic shopping sites (Kashyap & Maurya, 2013). Entrepreneurs accept that it is a very practical method for buyers and sellers to meet on the Internet, and in the first stages of their venture they set up websites for their products without waiting. It is now possible to see brand new e-commerce models on the Internet. It is seen that e-commerce models with different scenarios have been developed, such as coupon sites, auction sites, sale of opportunity products in a limited time, sale of a limited number of discounted products, free shipping of giveaway products in return for comments and sale of second-hand products (Mazzarol, 2015). Some of these have achieved great success and have become widespread throughout the world. It is no longer necessary to make a physical effort to purchase a work of art from the private collection of a very famous art gallery. It is also possible to pre-order a new Apple iPhone before it is released. In short, the world is no longer the same as before. Therefore, the business world is gradually eliminating old routines and borders are disappearing with Internet, e-commerce and information technologies. Especially for successful digital entrepreneurs, geographical boundaries do not matter.

E-commerce successfully brings together vendors, suppliers, dealers, customers and intermediaries over the Web in an easy and practical way. Many companies supplying goods no longer matter where in the world they are located. A company that requests goods can discover the supplier company that sells the product or raw material it needs and can request the desired amount of goods via the Internet. Communication and coordination between the main company headquarters and dealers can be carried out seamlessly over the Internet. Companies that carry out their activities over the Web can also access customer feedback more easily and quickly resolve problems by identifying more attainable business strategies. Considering customer loyalty to the products of one company, it is more possible to respond quickly to customer feedback, and this could increase the prestige and awareness of the company's products. This quick response could increase rapidly customer satisfaction, and it leads to customer loyalty and trust (Lafley & Martin, 2017). Thus, the business volume of that company could grow in a very short time.

Confidentiality, reliability, measurability, security, etc. were the worries that companies hesitate to conduct their businesses over the Internet. However nowadays, the concerns of the companies are decreasing day by day and the problems related to these worries are being resolved in a more permanent way. When companies carry out their activities on the Web, they can allocate more time to their main activities due to the few disruptions. Since the time management of such enterprises is realized in the most efficient way, they can allocate more time to customer relations and optimize their organizational processes by using their limited resources at the optimum level. On the other hand, the main purpose of establishment of the business is to bring profit, and thanks to e-commerce goods can be easily bought and sold in a most practical manner (Savrul et al., 2014). In summary, the e-commerce system has recently become indispensable for businesses to discover new opportunities, perform the analysis of business requirements correctly and determine the right entrepreneurial strategies.

Digital Workplace Entrepreneurship

Digital entrepreneurship is a technology-oriented type of entrepreneurship where entrepreneurship uses its continuous self-renewal and development motivation to benefit existing businesses. Digital workplace entrepreneurship is often described as the process of inventing new technological products. Digital workplace entrepreneurship is effective in establishing digital businesses and adopting digital technologies by existing entrepreneurs. In short, digital workplace entrepreneurship allows entrepreneurs to produce new products in their own venture business and helps them to keep up with the new era by eliminating digital deficiencies in other businesses. In other words, digital initiatives can ensure that the processes of existing businesses adapt to advanced technology by digitally renewing them (Attaran et al., 2019).

Although digital workplace entrepreneurship is an area that is not preferred and is avoided by many entrepreneurial candidates because it requires intense technical expertise, knowledge and skills in entrepreneurship, it is now a highly sought-after type of entrepreneurship after the serious economic crisis and pandemic that occurred in the 2020s (Freitag et al., 2020).

There are many right things to do in order to survive in societies, to ensure the sustainability of economies and even to meet the most basic needs of people. By adapting digital systems in the most efficient way to human life, both at the individual level and at the business level, entrepreneurial requirements could be met easily. Successful digital enterprises support economic development by establishing a new digital business and benefit from the current features of digital technologies in the most efficient and effective way (Enkhjav et al., 2021). There are two things that are essential for many digital ventures to be successful. These are to start the venture with lower initial costs and to find wider access to foreign markets.

Recent international scientific research shows that the proportion of people among successful digital workplaces entrepreneurs in the European Union (EU) is quite low. According to these studies, only 20% of digital enterprises were started in 2019, and digital enterprises divided by total enterprises have been increased year by year since 2019. Moreover, it is observed that there is no visible increase or decrease in these rates in a period of approximately 5 years (Dincă et al., 2019).

When women's digital enterprises are compared to all enterprises, the situation is much worse. As the need for digital systems increases in the new world order with the developing challenging environmental conditions, businesses and enterprises that cannot adapt to this will tend to disappear. If women are not successful in integrating into digital systems, the rate of female entrepreneurship will decrease rather than increase. Especially considering the concept of digital transformation, which has become more important with the COVID-19 pandemic, women entrepreneurs need to take very radical steps regarding digital workplace entrepreneurship (Južnik Rotar et al., 2019).

There are several reasons why women lag behind men in digital workplace entrepreneurship. One of them is the lack of people to be role models for women. Another is the lack of digital skills development and reluctance for digital subjects in women. In many countries, most women do not even have knowledge of computer and Internet usage, let alone digital development (Južnik Rotar et al., 2019).

While digital entrepreneurship is an opportunity to help convince individuals from all walks of life to start entrepreneurship, it is also a type of entrepreneurship that can pave the way for potential successful entrepreneurs from disadvantaged groups where state support for entrepreneurship is insufficient (Nicola et al., 2020).

If today's businesses and digital enterprises aim to survive in economies, digital entrepreneurship skills of individuals, especially women and youth, should be developed rapidly by digital training. To sustain success of initiatives, to meet new requirements in complex business environment and to improve digital workplace entrepreneurship, entrepreneurs should be supported by the regulatory environment by gathering government support and financial incentives.

The Benefits of Digital Workplaces to Employees

Physical workplaces are working systems that take businesses out of their comfort zone. Digital workplaces, on the contrary, ensure that employees stay in their comfort zone. Digital workplaces give the employees the opportunities to work independently in terms of time and place and give a space for freedom. Digitalization of businesses is closely related with employing the right people who are suitable for the digital workplace business model (Enkhjav et al., 2021).

Digital workplaces are important because they cause enterprises to develop an increasing number of innovative products and services. Digital workplaces accelerate innovation and enable more efficient and innovative entrepreneurial activities. In the new digital era, considering that the way to provide competitive advantage in economies leans to innovative approaches (Dery et al., 2017), it is now inevitable for businesses to implement digital workplace models. Digital workplaces give entrepreneurs and businesses an advantage of acting interactively by increasing social cooperation with employees and changing the way they do business (Hamburg, 2019).

By the increasing importance of social networks, change must be innovative and interactive at all business levels (Dery et al., 2017). In today's social media age, companies now need to have more widespread interaction with both internal employees and external stakeholders. The business world is now surrounded by the rules set by the digital and social world. Competitive advantage in economies and the success of businesses in economies is only possible with the success of digital transformation.

It is essential for businesses to successfully integrate their digitalization processes into their corporate culture and ensure that employees adopt digital changes simultaneously because digital usage habits and the advantages of social media have already become an integral part of human life. The digital habits that people acquire in their daily routines should now be used to increase productivity in their working lives. Managers should transform work environments into digital workplaces by working independently of time and place. Digital workplaces lead to saving time and cost by making the organizational processes of businesses faster (Hamburg, 2019). With increased employee interaction in digital workplaces, it enables employees to access information more easily by the socialization. In this way, digital workplaces allow them to develop their expertise and gain digital workplace advantages and social cooperation.

The digital workplace provides flexibility for employees to access information and work whenever and wherever they want. Digital workplaces help build a team that works more effectively within the company and allow the whole team to focus on the same goal. Digital workplaces support the improvement of productivity by managing all social network competencies from a stable online platform (Attaran et al., 2019). Digital workplaces offer an integrated and social collaboration system that increases the efficiency of the end user and reduces operational costs. Digital workplaces reduce the burden of information technologies resources managing different social network systems and provide employees and users with better communication, data sharing, reporting and connectivity.

The Benefits of Digital Workplaces to Entrepreneurs

After the 2000s, information technologies and digital technologies have been developed and the entrepreneurs have many opportunities to both open up to new markets and they carry out their activities with more affordable financing by the development of these technologies. Therefore, it could be argued that the improvements in digital technologies have positive impacts on entrepreneurs. In today's economies, information and digital technologies have a crucial role and sustain a competitive advantage in the economies. A good analysis of the opportunities that electronic commerce will offer to entrepreneurs and customers depends on a good understanding of traditional marketing functions and some useful suggestions of electronic commerce and digital workplaces for these functions.

Many entrepreneurs and customers do not have enough information about the promise of digital workplaces. The digital workplace is not only a mass communication tool, but are also used for different marketing purposes, from online sales to promotions. While technological change threatens all kinds of businesses and entrepreneurs, it offers a variety of entrepreneurial opportunities as well. In order to be successful (Hamburg, 2019), the important thing for entrepreneurs is to define the new commercial strategies and organizational structure that fits new technological aspects and to fulfill the requirements of the new digital era.

Entrepreneurs can increase the coordination with their customers, improve data flow and reduce transaction costs through digital workplaces and information technologies. In addition, digital workplaces reduce the cost of collecting information about potential buyers and sellers. An ideal digital workplace reduces costs and increases the quality of products and services. Digital workplaces provide the opportunity to reach new buyers and sellers. It also allows businesses to develop new methods for selling existing products. The offers of the digital workplaces should be able to attract the attention of entrepreneurs:

- Web technology should be able to ensure that online transactions are processed correctly.
- Support services should accelerate online transactions and sales.
- Digital workplaces should be safe with the operational method.
- E-commerce is the production, advertising, marketing and selling of goods and services through an online network. A quality e-commerce system could be established in digital workplaces.

In the electronic environment, movable and immovable physical products are traded over open and closed online networks. Services such as data services, information services, finance, law, health, education and transportation can be traded over the Internet. Transmission of video, written text or audio, monitoring of production processes, ordering processes, financial transactions such as banking, fund transfers, public procurement, tenders, stock exchange, etc. can be completed through the Internet as well. Many transactions under the scope of e-commerce could be done via the Internet. Digital workplaces are common in many sectors, and an increasing number of businesses prefer to change their physical workplaces to digital ones day by day (Kiron et al., 2016).

The purposes of digital workplaces are:

- Setting new revenue channels
- Reducing costs
- Reducing time consumed in business processes and the production time of the products
- Being accessible and facilitating communication
- Ensuring customer loyalty and continuity
- Increasing the market share

According to 2020 TEI data, it is stated that IBM Connections provides a 168% ROI after switching to the digital workplace system with Forrester's IBM Connections Social Collaboration experience (Cohen et al., 2019). However, after the transition to the digital workplace system, a 20% decrease in IT operation costs, a 5% decrease in employee wear and an increase in end-user productivity was observed (Meske et al., 2019). In addition, within a short period (almost in 1 year), a return on the digitalization investment had been received.

Digital workplaces increase information sharing within the company and accelerate decision processes. They also make business experiences in the company available to the sales teams and help to establish a fast and effective relationship between the customers, the sales team and the customer service team. In digital workplaces, it is possible to plan business processes that are suitable for approval by receiving customer feedback quickly. In digital workplaces, it is possible to quickly plan business process configurations in accordance with customer demands and expectations and to increase the efficiency of business processes easily.

In summary, digital workplace transformation is an important digital solution that provides value to every department of the company in business processes that need to be integrated into all areas of businesses, such as project management. Digital workplaces offer significant opportunities to entrepreneurs and small businesses. A brief history of digital workplaces shows people the most successful examples of entrepreneurs. By making use of digital workplaces, new entrepreneurs and small businesses have also had the opportunity to sell goods and services directly to customers through e-commerce, and to do business and have customers around the world as part of the supply chains of large companies. It is expected that the developments in the field of digital workplaces will continue in the near future, and these improvements aim to solve the problems of technological infrastructure and cybersecurity issues.

The Challenges of Digital Workplace Management

The challenges that can lead to serious negativities in digital workplaces are not just difficulties arising from a single use of digital tools. These difficulties are usually those arising from the separate use of different kinds of digital tools that serve multiple uses. Although a digital platform may offer certain solutions and advantages for solving a challenge, it may lack certain important functions that enable basic operations to be carried out in the digital workplace (Colbert et al., 2016). In such cases, new digital tools are still required for the businesses to overcome the other problems. Partial solutions reached by different digital tools in the business complicate the workflows in the digital workplace and even lead to a dead end.

For instance, a highly effective digital sales tool that monitors how a potential customer reads a set offer for a product or service on the digital platform actually harms the workflow and thus the workplace, since it only offers a solution for a certain part of the product life cycle (Aleksandrova et al., 2019). Because the proposal is poorly offered, employees cannot access the templates, images or necessary disclaimers in the digital sales tool, and a disconnection occurs during the proposal-reading process. Moreover, this harms the workflow, which in turn harms the business or the enterprise.

Another challenge of digital workplace management is related to the effective use of the digital tools of the workplace by the employees. When business owners and managers invest in new digital tools, they should strive to make their employees dependent on these digital tools. If employees do not have enough knowledge and skills to use these digital tools effectively, managers should provide employees with various trainings on the features and effective use of these digital tools. However, most employees show resistance to new technologies in the first place and prefer to stick to the old digital platforms that they use and are comfortable using for the continuation of their work. That is, adapting and exploring a new technology or digital tool is often high on employees' priority lists.

Furthermore, another problem that employees experience with digital tools in digital workplaces is that the digital tool each employee prefers to use is different, and employees generally find distinct tools practical or unpractical. In a digital workplace, project teams or experts in various departments can carry out their work on more than one digital platform. For example, the digital office in the United States may prefer to use Microsoft Teams to communicate, while the digital office in Europe may prefer the Slack program (Maedche et al., 2019). Therefore, identifying a single type of digital tool or platform may not always have positive results for the workplace. Allowing each employee to use the digital tool they prefer to use as much as possible could help in achieving success in digital workplace management. In this way, employees will feel more free thanks to the digital tools they prefer to use, and they could work more effectively and collaborate efficiently with other employees because the most effective coordination in the digital workplace can be achieved with the adaptation and satisfaction of employees to use digital tools. In digital workplaces where employee preferences are considered, it is almost impossible to fail in the integration and practical use of digital tools.

Many digital tools are being developed to increase productivity and offer opportunities to improve employee workflows. However, although working on more than one project and communicating instantly with other employees in a coordinated manner seems quite easy on paper, thanks to digital tools, it is extremely difficult to achieve this in practice. Because when many projects are started on more than one digital platform, the employees feel pressure, and the stress factor can cause various failures by distracting them even when they are working on a project that they could easily succeed in ordinarily.

Problems that arise in digital workplaces are often caused by a lack of coordination. As the conversation streams, employees are inevitably distracted by all the clutter, skimming emails, receiving task notifications in two different project managements and then searching intranet folders for content before working in Microsoft Office (Maedche et al., 2019). Switching between multiple applications is a common problem in digital workplaces and can hinder workflows and frustrate employees with failures. All this confusion has holistic consequences. These conclusions are that time wastage and hidden costs increase in the digital workplace due to complexity.

Choosing Appropriate Digital Tools in the Digital Workplace

According to the forecasts for global information technology spending, the digital tools market will continue to grow steadily, and investments in digital tools will continue to increase day by day. Therefore, it will be inevitable for businesses to adapt to digital processes over time. It is vital for each company to choose the right digital tools suitable for themselves and the industry they are in and integrate them into their business processes. When conducting the analysis and market research required for the discovery of the right digital tools, businesses should consider productivity and, most importantly, the end-user experiences. End users for companies are employees or experts in various departments. Hence, only if there are employees who are satisfied with the digital tool they use in a business and have a collaborative approach to adapting new technologies to their work is it possible to talk about the existence of a successful digital workplace in that business.

Repetitive frustrating tasks and stereotypical job descriptions make employees most unhappy in digital workplaces. For example, in a survey of nearly 20,000 office workers in nearly 15 countries, "data entry" was described as the world's most disliked job description. Following data entry, the job descriptions of "managing e-mail traffic" and "filing digital documents in the right folders" lead the list of most disliked jobs. In addition, 52% of millennials who responded to the survey argued that they can be more productive if they are given fewer administrative tasks (Murawski & Bick, 2017).

In digital workplaces, it is possible to form a better work environment with less frustration and higher productivity. For this, internal business processes should be well and clearly defined, and job descriptions should be shared with employees and should be developed by considering their wishes and expectations. For instance, employees should be consulted on how overly complex processes can be made more practical with the newly introduced digital tools in the company or how to improve business processes and set more value for the company by which digital tools should be debated in performance evaluation meetings. It is necessary to try to reach a decision with employees regarding which is the best practical digital tool for achieving company success (Dery et al., 2017). Employees should be asked what administrative tasks they spend the most time on and look for ways to automate manual tasks, such as document preparation, with digital tools to aid productivity among employees.

To improve the core practices of companies and the way people work, it is important to purchase user-friendly digital tools that can be connected seamlessly. Companies moving to digital workplace models often take advantage of Microsoft Office Suite, document management systems like iManage or SharePoint, CRMs like Salesforce and security and identity management applications like Azure (Vom et al., 2018). These package programs include facilitating digital systems with various usage purposes that help businesses make the most of digital technologies.

To ensure employee satisfaction and productivity in the digital workplace, it is important to keep distractions to a minimum. Digital tools and advanced technology used within the company either have the effect of distracting employees or, on the contrary, have the potential to positively affect the internal workflow. What needs to be done to ensure that the new digital tools included in the company are useful is possible by making sure that the employees use the newly added technology correctly. To illustrate, digital solutions like Templafy benefit workflows, as they eliminate the need for employees to switch between applications when preparing presentations and documents. Through Templafy, employees can access the latest images, text elements and document templates directly from their favorite applications, such as Microsoft PowerPoint, Word or Outlook (Koceska & Koceski, 2020). A solution that strengthens the brand image on an international scale, Templafy seamlessly automates repetitive tasks without interrupting the workflow. Templafy also provides job descriptions of employees. It records company information and company-related data in documents and thus contributes to the legal compliance of the brand.

In short, with increasing digital platforms, businesses have the opportunity to be more productive than ever before; however, it is very difficult to ensure that the digital tools used in digital workplace management are used for the benefit of all entrepreneurial activities. Ensuring the most efficient use of digital platforms in digital workplaces is possible by believing that tools will make the lives of employees easier. Most of the employees would like to adapt to a digital tool, and this is one of the most serious obstacles to employee productivity in digital workplaces.

Conclusion

Today, with increasing number of digital tools, businesses have the opportunity to be more productive and successful than ever before. However, it is not enough just to have advanced technological tools to achieve business success. Enterprises and businesses should ensure that the digital tools required in digital workplace management are used for the benefit of entrepreneurship activities by all employees to increase productivity in the digital workplace and to achieve success in entrepreneurial activities.

The digital workplace is a very essential workplace in all processes of enterprises and businesses, especially regarding project management and intrapreneurship activities because digital technologies are technologies that add value to every process of enterprises and businesses and provide crucial digital solutions to business problems. Digital workplaces, on the other hand, are workplaces where efficiency is increased in business processes by intensive use of these technologies. Entrepreneurs are in high demand for digital workplaces that save labor and time, value people and aim to complete the work for the lowest cost. Considering that the competition in almost every sector is increasing and the sectors are very saturated in terms of both suppliers and manufacturers, it is very difficult to have a share in the sector by starting a new venture. At this point, digital workplaces are a good opportunity for entrepreneurs, considering the benefits and conveniences they provide.

References

Aleksandrova, S. V., Vasiliev, V. A., & Alexandrov, M. N. (2019). Integration of quality management and digital technologies. In *2019 international conference quality management, transport and information security, information technologies (IT&QM&IS)* (pp. 20–22). IEEE.

Attaran, M., Attaran, S., & Kirkland, D. (2019). The need for digital workplace: Increasing workforce productivity in the information age. *International Journal of Enterprise Information Systems, 15*(1), 1–23. https://doi.org/10.4018/IJEIS.2019010101

Cohen, Y., Naseraldin, H., Chaudhuri, A., & Pilati, F. (2019). Assembly systems in industry 4.0 era: A road map to understand assembly 4.0. *International Journal of Advanced Manufacturing Technology, 105*(9), 4037–4054. https://doi.org/10.1007/s00170-019-04203-1

Colbert, A., Yee, N., & George, G. (2016). The digital workforce and the workplace of the future. *Academy of Management Journal, 59*(3), 731–739. https://doi.org/10.5465/amj.2016.4003

Dery, K., Sebastian, I. M., & van der Meulen, N. (2017). The digital workplace is key to digital innovation. *MIS Quarterly Executive, 16*(2).

Dincă, V. M., Dima, A. M., & Rozsa, Z. (2019). Determinants of cloud computing adoption by Romanian SMEs in the digital economy. *Journal of Business Economics and Management, 20*(4), 798–820. https://doi.org/10.3846/jbem.2019.9856

Enkhjav, T., Szira, Z., & Varga, E. (2021). Reconsidering HR competency models: Entrepreneurship and digital competency. In *Technology transfer: Innovative solutions in social sciences and humanities*, 12–14. Retrieved from SSRN https://ssrn.com/abstract=3853543

Freitag, M., Kinra, A., Kotzab, H., Kreowski, H. J., & Thoben, K. D. (Eds.). (2020, December 2–3). Subject-oriented business process management. The digital workplace-nucleus of transformation. In *Proceedings of the 12th international conference, S-BPM ONE 2020*, Bremen, Germany. 1278(1), 234–256. Springer Nature.

Ghosh, S., Hughes, M., Hughes, P., & Hodgkinson, I. (2021). Corporate digital entrepreneurship: Leveraging industrial Internet of things and emerging technologies. *Future of Business and Finance, 183*, 183–207. https://doi.org/10.1007/978-3-030-53914-6_10

Hamburg, I. (2019). Implementation of a digital workplace strategy to drive behavior change and improve competencies. *Strategy and Behaviors in the Digital Economy, 2*(1), 19–32.

Južnik Rotar, L., Kontošić Pamić, R., & Bojnec, Š. (2019). Contributions of small and medium enterprises to employment in the European Union countries. *Economic Research-Ekonomska Istraživanja, 32*(1), 3296–3308.

Kashyap, R., & Maurya, S. K. (2013). Trends of retailing in e-commerce – Product and services. *Global Journal of Enterprise Information System, 5*(2), 40–47.

Kiron, D., Kane, G. C., Palmer, D., Phillips, A. N., & Buckley, N. (2016). Aligning the organization for its digital future. *MIT Sloan Management Review, 58*(1), 1–30.

Koceska, N., & Koceski, S. (2020). The importance of Enterprise Collaboration Systems during a pandemic. *Journal of Applied Economics and Business, 8*(4), 35–41.

Lafley, A. G., & Martin, R. L. (2017). Customer loyalty is overrated. *Harvard Business Review, 95*(1), 45–54.

Maedche, A., Legner, C., Benlian, A., Berger, B., Gimpel, H., Hess, T., . . . Söllner, M. (2019). AI-based digital assistants. *Business and Information Systems Engineering, 61*(4), 535–544. https://doi.org/10.1007/s12599-019-00600-8

Maier, S., & Nair-Reichert, U. (2007). Empowering women through ICT-based business initiatives: An overview of best practices in e-commerce/e-retailing projects. *Information Technologies and International Development, 4*(2), 43–60.

Mazzarol, T. (2015). SMEs engagement with e-commerce, e-business and e-marketing. *Small Enterprise Research, 22*(1), 79–90. https://doi.org/10.1080/13215906.2015.1018400

Meske, C., Wilms, K., & Stieglitz, S. (2019). Enterprise social networks as digital infrastructures-understanding the utilitarian value of social media at the workplace. *Information Systems Management, 36*(4), 350–367. https://doi.org/10.1080/10580530.2019.1652448

Murawski, M., & Bick, M. (2017). Digital competences of the workforce – A research topic? *Business Process Management Journal, 23*(3), 721–734. https://doi.org/10.1108/BPMJ-06-2016-0126

Nicola, M., Alsafi, Z., Sohrabi, C., Kerwan, A., Al-Jabir, A., Iosifidis, C., . . . Agha, R. (2020). The socio-economic implications of the coronavirus pandemic (COVID-19): A review. *International Journal of Surgery, 78*, 185–193. https://doi.org/10.1016/j.ijsu.2020.04.018

Savrul, M., Incekara, A., & Sener, S. (2014). The potential of e-commerce for SMEs in a globalizing business environment. *Procedia – Social and Behavioral Sciences, 150*, 35–45. https://doi.org/10.1016/j.sbspro.2014.09.005

Schallmo, D., Williams, C. A., & Boardman, L. (2020). *Digital transformation of business models – Best practice, enablers, and road map.* World Scientific. Digital Disruptive Innovation, 119–138.

Vom Brocke, J., Maaß, W., Buxmann, P., Maedche, A., Leimeister, J. M., & Pecht, G. (2018). Future work and enterprise systems. *Business and Information Systems Engineering, 60*(4), 357–366. https://doi.org/10.1007/s12599-018-0544-2

PART III

New strategic approaches to the digital workplace

14

DIGITAL SUSTAINABILITY FOR WORKPLACE STRATEGIES

Esra Sipahi Döngül and Luigi Pio Leonardo Cavaliere

Introduction

In parallel with the developments in information and communication technologies, working environments are rapidly digitized. The rate of digitization of working environments is largely determined by the rate of individual Internet usage. According to the Turkish Statistical Institute, the proportion of households with broadband Internet access increased from 30% in 2009 to 82.5% as of 2018. In other words, four out of five households in Turkey have high-speed Internet access. Approximately 45% of 16–74-year-olds who use the Internet say they use e-government services, while 30% of these individuals are found to be shopping online.[1] In the light of these data, it is seen that there is a tremendous supply/demand for the services offered by both public- and private-sector organizations over the Internet.

While these developments are happening in the Internet world, organizations are also affected by technological changes occurring in their external circles. With digitalization, virtual dimensions are added to traditional business processes, organizational forms of communication and workspaces.[2] As a result of this transformation, traditional intranet systems are rapidly being replaced by digital intranet systems. While the Internet is a communication network that allows computers to communicate with each other around the world, an intranet is a private communication network that enables only computers within an organization to communicate with each other.[3]

In traditional intranet systems, information and documents that go through a hierarchical approval process are shared with the employees. Communication is carried out by the organization from one center and in one way. Therefore, employees constitute only the passive (receiving) part of internal communication. So, horizontal communication and cooperation opportunities between employees

DOI: 10.4324/9781003283386-17

are not available in traditional intranet systems. On the other hand, the new generation of social intranet systems (a) offers opportunities such as being able to work on common documents among employees regardless of distance, (b) to discuss in forums, (c) to create wikis, (d) to access corporate applications on a power-by-powers basis and (e) to communicate instant chat.

As is known, successive technological inventions after the Industrial Revolution paved the way for many developments.

> Information technologies, which are one of the important development sites of the 20th and 21st centuries, have created an explosion of knowledge that will repeatedly multiply the knowledge of the past centuries, enabling the information produced to be managed by information control tools and transmitted by Internet technology to reach a wide audience.[4]

Literature background

It is demonstrated that the digitization of communication technologies has positive and negative effects on all layers of social structure in different dimensions. The effects of these on groups demanding social transformation are explained in the context of giving new tools to social movements. On the other hand, it is also claimed that the actions put forward by digital communication technologies do not contribute to the real forms of social struggle that help individuals satisfy themselves.

As organizations implement "digital technologies" – which in this context really means computers and other information technology – people's jobs change. For example, imagine factory workers putting down their hammers and lathes and instead using computer-controlled equipment. According to the Brookings report, such change is at the heart of digitalization (Bloomberg, 2018).

Today, even if the format and content change thanks to technology, the office work of organizations continues, but the workplaces gradually disappear. Jobs can be done anywhere; all kinds of office activities, such as inventory inspections, inventory controls, employment policies, business analysis and control of end-of-term accounts, are carried out without being connected to a certain office via Internet connection in a computer environment. To mention the specific characteristics of new offices, i.e., contemporary offices, there are no physical boundaries in contemporary offices because in large institutions, strong communication between experts and units is required to solve complex problems faster. With developing technology, business areas become more comfortable areas. With the concept of digital archives, the needs in the field of study can be analyzed more clearly. It provides easier and faster access to all documents. In addition, space is saved and all the requested documents can be accessed with just a few clicks. The digital archive system, which attracts the attention of people who are aware of business management, allows the work to progress faster.

Although digitalization and technology have entered our lives very quickly, it is not possible to expect this transformation to take place in a very short time, as it has at different times in the history of the world. This is also a process of management and evolution of a great sociological, cultural and economic change. Considering the features that institutions and organizations should have in order to minimize the compliance problems they will encounter in this digitalization process and also it is necessary to determine the competencies that will adapt to the digitalization of the workforce, to develop solutions that will reveal special differences in the workforce, and to start using the necessary tools by being aware of the risks that this process will pose to us which is extremely important.

The internal control that has passed Fordism into the crisis is as follows:[5]

- With the development of technology, the labor-intensive character of new goods declines, and as a result the importance of cheap labor policies in dependent countries in the size of the economic system decreases.
- The lack of quality control and the poor quality of the business structure aggravate this problem.
- The spread of production around the world and therefore the increase in transportation, coordination and management costs.
- Increased bureaucracy density slows decision-making processes.
- High costs of public services and social policy practices.

Neo-Schumpeter approach

The basic assumption of this approach is that capitalism has the nature of a systemic and cyclical crisis. Similar to the "accumulation regime" and "accumulation mode" of regulators, neo-Schumpeterists manifest themselves as a "techno-economic paradigm" and "social-institutional infrastructure", respectively. The most noticeable difference between the two approaches is that neo-Schumpeterists explain the "circular flow" of capitalism directly with the phenomena of "technology" and "technological standards".[6]

This approach was first demonstrated in the 1980s by the ideas put forward by Freeman, Perez and colleagues based on the "technological discovery (innovation)" concept that formed the backbone of Joseph Schumpeter's work.[7]

This way of working, defined as "typical work", has been transformed by the move away from factory-style production, and the number of workers working in a fixed workplace has gradually decreased under the strategies of resilience and removal.[8]

Another development that creates the need for changes in the concept of the workplace has been the emergence and dissemination of removal strategies that envisage the removal of the worker from the workplace and the work outside the workplace.[9]

In response to the Fordism that came up with the production system designed by Henry Ford by combining with the principles of scientific management, it can be argued that the first point of origin of post-Fordism is also the auto-industrial sector and that post-Fordism emerged with flexible production and management techniques developed by applying it with the mentioned sector focus.[10]

Future of the workplace: virtualization

Virtual workplace

Considering that traditional offices are being replaced by virtual offices today, the concepts of office and virtuality need to be considered together.[11]

Another concept related to virtual office is virtual collaboration. Virtual collaboration refers to cooperation with information and communication technologies, developed for geographically dispersed groups that either never have or are limited in face-to-face communication. In this context, the virtual workplace refers to an environment where geographically dispersed employees use communication and information technologies to perform a specific organizational task. By creating a virtual collaborative workplace, organizations can benefit from both the creative synergy of teamwork and the positive benefits of information and communication technologies. The main reasons behind the transition of organizations from face-to-face communication to virtual collaboration are as follows:[12]

- Increasing prevalence of printed and horizontal organizational structures
- Increased cooperation and competition between organizations
- Transformation from production-based business environments to service- and knowledge-based business environments
- Globalization of commercial and corporate activity

Another concept related to virtual office is virtual organization. To reduce costs and increase flexibility, virtual organization refers to project type (temporary) organizations run by independent businesses, workgroups or employees, interconnected by advanced computer networks and communication technologies.

These organizations try to network between suppliers, manufacturers and management to achieve specific purposes.[13]

A virtual organization refers to a type of business in which complementary resources owned by several businesses working together is integrated around the effort toward a particular product. Virtual organizations are designed to implement three types of competence:[14]

- Quickly creating or gathering productive resources
- Creating or gathering productive resources frequently and simultaneously
- Creating or combining a wide range of productive resources (such as research, manufacturing and design)

Today, after establishing the necessary technological infrastructure, any organization can carry out its organizational and administrative activities effectively in the virtual environment. Millions of people can now carry out office activities through electronic tools independently of time and space and with great flexibility.

Telework, teleworking and virtual offices offer professional information workers great freedom in their work. In this context, several unique qualities of virtual office and virtual work concepts can be expressed as follows:[15]

- Access: It is the ability to access information and share the information that is reached that ensures the efficiency of virtual office activities. Electronic bulletins, documents, programs, interfaces and databases are areas of information available on the Internet, and the presence of a computer and Internet connection are sufficient to reach all these information banks.
- Computers: The use of computers as an information and communication tool in virtual offices leads to radical changes in the way office workers perform their work, and as a result traditional physical offices are replaced by virtual offices.
- Virtual offices: These provide organizations and employees with more effective communication with customers, colleagues, family members and friends. Virtual offices, on the other hand, enable the sharing of documents, pictures and graphics; increase the effectiveness of document management; and provide employees with the opportunity to discuss and share their knowledge on any subject.[16]
- Working from home: Working from home involves working at home, outside the traditional office, connecting with the central workplace through computers and communication technologies. This type of work has a fully independent work environment.
- Tele-central work: Tele-centers are offices away from the main center of the enterprise and connected to this main center by information and communication tools. Workstations in these offices can be permanently allocated to specific employees or allocated to the sharing of several employees.
- Mobile office: A mobile office is an organization of mobile vehicles equipped with information and communication technology for jobs that require mobility. Applications have been launched in Turkey in this direction, and the best example of this is the use of portable computers called tablet PCs for inspection purposes by traffic police.
- Common office: It is not possible to take full advantage of office spaces in the traditional workplace. Office spaces may remain empty due to employee conditions, such as leave, illness and personnel or technical service personnel who spend a significant part of their time in customer offices. For this reason, businesses are moving to the practice of co-office, preferring a more economical alternative.

TABLE 14.1 Technologies used in a virtual office environment[17]

Technology	Functions of technology
Laptop computers	They give flexibility to the environment in which the work is performed.
High-speed modems	Computers far from each other work as fast as computers in the office to retrieve documents.
Fax machines	Thanks to fax machines, documents in a printed environment can be sent anywhere.
Voice mail	Voice communication makes it possible to communicate with the receiving party, although it is not accessible during the call.
Cellular data network	Provides flexibility in places where data communication takes place.
E-post	It allows the transmission of documents and text messages without the need to know where the recipient is located.
ISDN (Integrated Services Digital Network)	It enables voice communication and data transfer over the same phone line at the same time. For example, on the phone with the working customer when talking, the customer can review the record.
Cellular phones	It makes real-time conversations possible without the need to know where the recipient is located.
Pagers	It makes instant contact possible at a low cost.
PCS (personal communications systems)	It enables telework with a low-cost phone call.

In addition to the information and communication technologies provided in Table 14.1, computers are one of the most relevant information technologies. A computer is a digital electronic machine that can be programmed to carry out sequences of arithmetic or logical operations (computation) automatically.

New concepts based on virtual workplace

Crowdworking

Mass work, which is blessed with the claim that it will improve the competitive environment in favor of small businesses and create a more democratic environment in business life and thus spreads rapidly, is a new concept that technology adds to the working life.[18]

According to a report by the Turkish Banks Association, as of March 2018, the "total number of employees in the banking sector" compared to the same period of the previous year decreased from 196,758 to 193,177, a decreased of 3,581 people (1.8%). In 2015, the number of employees had decreased by 8,028, from 201,205, and employment contracted by 4%. The same trend is seen in the number of branches. The number of branches decreased by 244 compared to the same month of the previous year, that is, March 2017. The picture emerging in the sector in terms of the number of branches between 2014 and 2018 is as follows: The number of branches decreased from 11,223 in 2014 to 10,510 in March 2018. In other words, from 2014 to March 2018, a total of 713 branches, or 6.4% of businesses, were closed.[19]

The COVID-19 pandemic naturally accelerated the transition to remote working. Despite all its disruptive aspects, communication with platforms such as Teams, Zoom, etc. through remote meetings has almost become a custom.

The future of digital workspace security

The emergence of unprecedented challenges, such as the COVID-19 pandemic, has made it clear that organizations need to change the way their employees work. As companies go through the transformation process, conversations shift from traditional organizational solutions to digital workspace solutions. They want to adopt and use IT solutions while maintaining workflow and increasing productivity.[20]

Result

Companies are constantly pushing for success. For those who succeeded in the transformation, the old field plan and the defeated technique came together. They called it the next generation that offers experience and technology as a whole, but digital business can make me successful in business.

With access to specialized support mechanisms to address growing digital workplace issues, a digital workplace company that enables employees to work collaboratively, agilely and securely can stand out in a competitive environment. Today, the steps to be taken to ensure business continuity are possible with the right infrastructure, remotely, of our workforce in future crises, such as the COVID-19 pandemic.

In this sense, it is imperative that strategies and guidelines for remote operation of the network are accurately determined and implemented, emphasizing end-user requirements across devices, connectivity, bandwidth capacity, security and collaboration tools to ensure business continuity.

The change initiated by the developments in information and communication technologies in the last quarter of the 20th century globalization of working life, the emergence of an intense competitive environment and the importance of customer satisfaction has led to the emergence of knowledge-based businesses (Kış, 2009).

Virtual office, which is discussed together with other concepts, such as virtual business, virtual organization and telework, is a reflection of information society conditions on office work. Intellectual capital gained importance in the information society; information workers emerged and the work done became knowledge intensive. The engine power of this development has also been generated by advances in information and communication technologies. To have the skills of information and communication technology, mental and intellectual skills and advanced intellectual capacity are considered some of the main characteristics of knowledge workers. Information workers refer to the class of employees who do not need to be connected to a closed space in order to do their jobs and who can produce, process and distribute information wherever they are. In this context, information workers are now able to carry out their work at any time in their daily lives and in any place by moving beyond the boundaries of traditional offices. Of course, the transformation from traditional offices to virtual offices is still ongoing. In particular, it can be said that this transformation can be realized more quickly and effectively in developed industrial societies that have made progress in the transition from industrial society to information society. The enormous opportunities of the Internet in professional and civilian life are irreversibly changing the social structure and the business world. It can be said that future advances in information and communication technologies will increase the distance that digital offices and virtual work can travel.

Notes

1 TUIK. (2018). *Hanehalkı bilişim teknolojileri (BT) kullanım araştırması*. https://data.tuik.gov.tr/Bulten/Index?p=Hanehalki-Bilisim-Teknolojileri-(BT)-Kullanim-Arastirmasi-2018-27819
2 Metin, F., & Medeni, T. D. (2016). Measuring organisational readiness for successful online knowledge sharing. *ADAM Akademi Sosyal Bilimler Dergisi, 6*(1), 129–155.
3 Aziz, A., & Dicle, U. (2017). *Örgütsel iletişim*. Hiperlink Yayınları.
4 Karagözoğlu Aslıyüksek, M. (2016). Bilgi Teknolojileri ve Dijitalleşmenin Türkiye'de Bilgibilim Literatürüne Yansıması: Bilgi Dünyası Dergisi Örneği (2000–2014). *Bilgi Dünyası, 17*(1), 87–103. http://bd.org.tr/index.php/bd/article/view/480/565
5 Belek, İ. (1999). *Postkapitalist Paradigmalar: Postkapitalizm, Endüstri Ötesi Toplum, Post-Fordizm, Esnek Uzmanlaşma, İkinci Endüstriyel Bölünme, Enformasyon Toplumu, Disorganize Toplum*. Sorun Yayınları. s.169.
6 Amin, A. (1994). Post-Fordism: Models, fantasies and phantoms of transition. In *Post-Fordism* (p. 1). Studies in urban and social change. Published by Blackwell with The International Journal of Urban and Regional Research.
7 Amin, Post-Fordism: Models, fantasies, 12.
8 Hamblin, H. (1995). Employees' perspectives on one dimension of labour flexibility: working at a distance. *Work, Employment & Society, 9*(3), 477–478.
9 Hamblin, Employees' perspectives, 478.
10 Parlak, Z. (1999). *Yeniden Yapılanma ve Post-Fordist Paradigmalar*. Marmara Üniversitesi İ.İ.B.F. Çalışma Ekonomisi ve Endüstri İlişkileri Bölümü, Bilgi Dergisi, 83–102
11 http://zmyo.beun.edu.tr/yukle/notlard/isletme/1-donem/%5bziy-107-emel-kesim%5d-buro-yonetimi.doc
12 Hossain, L., & Wigand, R. T. (2004). ICT enabled virtual collaboration through trust. *Journal of Computer Mediated Communication, 10*(1).
13 Kış, E. (2009). *Geleneksel ve sanal ofislerde iş doyumu: Bir alan araştırması* [Yayımlanmamış Yüksek Lisans Tezi, Gazi Üniversitesi Eğitim Bilimleri Enstitüsü Büro Yönetimi Eğitimi Anabilim Dalı].
14 O'Leary, D. E., Kuokka, D., & Plant, R. (1997). Artificial intelligence and virtual organizations. *Communications of the ACM, 40*(1), 52–59.
15 Tutar, H. (2006). *Yönetim bilgi sistemi*. Seçkin Yayıncılık.
16 Kış, E. (2009). *Geleneksel ve sanal ofislerde iş doyumu: Bir alan araştırması* [Yayımlanmamış Yüksek Lisans Tezi, Gazi Üniversitesi Eğitim Bilimleri Enstitüsü Büro Yönetimi Eğitimi Anabilim Dalı].
17 Davenport, T. H., & Pearlson, K. (1998). Two cheers for the virtual office. *Sloan Management Review*, 51–65.

18 Howcroft, D., & Bergvall-Kåreborn, B. (2019). A typology of crowdwork platforms. *Work, Employment and Society, 33*(1), 22.
19 TBB. (2018). *Mart 2018 – Banka, Çalışan ve Şube Bilgileri*. www.tbb.org.tr/tr/bankacilik/banka-ve-sektor-bilgileri/istatistiki-raporlar/59
20 www.affde.com/tr/the-future-of-todays-workplace-the-digital-workplace-solutions.html; https://en.wikipedia.org/wiki/Computer

References

Amin, A. (1994). Post-Fordism: Models, fantasies and phantoms of transition. In *Post-Fordism* (p. 1). Studies in urban and social change. Published by Blackwell with the International. Journal of Urban and Regional Research.

Aslıyüksek, K. M. (2016). Bilgi Teknolojileri ve Dijitalleşmenin Türkiye'de Bilgibilim Literatürüne Yansıması: Bilgi dünyası dergisi örneği (2000–2014). *bilgi dünyası, 17*(1), 87–103 [Reflection of information technologies and digitalization in the information literature in turkey: Information world journal example (2000–2014). *Information World, 17*(1), 87–103]]. http://bd.org.tr/index.php/bd/article/view/480/565

Aziz, A., & Dicle, U. (2017). *Örgütsel İletişim*. Hiperlink Yayınları [Organizational communication. Hyperlink Publications].

Belek, I. (1999). *Postkapitalist Paradigmalar: Postkapitalizm, endüstri Ötesi toplum, post-Fordizm, Esnek Uzmanlaşma, İkinci endüstriyel Bölünme, enformasyon Toplumu, disorganize toplum* (p. 169). Sorun Yayınları [Postcapitalist paradigms: Postkapitalism, trans-industrial society, post-Fordism, flexible specialization, second industrial division, information society, disorganized society. Issue Publications].

Bloomberg, J. (2018). *Digitization, digitalization, and digital transformation: Confuse them at your peril*. http://www.forbes.com/sites/jasonbloomberg/2018/04/29/digitizationdigitalization-and-digital-transformation-confuse-them-at-yourperil/#3f4222a72f2c

Davenport, T. H., & Pearlson, K. (1998). Two cheers for the virtual office. *Sloan Management Review*, 51–65.

Eser-Ay, S. (2017). *Dijital İşyerinin Kalbi Dijital Çalışma Portalında Atıyor*. Retrieved from http://knowizz.com/blog/2017/10/27/dijital-isyerinin-kalbidijital-calisma-portalinda-atiyor/

Hamblin, H. (1995). Employees' perspectives on one dimension of labour flexibility: Working at A distance. *Work, Employment and Society, 9/3*, 477–478.

Hossain, L., & Wigand, R. T. (2004). ICT enabled virtual collaboration through trust. *Journal of Computer-Mediated Communication, 10*(1).

Howcroft, D., & Bergvall-Kåreborn, B. (2019). A typology of crowdwork platforms. *Work, Employment and Society, 33*(1), 22.

Kış, E. (2009). *Geleneksel ve sanal ofislerde iş doyumu: Bir alan araştırması* [Yayımlanmamış Yüksek Lisans Tezi, Gazi Üniversitesi Eğitim Bilimleri Enstitüsü Büro Yönetimi Eğitimi Anabilim Dalı] [Job saturation in traditional and virtual offices: A field survey (Unpublished master's thesis, Gazi University Institute of Educational Sciences, Department of Office Management Education)].

Metin, F., & Medeni, T. D. (2016). Measuring organisational readiness for successful online knowledge sharing. *Adam Akademi, Sosyal Bilimler Dergisi* [ADAM Academy Journal of Social Sciences], *6*(1), 129–155.

O'Leary, D. E., Kuokka, D., & Plant, R. (1997). Artificial intelligence and virtual organizations. *Communications of the ACM, 40*(1), 52–59. https://doi.org/10.1145/242857.242871

Parlak, Z. (1999). *Yeniden Yapılanma ve post-Fordist paradigmalar*. Marmara üniversitesi İİİF. Çalışma Ekonomisi ve endüstri İlişkileri bölümü, bilgi Dergisi [Restructuring and post-Fordist paradigms. Marmara University, I.I.B.F. Department of Labor Economics and Industrial Relations, Information Journal], 83–102.

Spraggon, M., & Bodolica, V. (2007). Knowledge creation in small knowledge-based firms engaged in radical innovation generation. In *6th knowledge, economy and management international congress*. 2 radical İstanbul, 258.

TBB. (2018). *Banka, çalışan ve şube bilgileri* [Bank, employee and branch information]. http://www.tbb.org.tr/tr/bankacilik/banka-ve-sektor-bilgileri/istatistiki-raporlar/59. Retrieved October 18, 2021, from www.affde.com/tr/the-future-of-todays-workplace-the-digital-workplace-solutions.html. Retrieved October 7, 2021, from http://www.affde.com/tr/the-future-of-todays-workplace-the-digital-workplace-solutions.htmlhttp://zmyo. Retrieved October 6, 2021, from http://beun.edu.tr/yukle/notlard/isletme/1-donem/%5bziy-107-emel-kesim%5d-buro-yonetimi.doc. http://www.tuik.gov.tr/PreHaberBultenleri.do?id=27819

Türkiye Istatistik Kurumu. (2018). *Hanehalkı bilişim Teknolojileri (BT) kullanım Araştırması* [Household information technologies (IT) usage research]. https://data.tuik.gov.tr/Bulten/Index?p=Hanehalki-Bilisim-Teknolojileri-(BT)-Kullanim-Arastirmasi-2018-27819

Tutar, H. (2006). *Yönetim bilgi sistemi*. Seçkin Yayıncılık [Management information system. Distinguished Publishing].

15

DIGITAL TRANSFORMATION IN WORKPLACE STRATEGY

Huseyin Arasli and Furkan Arasli

Introduction

Globally, the digital revolution continues "at unprecedented speed" (European Union, 2019) and "transformative industrial and technological revolution" will be one of the keys to unlocking economic development of the EU in 2030 (European Commission, 2021). This digital transformation can be defined as "the realignment of, or new investment in, technology and business models to more effectively engage digital customers at every touch point in the customers' experience (Solis et al., 2014, p. 3). Presently, the fourth Industrial Revolution is possibly the most rapid in human history, building on earlier revolutions and utilizing the "full power" of modern digital technologies (Schwab, 2017).

Currently, businesses develop and depend on transformative strategies to cope with multifaceted challenges concerning this revolution. None of these businesses are entirely unaffected by the digital transferability of the world, and businesses require workplace strategies with an emphasis on the incorporation of high-tech developments to achieve survivability (Ismail et al., 2017). Digital transferability of the business world intonates the fundamental transformation of our world that has occurred as a result of the widespread adoption of digital technologies (Lanzolla & Anderson, 2010).

Building on this revolution, business leaders have prioritized digital transformation for businesses' digital transferability and is amongst the most complex dimensions of business strategies of our digitally-able world (Von Leipzig et al., 2017; Hess et al., 2016). This yielded the eminence of "digital technologies such as social media, mobile technology, analytics, or embedded devices to enable major business improvements including enhanced customer experiences, streamlined operations, or new business models" (Fitzgerald et al., 2014, p. 2). In the US and UK, "nearly

DOI: 10.4324/9781003283386-18

90% of business leaders [are] expecting IT and digital technologies to make an increasing strategic contribution to their overall business in the coming decade" (Hess et al., 2016, p. 2).

From an individualistic standpoint, digital transformation extends on the acts of the self where manifestation of digital transformation has had a dramatic change on how people present and communicate with each other. For instance, customers of a business are able to provide feedback or inquire about the business's way of doing things by posting publicly accessible comments on businesses' social media pages (Melancon & Dalakas, 2018). Belk (2013) identifies five significant changes associated with the digital age: the dematerialization of personal objects via images and videos; the new representation of our material existence via images and videos; the growing sharing of digital devices; the co-construction of the self via digital tools such as social websites and blogs; and a distributed memory in which human memories are digitalized.

Metaverse (formerly known as Facebook – a multinational technology business) furthered its digitalization by revolutionizing what may seem like a radical model. By introducing Metaverse (company), they are objectifying the formation of deeper connections between peoples' desires and a digital world by eventually carrying over the physical capabilities of businesses into virtual environments (Kraus et al., 2022).

From a business standpoint, technological improvements alter company models, altering not only the goods and services delivered but also the distribution channels and supply chains that support them. As such, integrating and using new digital technology is a critical issue for today's businesses and is expected to continue to be so in the future. Through this lens, businesses incorporate technologies into their work environments in order to transform their operations as a result of their digitalization initiatives. The Metaverse example was given on the basis of digital transformation allocating the possibility to create new products, organizational structures, or procedural automation over an immersive virtual platform (Ghaffary, 2021).

Digital transformability of businesses may affect many or all facets of businesses operating today and tomorrow. Given its multifaceted nature, digital transformation initiatives must be well internalized within the departments and operations of businesses on a continual basis. Otherwise, challenges are likely to emerge, and divisive strategies may fail to benefit the business. When done correctly, customer-centered businesses may benefit from transformative qualities of digitalization that may centrifugally enhance their customer experiences, work environment–related processes, overall decision-making, and organizational structures where their brick-and-mortar and digital presences may complement one another (Kraus et al., 2021; Hokkanen et al., 2020).

Contrarily, its depth may challenge its application. It requires ceaseless investigation (i.e., Schuchmann & Seufert, 2015). In line with the Metaverse example, Blockbuster's bankruptcy and the sale of the *Washington Post* to Amazon indicate the passage of market leadership from non-adaptive models to digitally adaptive giants like Amazon (Hess et al., 2016). Given this, businesses must adapt to their environment concerning market competition, relationships with customers, user experiences, markets they operate within, and consumer demands before implementing their expansions with digital transformation strategies (Gallan et al., 2021; Lucas et al., 2013). These expansions include tools and methods such as traditional web technologies, cloud and mobile services, big data, Internet of Things, and artificial intelligent automations (Zaoui & Souissi, 2020).

Bridging the Past and Present: Mechanisms of Digital Transformation

Essentially, fundamental mechanisms of digital transformation and the framework constitutes human-centric processes. Transformation is the key to implementing successful digital transformation strategies and refers to bridging past experiences. Customer-centric businesses often face the challenge of having to adapt to internal and external changes. From this perspective, workplace strategies encompass people, data, insights, actions, and outcomes (i.e., Chamorro-Remuzic, 2021).

In such workplaces, interactions between employees and customers can be captured as digital records to generate valuable data. Analytics can be used to analyze the data and provide key insights (e.g., customer perceptions, feedback, behaviors, and demographic details). In other words, interactions can be well transformed into digitized data to capture customer thought processes.

The bridge between generated data and meaningful insights relies on human-centric interpretivisms (Agrawal et al., 2018). Thus, both traditional and digital strategies involve human-centric approaches and require the so-called human touch. Indeed, the rapid pace of the digital revolution (European Union, 2019) requires more than just raising funds or collecting more data.

Thereupon, it cannot represent a static, irrefutable truth and contain a constant facticity. By and of themselves, they can be considered momentary findings. In this sense, the mechanisms of digital transformation strategies can be viewed as a funnel that allocates strategic flow, and management can draw back to the people phase to re-litigate and re-interpret their customers' perspectives. In this way, customer-centric businesses can understand what their customers want. Understanding the moment is critical because constant change is often intertwined in unprecedented times, such as those brought about by the COVID-19 pandemic (Amankwah-Amoah et al., 2021) or difficulties in attracting qualified employees (e.g., Weber et al., 2022).

Indeed, such problems as attrition have been around for some time; yet studies of traditional strategies have highlighted their possible antecedents from the human-centered perspective of scholars. Bridging past and present, the mechanisms of digital transformation strategies work together with four transformative dimensions of the digital transformation framework to assess an organization's capabilities in its "present." These dimensions capture the technological, financial, structural, and value-added changes of businesses (Ismail et al., 2017). Technology use addresses a business's attitude toward new technologies and its capabilities. Value creation evolves as new technologies are adopted in the workplace. The introduction of new products and services into the structures or work environments of companies affects their sales and profitability. Hence, new technologies need fundamental changes in organizational structure, procedures, and capacities. A company's capacity to fund a digital transformation, as well as its need to act in reaction to a deteriorating core business, are both included in the financial dimension.

Digital Transformation in Workplace Strategy

Employees and work environments are critical for operational expansion (e.g., Ahmad & Abu Seman, 2018). If digital transformation strategies are not continuously applied, employees will be challenged with accessing business-relevant information, collaboration, and customer engagement. Thus, it becomes difficult to keep track of files and communication streams (Hicks, 2019).

Pertaining to revolution, businesses utilizing their human capital would generally want to reiterate their successful structures and evolve transformative mechanisms to adapt to the current digital revolution. In line with the considerations for the fourth Industrial Revolution and addressing the utilization of their human capital, Table 15.1 exemplifies businesses with successful digital transformation strategies.

TABLE 15.1 Examples of digital transformation strategies of businesses

Business	Service type	Digital transformation strategies	Result of DTS	Sources
UPS	Shipping	Big data analytics and artificial intelligence	Achieved faster delivery and real-time packaging goals	Belka (2021)
McDonald's	Fast food	Customer experience delivery with AI drive-thru and app experiences	Reduced customer experience gap	Barsky (2022)
Domino's	Fast food	Customer engagement systems through app services	Led to substantial profitability	Purdy (2017)
Netflix	Video streaming service	Streaming, app experiences, and recommendation algorithm	Increased customer experience and profitability	Yu and Shan (2020)
Spotify	Music streaming service	Agile structure with behavioral prediction algorithms	Increased market share and profitability	Davis and Aggarwal (2020)

According to the UK's Office for National Statistics, "85 percent of currently homeworking workers are expected to share their time between their usual place of work and remote working in the future" (Casey, 2021, p. 9). Similarly, Kroop et al. (2021) mentions that most mid-size businesses are likely to applicate this hybrid approach. As we go deeper with the revolution, improving employees' performance proves to be evermore crucial for survivability, and expansion of businesses currently requires hybrid workplaces. So far, the COVID-19 pandemic has enhanced the digitalization of the world and many pre-COVID-19 "strategies were thrown out the window" (Tabrizi, 2020).

As a result, post-COVID-19 procedures are likely to center digital transformation strategies in the workplace (Savić, 2020). By leveraging digital transformation strategies, businesses applicate technologies such as instant messaging, online meetings, cloud-based information management (like Box), social media tools, and hybrid collaboration platforms. These applications allow employees to adequately perform their tasks and help with bridging their needs at work. Additionally, they also provide remote access for troubleshooting and support requests and automate monotonous tasks and workflows (like seamlessly storing documents in the cloud). It should therefore be clear that the hybrid workplaces of the current business world deem digitalization strategies to be highly important (Miller, 2016).

Digital Transformation Strategies: Practical and Scholarly Companionship

To conclude Chapter 15, this section extends on the stated gray literature and synthetization of scholarly works. With it, the authors introduce their framing on the existent discussion for practical and scholarly companionship and make note of topical scarcities. It is clear that lenses on digital transformation and relevant strategies exist (i.e., Nadkarni & Prügl, 2021; Rêgo et al., 2021; Schneider & Kokshagina, 2021; Vial, 2021; Matt et al., 2015). However, criticality of hybrid workplaces, changing nature of the transferability, importance of employee performance, and importance of conducting research across organizations, sectors, and industries were discussed to lay the scarcities concerning the possible antecedents and consequences of digital transformation strategies in the workplace.

Argumentatively, most academic research on digital transformation focused on providing guidance on specific components of the process rather than offering a holistic view of the adoption of the process (Hansen & Sia, 2015), and their overall impact on the digital transformation processes requires investigation (Albukhitan, 2020). Given the timely length of transformational strategies, one may ask, "who is to manage these changes within workplaces?" and "should there be a specific position for the strategic management of digitalization in the workplaces?" In our passages we emphasized the importance of understanding the hybrid nature of current workplaces as deemed necessary during and after COVID-19-related procedures. Ismail et al. (2017) noted the need of investigating the role of the chief digital officer (CDO), and we extend that to suggest the scholarly enquiry on its effectiveness across contexts (e.g., Western and Eastern perspectives).

Building up on the timeliness, further research on small and medium-level businesses is needed to implicate contextual, sectoral, and industrial insights for practical companionship (Belitski & Liversage, 2019). Contextually speaking, technologically advanced sectors and industries are more likely to experience sustainable technology adoption. However, the non-static nature of transferability does not differentiate businesses just because they are within technologically developed contexts (e.g., Blockbuster). Another point of consideration can be made for small- and medium-level businesses as they differ in their capitals, services, and survivability (Liu et al., 2020). As such, changes in the skills required for digital transformation and their success are dependent on the characteristics of businesses and their contexts.

Conclusion

In line with the literature and calls from the industry, the human-centric nature of businesses should be further investigated. Depending on where the company is located, retaining technologically abled employees may be difficult. Digital transformation strategies bridge traditional, digital, and the current form of hybrid work environments that are not entirely "physical." In that sense, studies concerning these strategies may investigate the hybrid nature of businesses. Such studies may contribute to the literatures of value co-creation (Zhang et al., 2020), employees' behavioral intentions (Parvez et al., 2022), mistreatment (Zhou et al., 2021), and commitment of employees (Arasli et al., 2021).

Multidisciplinary approaches may centralize digitalized delivery of health care services for travelers. WHO (2021) mentions the importance of digital health as it "expands the concept of eHealth to include digital consumers, with a wider range of smart-devices and connected equipment" (p. 39). Among its digital delivery, telemedicine regards "the provision of health services, where distance is a critical factor, by all health professionals using information and communication technologies . . . with the goal of promoting the health of individuals and communities."

In line with the digital revolution, Wong and Hazley (2020) mention how the health care industry would facilitate the creation of health care tourism by modernizing client transportation, particularly during an initial visit and subsequent follow-up. Technology is extremely important and beneficial for health tourism, especially in terms of strengthening operative care processes, both from a medical perspective and in terms of customer service (Medical Tourism Magazine, 2020). The health care industry combines the tenets of tourism with the capabilities of communication and technology. Pertaining to the multidisciplinary nature of health services, health tourists who "seek and receive health, medical and/or wellness services for different reasons" (p. 268) may be investigated alongside digital transformation strategies and digital tools (e.g., smart apps).

Hence, digital health "encompasses" knowledge and practice associated with the development, and use of digital technologies to improve health" (WHO, 2021, p. 39). These technologies "will imply the combination of properly using technologies, aligned with integrated working processes and skilled professionals" (Lapão, 2019, p. 1). As previously discussed, people and data are carved into digital transformation strategies where matters related to data security became evermore critical businesses are likely to lose their customers' trust with the impeachment of their personal information and data (Blackburn et al., 2020).

Businesses must establish protocols for designing, implementing, reviewing, and modifying digital transformation strategies and have sufficient staff for both the initial phase and the ongoing implementation of the strategy. Management often plays the vital role of monitoring, evaluating, and adjusting the performance levels of employees. It is critical to have clear protocols in place to ensure that expectations are being met and that appropriate action can be taken immediately when they are not. This includes developing procedures and criteria for measuring organizational progress, as well as defining remedial actions and the frequency of reassessments (Arasli et al., 2019). Given the role of management, influences of leadership styles may be investigated across contexts and provide an industry-specific knowledge base (Arici et al., 2021).

Traditionally, leadership training has focused on honing one's interpersonal and organizational communication skills. To be successful in today's world of digital transformation, leaders must sharpen their transformational skills and develop into "tech visionaries." To elaborate, top management support is essential for transferability of employees' efforts and for interpretation and implementation of insights via analytics Nadkarni and Prügl (2021). Upper management may request further training on digitalization-related problems, such as media exposure and transparency. Leaders today face far greater public scrutiny than their traditional forefathers because of the pervasiveness of information and the quick dissemination of data (through smart phones, viral repercussions of social media, etc.). Nadkarni and Prügl (2021) investigate the importance of understanding the influence and implications of strategies on leadership calls for the investigation of paradigmatic shifts on digital transformation strategy (El Sawy et al., 2016).

Because digital transformation activities affect the entire business, internal cooperation, therefore, is critical. Bottom-to-top and top-to-bottom viewpoints may be investigated to reveal possible similarities, contracts, and practical implicativeness for industries. In this chapter, the authors provided a general look at the business world. While a bird's-eye view may be useful in understanding the overview of the current differences among industries, it may pose a challenge in the application of a generally agreeable truth. As such, scholarly worldviews (e.g., constructivist, interpretivist, pragmatic, and transformative approaches) may aid in the exploration and investigation of the aforementioned topicalities that may aid in our understanding for practical and scholarly companionship (Creswell & Creswell, 2017). It is with this virtue that, authors of this chapter suggest the investigation of multifaceted viewpoints where both preliminary, methodological, review, and empirical studies may help discover possible resolves concerning the complexities of digital transformation strategies in the workplaces.

References

Agrawal, A., Gans, J., & Goldfarb, A. (2018). *Prediction machines: The simple economics of artificial intelligence.* Harvard Business Press.
Ahmad, N., Shamsuddin, A., & Abu Seman, N. A. (2018). Industry 4.0 implications on human capital: A review. *Journal for Studies in Management and Planning, 4*(13), 221–235.
Albukhitan, S. (2020). Developing digital transformation strategy for manufacturing. *Procedia Computer Science, 170,* 664–671.
Amankwah-Amoah, J., Khan, Z., Wood, G., & Knight, G. (2021). COVID-19 and digitalization: The great acceleration. *Journal of Business Research, 136,* 602–611.
Arasli, H., Alphun, C., & Arici, H. E. (2019). Can balanced scorecard adoption mediate the impacts of environmental uncertainty on hotel performance? The moderating role of organizational decision-making structure. *Journal of Hospitality Marketing & Management, 28*(8), 981–1009.
Arasli, H., Cengiz, M., Arici, H. E., Arici, N. C., & Arasli, F. (2021). The effect of abusive supervision on organizational identification: A moderated mediation Analysis. *Sustainability, 13*(15), 8468.
Arici, H. E., Arici, N. C., Köseoglu, M. A., & King, B. E. M. (2021). Leadership research in the root of hospitality scholarship: 1960–2020. *International Journal of Hospitality Management, 99,* 103063.
Barsky, N. (2022, January 25). McDonald's digital transformation special sauce is curiosity. *Forbes.* www.forbes.com/sites/noahbarsky/2022/01/25/mcdonalds-digital-transformation-special-sauce-is-curiosity/?sh=30ba3d47e986.
Belitski, M., & Liversage, B. (2019). E-Leadership in small and medium-sized enterprises in the developing world. *Technology Innovation Management Review, 9*(1), 64–74.
Belk, R. W. (2013). Extended self in a digital world. *Journal of Consumer Research, 40*(3), 477–500.
Belka, A. (2021, October 30). *5 Examples of digital transformation – customer success guide.* 5 Digital Transformation Examples. What is it & benefits | Digital product design and development company Boldare. www.boldare.com/blog/5-examples-of-digital-transformation/#what-is-digital-transformation?-examples-of-digital-transformation-are.
Blackburn, S., LaBerge, L., O'Toole, C., & Schneider, J. (2020, April 22). Digital strategy in a time of crisis. *McKinsey Digital.*
Casey, A. (2021, June 14). *Business and individual attitudes towards the future of homeworking, UK.* Office for National Statistics. Business and individual attitudes towards the future of homeworking, UK – Office for National Statistics. www.ons.gov.uk/employmentandlabourmarket/peopleinwork/employmentandemployeetypes/articles/businessandindividualattitudestowardsthefutureofhomeworkinguk/apriltomay2021.
Chamorro-Premuzic, T. (2021, November 23). The essential components of digital transformation. *Harvard Business Review.* https://hbr.org/2021/11/the-essential-com ponents-of-digital-transformation.
Creswell, J. W., & Creswell, J. D. (2017). *Research design: Qualitative, quantitative, and mixed methods approaches.* Sage Publications.
Davis, J., & Aggarwal, V. A. (2020, July 21). How Spotify and TikTok beat their copycats. *Harvard Business Review.* https://hbr.org/2020/07/how-spotify-and-tiktok-beat-their-copycats.

El Sawy, O. A., Kræmmergaard, P., Amsinck, H., & Vinther, A. L. (2016). How LEGO built the foundations and enterprise capabilities for digital leadership. *MIS Quarterly Executive, 15*(2).

European Commission. (2019). *Digital transformation.* https://ec.europa.eu/growth/industry/policy/digitaltransformation_en

European Commission. (2021). *State of the union: Commission proposes a path to the digital decade to deliver the EU's digital transformation by 2030.* https://ec.europa.eu/commission/presscorner/detail/en/ip_21_4630

Fitzgerald, M., Kruschwitz, N., Bonnet, D., & Welch, M. (2014). Embracing digital technology: A new strategic imperative. *MIT Sloan Management Review, 55*(2), 1.

Gallan, A. S., Kabadayi, S., Ali, F., Helkkula, A., Wu, L., & Zhang, Y. (2021). Transformative hospitality services: A conceptualization and development of organizational dimensions. *Journal of Business Research, 134,* 171–183.

Ghaffary, S. (2021, November 24). Why you should care about Facebook's big push into the metaverse. *Vox.* Retrieved February 4, 2022, from www.vox.com/recode/22799665/facebook-metaverse-meta-zuckerberg-oculus-vr-ar

Hansen, R., & Sia, S. K. (2015). Hummel's digital transformation toward omnichannel retailing: Key lessons learned. *MIS Quarterly Executive, 14*(2).

Hess, T., Matt, C., Benlian, A., & Wiesböck, F. (2016). Options for formulating a digital transformation strategy. *MIS Quarterly Executive, 15*(2).

Hicks, M. (2019). Why the urgency of digital transformation is hurting the digital workplace. *Strategic HR Review, 18,* 34–35. https://www.emerald.com/insight/content/doi/10.1108/SHR-02-2019-153/full/pdf?title=why-the-urgency-of-digital-transformation-is-hurting-the-digital-workplace

Hokkanen, H., Walker, C., & Donnelly, A. (2020). Business model opportunities in brick and mortar retailing through digitalization. *Journal of Business Models, 8*(3), 33–61.

Ismail, M. H., Khater, M., & Zaki, M. (2017). Digital business transformation and strategy: What do we know so far. *Cambridge Service Alliance, 10,* 1–35.

Kraus, S., Durst, S., Ferreira, J. J., Veiga, P., Kailer, N., & Weinmann, A. (2022). Digital transformation in business and management research: An overview of the current status quo. *International Journal of Information Management, 63,* 102466.

Kraus, S., Jones, P., Kailer, N., Weinmann, A., Chaparro-Banegas, N., & Roig-Tierno, N. (2021). Digital transformation: An overview of the current state of the art of research. *SAGE Open, 11*(3), 21582440211047576.

Kroop, B., Smith, A., & Cain, M. (2021, October 4). How to build digital dexterity into your workforce. *Harvard Business Review.* https://hbr.org/2021/10/how-to-build-digital-dexterity-into-your-workforce.

Lanzolla, G., & Anderson, J. (2010). The digital revolution is over. Long live the digital revolution! *Business Strategy Review, 21*(1), 74–77.

Lapão, L. V. (2019). The future of healthcare: The impact of digitalization on healthcare services performance. In *The internet and health in Brazil* (pp. 435–449). Springer.

Liu, C., Van Wart, M., Kim, S., Wang, X., McCarthy, A., & Ready, D. (2020). The effects of national cultures on two technologically advanced countries: The case of e-leadership in South Korea and the United States. *Australian Journal of Public Administration, 79*(3), 298–329.

Lucas Jr, H., Agarwal, R., Clemons, E. K., El Sawy, O. A., & Weber, B. (2013). Impactful research on transformational information technology: An opportunity to inform new audiences. *MIS Quarterly,* 371–382.

Matt, C., Hess, T., & Benlian, A. (2015). Digital transformation strategies. *Business & Information Systems Engineering, 57*(5), 339–343.

Medical Tourism Magazine. (2020). *Trends in healthcare digital revolution*. Retrieved February 10, 2020, from www.magazine.medicaltourism.com/article/trends-health care-digital-revolution.

Melancon, J. P., & Dalakas, V. (2018). Consumer social voice in the age of social media: Segmentation profiles and relationship marketing strategies. *Business Horizons, 61*(1), 157–167.

Miller, P. (2016). How to create a digital workplace. *Harvard Business Review*, 1–8.

Nadkarni, S., & Prügl, R. (2021). Digital transformation: A review, synthesis and opportunities for future research. *Management Review Quarterly, 71*(2), 233–341.

Parvez, M. O., Arasli, H., Ozturen, A., Lodhi, R. N., & Ongsakul, V. (2022). Antecedents of human-robot collaboration: Theoretical extension of the technology acceptance model. *Journal of Hospitality and Tourism Technology, 13*(2), 240–263. https://www.emerald.com/insight/content/doi/10.1108/JHTT-09-2021-0267/full/html

Purdy, C. (2017, March 22). Domino's stock has outperformed Google, Facebook, Apple and Amazon this decade. *Quartz*. https://qz.com/938620/dominos-dpz-stock-has-outperformed-google-goog-facebook-fb-apple-aapl-and-amazon-amzn-this-decade/.

Rêgo, B. S., Jayantilal, S., Ferreira, J. J., & Carayannis, E. G. (2021). Digital transformation and strategic management: A systematic review of the literature. *Journal of the Knowledge Economy*, 1–28.

Savić, D. (2020). COVID-19 and work from home: Digital transformation of the workforce. *Grey Journal (TGJ), 16*(2), 101–104.

Schneider, S., & Kokshagina, O. (2021). Digital transformation: What we have learned (thus far) and what is next. *Creativity and Innovation Management, 30*(2), 384–411.

Schuchmann, D., & Seufert, S. (2015). Corporate learning in times of digital transformation: A conceptual framework and service portfolio for the learning function in banking organisations. *International Journal of Corporate Learning (iJAC), 8*(1), 31–39.

Schwab, K. (2017). *The fourth industrial revolution*. Currency.

Solis, B., Li, C., & Szymanski, J. (2014). The 2014 state of digital transformation. *Altimeter Group, 1*(1), 1–33.

Tabrizi, B. (2020, October 15). Put employees at the center of your post-pandemic digital strategy. *Harvard Business Review*. https://hbr.org/2020/10/put-employees-at-the-center-of-your-post-pandemic-digital-strategy.

Vial, G. (2021). Understanding digital transformation: A review and a research agenda. *Managing Digital Transformation*, 13–66.

Von Leipzig, T., Gamp, M., Manz, D., Schöttle, K., Ohlhausen, P., Oosthuizen, G., . . . von Leipzig, K. (2017). Initialising customer-orientated digital transformation in enterprises. *Procedia Manufacturing, 8*, 517–524.

Weber, E., Büttgen, M., & Bartsch, S. (2022). How to take employees on the digital transformation journey: An experimental study on complementary leadership behaviors in managing organizational change. *Journal of Business Research, 143*, 225–238.

WHO. (2021). *Global strategy on digital health 2020–2025*. World Health Organization. Licence: CC BY-NC-SA 3.0 IGO.

Wong, B. K. M., & Hazley, S. A. S. A. (2020). The future of health tourism in the industrial revolution 4.0 era. *Journal of Tourism Futures, 7*(2), 267–272. https://www.emerald.com/insight/content/doi/10.1108/JTF-01-2020-0006/full/html

Yu, H., & Shan, J. (2020, July 17). Netflix is managing expectations while winning the streaming war. *Forbes*. www.forbes.com/sites/howardhyu/2020/07/17/netflix-is-managing-expectations-while-winning-the-streaming-war/?sh=4cc4d2176aa2.

Zaoui, F., & Souissi, N. (2020). Roadmap for digital transformation: A literature review. *Procedia Computer Science, 175*, 621–628.

Zhang, T., Lu, C., Torres, E., & Cobanoglu, C. (2020). Value co-creation and technological progression: A critical review. *European Business Review, 32*(4), 687–707. https://www.emerald.com/insight/content/doi/10.1108/EBR-08-2019-0149/full/html?casa_token=IQGZ6GSGS7EAAAAA:eMJy9GIhbvb_4N2ua5rXV36hkE56_YbgBYHXrXO-DOcGTKVeCUzWSiQ93NY_0kilH3J6ATn5MezigFBJAoPofyBPSPKVJTIlVIYr7N5ylmkZVmk2wXUg

Zhou, Y., Mistry, T. G., Kim, W. G., & Cobanoglu, C. (2021). Workplace mistreatment in the hospitality and tourism industry: A systematic literature review and future research suggestions. *Journal of Hospitality and Tourism Management, 49,* 309–320.

16

DIGITAL TRANSFER MANAGEMENT IN THE WORKPLACE

Sneha Saha and Ridhima Shukla

In the post-pandemic world, the global economy is in transition to a knowledge economy, which is the latest development in global economic restructuring. The key component in the knowledge economy is technologies and digital transfer management (DTM) systems that are viewed as productive assets. Keeping up with the pace of ever-evolving technology and the ongoing pandemic, the workplace nowadays is not merely a physical space for employees to occupy during regular office hours. The workplace has to efficiently transform into digital management to connect with employees working remotely and function in full capacity. Digital transfer management is one in which employees are free of physical movements and can seamlessly access and exercise online organizational activities under any conditions irrespective of their work location and inclusive of data protection.

The world economy is in the fourth technological revolution based on a variety of intelligent networked adaptive production solutions systems. However, fundamental changes in information management are needed to take advantage of all the benefits of Industry 4.0. McKinsey & Company defines the term "Industry 4.0" as manufacturing digitization with virtually all sensors built in, analysis of product components and manufacturing plants, ubiquitous cyber-physical systems, and all related data (McKinsey & Co., 2015). The umbrella of digital transformation encompasses a wide variety of technologies, including applications and software, networking capabilities, AI, machine learning, augmented and virtual reality, the Internet of Things (IoT), sensing technology, video-based analytics, the cloud, and beyond.

Impacts of new technologies in the workplace must include three major components: the process of digitization itself, the organizational culture into which it is being introduced, and the process of embedding the technology in the context – the implementation process. Further, research supports the inherent interrelatedness of the three components (Bikson & Eveland, 1986; Stasz et al., 1986).

DOI: 10.4324/9781003283386-19

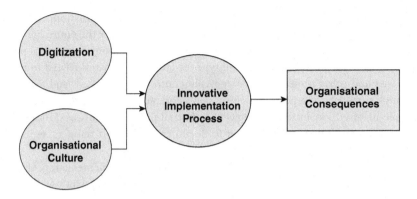

FIGURE 16.1   Understanding Organizational Digital Innovations

The practice of transferring electronic or analogue data from one computer to another utilizing computer techniques and technology is known as data transfer. The technique permits digital or analogue communications and data movement between devices by transferring data in bits and bytes through a digital or analogue media. Digital transfer utilizes various communication medium formats to move data between one or more nodes. Transfer data may be of any type, size, or nature. Digital data transfer converts data into digital bit streams, for example, data transfer from a remote server to a local computer is a type of digital data transfer.

Digital information transfer occurs multiple times during a work life cycle – meaning the information transfer is moved from one location to another, either within the same organization or even between organizations. Each transfer complicates the information management and the challenges to maintain a "single version of the truth". The challenge of digital transfer management is the same in all cases, i.e., ensuring the receiving party understands the process information well enough to implement it successfully to get the work done. The solution is to maximize speed accuracy and cost efficiency to digitize the information transfer. The solution includes forwarding digital transfers to other units within a correct timeline.

Recent practices of various workplaces in terms of competitive strategies shows the implementation and reconfiguration of tasks and processes keeping DTM in mind. In their approach to information management, it is important to measure the value of intangible assets (such as goodwill, brand recognition, and intellectual property) and create a digitized knowledge base.

DTM Case Example – Atrineo AG & Atriflow

Atrineo AG (n.d.) has developed a data management and software solution (Atriflow) specifically tailored for the forwarding industry. The development of this software solution is based on more than 25 years of work experience in the field of knowledge and technology transfer, leading to a solution that considers the special needs of the scientific institution in the best possible way.

This new solution makes it easy to combine relevant information, data, and documents from the handover area into one system. Consider the entire life cycle of ongoing and completed transfer cases, projects, collaborations, intellectual property rights, and spin-offs. Similarly, all types of tasks and activities related to transfer cases and other projects can be centrally controlled, processed, and evaluated through personalized reports. This gives you a complete picture of all transfer cases, people involved, organizations, projects, industrial property rights, and more. The new software solution makes it easier to document and report transfers, especially to different users.

Digital data management includes the definition and implementation of policies, practices, and procedures that facilitate the effective and efficient use of digital data. The elements of digital data management are:

- Optimal storage of digital data in computer memory for on-demand search
- Protection of digital data so it can only be accessed by authorized users
- Efficient access to specific data items without impacting computer performance
- Backing up data so you can access it in the event of a computer hardware failure
- Data retention over the years
- Transfering data between users or software applications that need it

Goals of DTM

Because today's world is characterized by continually changing data and rules, it is critical for a workplace to develop a competitive advantage; this, of course, necessitates having a good information management system in place. As technology advances, so does the process of transfer management. The usage of communication and media tools such as e-mail, cloud storage, short messaging, phone, and network infrastructure is considered as a support system for information transmission, particularly in the workplace.

DTMs is a developing set of principles, processes, organizational structures, and technological applications that enable people to share and leverage their knowledge in order to achieve workplace goals. The key point here is that the entire strategy is aligned with workplace goals. The following are the new goals and challenges for workplaces in terms of DTM:

- To define competence in terms of their work
- To plan the knowledge transfer and methods that will be most appropriate
- To assess the work environments in which this operation will be carried out
- In light of the actions, to create a library of expertise
- To create an action plan and identify the key players
- To complete the form and content of knowledge repositories
- To devise management tools, as well as to monitor, enhance, and measure results

DTM Case Example – Electronic Lab Notebook (ELN)

An electronic lab notebook (ELN) is often a key component to any such solution for the lab because it addresses numerous pain points across industries: collecting data efficiently and contemporaneously, standardizing the data that is collected, enabling collaboration and data reuse, and protecting intellectual property.

An ELN helps to preserve the digital thread of information throughout an organization, from research to development to manufacturing, transforming the concept of technology transfer (Hayward, 2019).

ELN acts as a central repository for many of the data generated and shared within the lab environment. ELN enables collaboration and retains knowledge, from planning and executing tasks to recording data and compiling reports.

Factors Influencing Digital Transfer

Digital transformation in workplaces is full of uncertainty and is considered as a testing time for both individuals and organizations alike. COVID-19 has worsened the situation all the more. In a recent review by Trenerry et al. (2021), many factors influencing DTM operating at different levels have been identified. Multiple individual-, group-, and organizational-level factors moderated by certain contextual factors seem to impact the overall digital transformation of workplaces. The researchers have pointed out that at the individual level, technology acceptance and adoption; perception and attitude toward transformation, skills, and abilities; workplace resilience; and adaptability play a key role in preparing the workforce for accepting changes.

Factors like team communication and collaboration and interpersonal relationships work at the group level. Likewise, leadership, human resources, and organizational culture and climate come into play at higher organizational levels. Different contextual factors, for example, gender, age, cultural background, work experience, skills and competencies, etc., moderate the relationship between a willingness to change and actual transformation at the employee and organizational levels.

An uncoordinated approach to match the organization's broader needs and objectives and digital transfer may have deleterious consequences, damaging not only the reputation but also the output of the organization. Hence, there must be effectively tailored practices in place to reengineer the entire system and make it workable.

Lacking a trained workforce may be an additional factor influencing effective digital management. Moreover, tedious processes of disparate or disjointed legacy IT systems have to be revamped by organizations to unlock the immense transformation potential.

Another pertinent factor influencing this transformation is cultural inertia. Individuals' innate preference of maintaining the status quo may lead them to resist any change for the better. This may become more problematic when leaders fail to recognize, within a stipulated time, that their organization's culture needs to change.

Despite the factors impacting the digital transformation, there are immense benefits of having digital workspaces.

Benefits of Digital Transfer

In the current times, the benefits for digital workplaces are manifold for all the stakeholders, especially the owners. It increases the flexibility in work schedules and in the work environment for employees, helping them strike a more cohesive work–life balance. Digital workplaces also lead to a decrease in operational costs and an increase in revenue generation. Additionally, it leads organizations to achieve their goals in an effective and efficient manner.

There are many benefits of DTM. The first being DTMs are objective and data-driven analyses for the employees. Second, DTMs are faster, economical, and more accurate. Third, the data sharing is happening in real time and is often on interactive dashboards. Fourth, automated reporting of the data is enabled by the processes of digital transfer. Fifth, because the transfer is happening using cloud-based platforms, employees can simply use plug-and-play add-ons to transfer and interact with the information.

Organizations are promptly and effectively shifting from hardware-based infrastructures to cloud-based applications in the post-pandemic world. This gives a more competitive edge to collaborate with stakeholders on a global scale and flexibility to their employees to access the information from any location. This equips the employees with the ability to use the right tool for carrying out the required tasks. Moreover, digital workplaces are not only unified, logical, and secure, they also provide employees with enhanced communication channels (whether they are based onsite or work remotely), portals for enhanced collaboration opportunities are more transparent because of automated processes and can strengthen organizational culture. A few more benefits are presented in Figure 16.2.

When organizations decide to go digital, there are immense benefits. Teams can connect through various innovative tools like video-conferencing software and

Employee Level	Organizational Level
• Personalized dashboards	• Collaboration with stakeholders
• Bookmarking	• Feedback generation and management
• Project management	• Effective decision-making
• Activity streams	• Strategic goal alignment
• User-friendly collaborative tools	• Widespread operational control
• Live feed and alerts	• Enterprise connectivity
• Knowledge sharing	• Efficient content management
• Support from seniors and juniors	• Reduced operational costs

FIGURE 16.2 Benefits of Digital Workspace for Employees and Organizations

instant-messaging platforms, or they may use different project-management and mind-mapping tools and hence can easily work collaboratively in geographically dispersed or proximate teams (Leonardi et al., 2013; Ellison et al., 2014; Anders, 2016). This has implicit as well as explicit benefits in that it facilitates task-related communication among team members increasing a swift flow of task-related information (Alshawi & Ingirige, 2003; Grudin, 2006).

Digital Workspace Case Example – AgilityPortal

AgilityPortal is a unified virtual platform that includes all applications, including an intranet, and enables employees to work more efficiently and collaboratively. A company's most valuable asset is its employees. AgilityPortal keeps the company running smoothly by connecting you with your customers and ensuring their satisfaction. The virtual platform is the only point of contact between a corporation's executive team and its customers in the real world.

Challenges and Opportunities for Effective Digital Transfer

Despite the benefits of having digital workspaces, many challenges face the organization to work remotely and effectively. In a survey conducted by RightScale (2017), lack of trained/expert staff, paucity of time and resources for implementing digital change, governance and control of information, and security concerns like phishing, hacking, or buffer overflow attacks, have been identified as pertinent challenges in DTM.

Of course, there can be issues with digitization. The majority of the issues revolve around the pervasiveness of technology and how it may interfere with other workplace patterns. Information overload is caused by the widespread distribution and availability of content (Rosencrance, 2016). Disagreements arise when people challenge one another through collaborative channels. Time wastage is a result of the incorporation of social network design patterns (like endless scrolling).

The future faces the "fate of newcomers" (Kelly, 2016) just by struggling to catch up. The progress and the main reasons are as follows. First, most of the key technologies that define life and competitiveness for the next 15–20 years have not yet been invented. Second, new technologies require endless updates, and users are constantly updated. Third, today, the technology obsolescence cycle is accelerating significantly (for example, phone applications are only relevant for a month on average).

In other studies conducted by Solis and Littleton (2017) and Adobe (2016) surveys of various organizations regarding the status of their digital workplace and mobile app usage found that only two-thirds of employees ever used their organization's mobile apps, whereas most of the organizations did not plan to launch or manage their own mobile apps. Almost 75% of organizations were found lacking a distinct understanding of digital touch points. Seventy percent of employees reported that their organization needed to strengthen their policies for making their workplaces digital.

While creating a digital workplace, organizations must identify specific measures that not only sustain connectivity and collaboration among the employees but also mitigate risks and enable compliance, particularly in the areas of governance, risk, and compliance (Priljeva, 2021).

The organizations may face difficulties in determining their guiding principles and aligning their focus with the organization's existing information management or information governance strategy. Therefore, for establishing good governance strategies, guiding principles need to be in place for effective DTM. Organizations must adhere to their best practices and translate the guiding principles to sustain ongoing development.

Another challenge could be in terms of defining the roles and responsibilities for effective management. To mitigate these, organizations must recognize their key individuals and create sustainable interaction models between them with well-defined governance measures and metrics for assessment and evaluation of the processes.

Effective DTM is difficult to achieve if the workforce is not trained enough. Organizations need to have policies in place for organizing regular training of their staff to help them gain necessary skill sets.

Organizations may at times lack the necessary channels for the smooth flow of information. Therefore, organizations need to systematically orchestrate the flow of information to and from different channels and must strictly avoid disconnected or loosely connected models where different groups make use of varied tools and communicate in silos. Another salient challenge with regard to information management could be related to the amount and kind of information rolled out for the public, which may be damaging or impair the organization's reputation and one-upmanship, throughput, or protection of confidential information. In case of a crisis where confidential information is circulated, organizations need to respond quickly, maintain a transparent stance, and be readily available for listening and initiating a dialogue with major stakeholders.

Strategies for Managing Digital Transfer

DTM is a sociocultural process of maneuvering firms toward new forms of functioning. This requires an imperative change in the skill sets to remain viable and hold their competitive edge over their competitors. Now, this digital transfer has moved beyond earlier conceptualizations of information technology or business process reengineering. Organizations must now engage in fruitful digital transfer processes that will entail a number of steps, like preparing the workforce or employees for digital transfer, planning and preparing the modules of such transfer, the actual administration of digital transfer, evaluation, and follow-up of the expected changes after successful implementation of digital transfer. There could be multiple methods of conducting ethical digital transfer; a few of those are as follows.

Analyzing and Reviewing the Existing Plans

First and foremost, organizations need to assess the effectiveness of existing DTM strategies. Finding out solutions or redressal of nonperforming assets must be prioritized. An in-depth analysis of the digital activity of the prospective competitors is essential and a precursor to ensuing transformation. SWOT analysis, identification of digital customers, and competitor analysis could be some of the ways to gather relevant information for bringing change to the existing policies and strategies.

Training Employees

There is ample evidence that suggests that having a digital workplace is demanding, as at times it may put more pressure and stress on employees. It may also blur the line between work and life, having a detrimental impact on employee well-being and work engagement. Therefore, for effective DTM, organizations must allocate resources to train their employees to be better adjusted to changed working scenarios. The organizations must train their workforce to be more adept and resilient in accepting the paradigmatic shift to the online working environment. A resilient workforce is not only an asset to the organization, it also provides productive, effective, and innovative solutions to overcome the challenges (Seidman, 2004).

Resource Allocation

Organizations must allocate resources not only for training their workforce for effective workplace adjustment and resilience building but must ensure that they segregate a budget annually for regularly organizing such skill-building workshops and training. Identification of training needs and inculcating required skill sets to the workforce may entail financial and other costs like time and resources, yet it is beneficial at many levels.

Identification and Removal of Obstacles

Effective digital transfer cannot take place unless and until organizations take cognizance of obstacles or roadblocks coming their way. These roadblocks may be attitudinal at the employee level or a lack of empathy at the organizational level. Timely identification and removal of all such obstacles is thus a prerequisite for optimizing organizational benefits.

Reworking Old Thinking Patterns

For digital transfer to be smooth and seamless, an end-to-end mindset where customer requirements, connections between tasks, ability to manage silos working remotely, and the outcome must be redefined and redesigned by organizations.

A process orientation about how to bring this change and mitigate any challenge faced therewith must be in tandem with both the requirements and implications for change. Transformative leadership will be the need of the hour when change is inevitable and welcome. Without effective redesigning of the workplaces, the transformation can only be just an incremental change and will not be beneficial in the long run.

Choosing the Right Infrastructure

Organizations focus more on saving their resources and optimizing productivity. For ensuring this the organizations can develop an infrastructure that offers maximum output with minimum cost and performance. They can look for cost-effective solutions that are scalable, secure, easily available, and high-performance solutions, like on-prem broker, cloud broker, or a hybrid structure, for their infrastructural needs (Cloud management, 2021).

Creating One-Stop Support Points

When the organizations are transferring to more digitized systems, support from top management gains prime importance. Therefore, various programs to identify potential new growth opportunities and specific goals for digitization must be carried out along with recruiting external resources for innovative developments. This would be required as an outcome because the digital transformation will involve substantial grassroot changes influencing customers, employees, organizational structures, and also the relationships with customers and other enterprises or partners. Creating a one-stop support point would thus be beneficial, as all the queries and their solutions can be identified at these support centers. Basically, the main task of this would be to troubleshoot the problems encountered during digital transformation.

There are immense opportunities for strategizing and implementing the change for digitization of the workspace. Only the organizations need to have a bird's-eye view and must be ready to welcome this change.

Data Environment in the Workplace Case Example – Avanade

Avanade excels at assisting clients in improving their business performance through strategy, technology, process, and change management. Avanade wanted to demonstrate its role as a leading digital innovator by applying this same expertise to internal operations and creating a modern workplace environment. It selected a suite of Microsoft technologies to help simplify business operations and foster a more engaging, productive workplace environment for employees.

Avanade took a three-tiered approach to workplace innovation, leveraging its people's talent as well as its technical expertise within the Microsoft ecosystem:

- Microsoft Office 365 provides a comprehensive set of cloud technologies, allowing employees to operate at scale and speed.
- OneDrive for Business and SharePoint Online provide employees with mobile access to information that is both convenient and secure.
- Avanade uses Microsoft PowerApps to create and publish curated content with little to no coding.

The Microsoft Office 365 ecosystem is the foundation of Avanade's digital workplace, giving employees the right tools for the right job at the right time. With greater accessibility, they are more productive and better able to serve and attract clients.

Implications of DTM in the Workplace

In the wake of COVID-19 and the increased call for information analytics in the workplace, management needs to shed the inhibition of sharing information. The workplace requires means of recasting information sharing as an enterprise necessity. Data analytics and transfer permit a higher method of gaining and obtaining digital information transformation. In the framework of development strategies, we need to consider such main aspects of digitization in the workplace:

Training: Creation of digital competencies centers and stimulation of applied research and development within the workplace; raising awareness in the business environment of new opportunities and the need for cooperation.

Technological Bandwidth: Development of high-speed and reliable data transmission networks for educational and analytical purposes; creation of pilot digital factories to popularize the digitalization process across the workplace.

Innovation: Creation of a new type of network technology transfer tools based on smart production with its combination with education; creation of specialized communication platforms for employees.

Conclusion

Effective digital transfer management is influenced by a multitude of factors and challenges that require close addressal and closure by both the employee and the organization. The organization must provide institutional support and acceptance to the slow and time-consuming change occurring at both levels. There may be multiple steps involved in the process of digital transfer management, like initiation, preparation, sensitivity review, and validation. To undergo the process successfully, efforts, acceptance, and immense resources are required by the organizations. Similarly, employees must be accepting and agile enough to adapt to the ever-evolving workplace more so in the post-COVID-19 era.

References

Adobe. (2016). *Driving competitive advantage with enterprise mobile app*. Retrieved January 16, 2022, from https://www.techrepublic.com/article/survey-spending-on-enterprise-mobile-apps-is-up-will-continue-to-increase-for-the-next-three-years/

Alshawi, M., & Ingirige, B. (2003). Web-enabled project management: An emerging paradigm in construction. *Automation in Construction, 12*(4), 349–364. https://doi.org/10.1016/S0926-5805(03)00003-7

Anders, A. (2016). Team communication platforms and emergent social collaboration practices. *International Journal of Business Communication, 53*(2), 224–261. https://doi.org/10.1177/2329488415627273

Atrineo AG (n.d.). *Transfer informations system – Technologies minds markets*. Retrieved January 15, 2022, from http://www.atrineo.com/transferinformationsystem.html

Avanade digital workplace case study. (n.d.). *Avanade*. Retrieved January 18, 2022, from http://www.avanade.com/en/clients/avanade-digital-workplace

Bikson, T. K., & Eveland, J. D. (1986). Evolving electronic communication networks: An empirical assessment. *CSCW '86*. Retrieved January 18, 2022. https://doi.org/10.1145/637069.637080

Cloud management. (2021, November 16). *Flexera Blog*. Retrieved January 15, 2022, from http://www.rightscale.com/blog/cloud-industry-insights/cloud-computing-trends-2017-statecloud-survey#cloud-workloads

Digital Workplace Software: Intranet software. (n.d.). *AgilityPortal*. Retrieved January 18, 2022, from https://agilityportal.io/

Ellison, N. B., Gibbs, J. L., & Weber, M. S. (2014). The use of enterprise social network sites for knowledge sharing in distributed organizations. *American Behavioral Scientist, 59*(1), 103–123. https://doi.org/10.1177/0002764214540510

Grudin, J. (2006). *Enterprise knowledge management and emerging technologies*. Paper Presented at the 39th Annual Hawaii International Conference on System Sciences. Los Alamitos, CA.

Hayward, S. (2019). Tech transfer: How ELNs are integral to data-based decision-making. *Pharmaceutical Processing World*. Retrieved January 17, 2022, from http://www.pharmaceuticalprocessingworld.com/tech-transfer-how-elns-are-integral-to-data-based-decision-making/

Kelly, K. (2016). *The Inevitable: Understanding the 12 technological forces that will shape our future*. Viking Press.

Leonardi, P. M., Huysman, M., & Steinfield, C. (2013). Enterprise social media: Definition, history, and prospects for the study of social technologies in organizations. *Journal of Computer-Mediated Communication, 19*(1), 1–19. https://doi.org/10.1111/jcc4.12029

McKinsey, and Company. (2015). How to navigate digitization of the manufacturing sector. *WhiteBook*. Retrieved January 11, 2018, from http://www.mckinsey.de/files/mck_industry_40_report.pdf

Priljeva, D. (2021). The role of technology in creating a culture of knowledge sharing. *Dan Priljeva's Website*. Retrieved January 15, 2022, from https://obie.ai/blog/the-role-of-technology-in-creating-a-culture-of-knowledge-sharing/

RightScale (2017). *State of the cloud report.* Retrieved January 15, 2022, from https://cdn2.
hubspot.net/hubfs/2582046/MSPs/RightScale-2017-State-of-the-Cloud-Report.pdf

Rosencrance, L. (2016). Real world visible light communication applications. *IoT Agenda.*
Retrieved January 15, 2022, from https://internetofthingsagenda.techtarget.com/
feature/Real-world-visible-light-communication-applications

Seidman, W. H. (2004). A behavioral approach to knowledge management. *Cutter IT Journal, 17*(12), 11–18.

Solis, B., & Littleton, A. (2017). *State of digital transformation.* Altimeter.

Stasz, C., Bikson, T. K., & Shapiro, N. Z. (1986). *Assessing the forest service's implementation of an agency-wide information system: An exploratory study.* The RAND Corporation,
N-2463-USFS. Retrieved on January 17, 2022, from https://nap.nationalacademies.
org/read/1860/chapter/15#252

Trenerry, B., Chng, S., Wang, Y., Suhaila, Z. S., Lim, S. S., Lu, H. Y., & Oh, P. H. (2021).
Preparing workplaces for digital transformation: An integrative review and framework
of multi-level factors. *Frontiers in Psychology, 12,* 620766. https://doi.org/10.3389/
fpsyg.2021.620766

17

THE EFFECTS OF THE PANDEMIC ON THE DIGITAL WORKPLACE

Latif Zeynalli and Aytan Zeynalli

Introduction

"You may not control all the events that happen to you, but you can decide not to be reduced by them" – the short excerpt penned by Maya Angelou reminds us that life is unpredictable and what happens around us is often not in our control, as COVID-19 has become a huge worry and complete surprise around the globe in recent years.

Since the beginning of 2020, COVID-19 has been one of the main topics of interest worldwide. With the global health crisis it caused and the number of infected people still increasing, it remains difficult to predict the full social and economic impacts of the pandemic (Nachit & Belhcen, 2020). Since the pandemic, as an international economic and life-threatening issue, has disrupted lives across all countries, entire economies are attempting to overcome it (Subramaniam et al., 2021).

COVID-19 was a newly identified virus first seen in Wuhan, the capital of central China's Hubei province, on December 31, 2019. COVID-19 is a globally declared pandemic viral disease that affects the upper and lower respiratory tracts and is caused by a novel coronavirus, a new strain of the virus that had not previously been identified in humans and was later designated SARS-CoV-2.

The virus rapidly spread from its origin in Wuhan to the rest of the world. Before it was declared a pandemic, people were allowed to travel globally, which led to the accelerated spread of the virus.

By the end of February 2020, nearly 90,000 people had been infected with the virus, resulting in more than 3,000 deaths (Deloitte, 2021). Only three months after the initial detection of COVID-19, was it declared a pandemic by the World Health Organization (WHO) in March 2020. By then, COVID-19 had spread with alarming speed, and it shook the world. The virus is spread from person to

DOI: 10.4324/9781003283386-20

person through direct contact and respiratory droplets. As of May 1, 2020, more than 3.27 million cases of COVID-19 had been reported in 187 countries and regions, resulting in more than 234,505 deaths. More than 1.02 million people had recovered from the disease (Kaushik & Guleria, 2020a). According to the data provided by WHO (2020), the mortality rate from COVID-19 has varied across countries, and estimates have ranged from 0.1% to 25% of the population.

Another study published in the *British Medical Journal* found that COVID-19 case mortality rates ranged from 2% to 3%, depending on the country or area (Cao et al., 2020). Even in the 20 most-affected countries, the mortality rates per 100,000 people as of March 1, 2021, ranged substantially from a high of 191 in Czechia to a low of nine in Nepal. In this scoring, the United Kingdom was second at 185, Italy third at 162 and the United States fourth at 157 (Johns Hopkins Coronavirus Resource Center, 2021).

According to the data provided by WHO, by November 1, 2021, the virus had infected over 246.6 million people globally, with more than 5 million fatalities (Weiss et al., 2020). By April 2021, the number of infections and deaths had accelerated, specifically in India, Brazil and parts of Africa and Asia, reaching daily record levels. By mid-September 2021, the more severe COVID-19 Delta variant had become a global concern and brought huge damage. This new variant alarmed the government for new policy initiatives and measures.

The rapid worldwide spread of COVID-19 led to a severe global economic downturn (Al-Mansour & Al-Ajmi, 2020). Because of this, countries all over the world implemented a variety of public health measures to prevent its spread, including social distancing (Fong et al., 2020).

Subsequently, governmental responses have focused on mitigation strategies, such as total lockdown, social distancing, travel and movement limitations, restricting group and mass gatherings and the closure of all non-essential activities. The main aim to implement social distancing is that governments will be able to "flatten the curve", i.e., achieve the significant decrease in the number of new cases related to the coronavirus from one day to the next to halt exponential growth and hence reduce the burden on medical services (John Hopkins University, 2020).

COVID-19 has exposed a significant threat to the global community in several ways, as it brought rapid shifts to remote work, hundreds of thousands of job losses due to business shutdowns and closures and new work hazards; these challenges have persisted throughout the pandemic. The pandemic has been labeled a transboundary crisis – a crisis that impacts all social system elements (Ansell et al., 2010).

With its significant impacts on work and work-related well-being, it has been described as "the most widespread and profound occupational health crisis in contemporary times" (Shoss, 2021).

Traditional ways of working encountered severe challenges. Strict government control measures led to many inconvenient working conditions. The COVID-19 pandemic has transformed how we work, with many employees working under isolating and complex conditions. To get over the challenges, companies started the implementation of new business models, are trying to run offices via a work-from-home (WFH) model through the usage of advanced technology. More discussion was made about how the pandemic has changed the future of work. COVID-19 had a similar impact on the world economy as the 2008 financial crisis; however, its long-term consequences were more severe. In significantly impacted areas and industries, such as education and health care, the influence on firm performance is more evident.

Work patterns changed in response to the pandemic, and the WFH model grew (Zou et al., 2020). However, with the rise of WFH, its corresponding side effects emerged. Compared to the traditional office work model, WFH requires people to have new online office competencies and skills and virtual work communication and cooperation skills. For this reason, companies need to respond quickly and embrace a COVID-19 strategy (Ahlstrom & Wang, 2020).

Furthermore, while working from home, the confidentiality of work data is essential. It requires developing and strengthening employees' WFH skills. According to the McKinsey report, COVID-19 altered worldwide labor markets in 2020. The short-term impacts were sudden and often severe: Millions of people lost jobs, and others rapidly adjusted to the WFH model as offices closed. The pandemic brought new behaviors for companies to adapt to. Going digital and the faster adoption of automation and AI, especially in work arenas, became the priority for companies. In a global survey conducted among 800 senior executives in July 2020, two-thirds said they were deploying digital advances, such as AI, either somewhat or significantly. As per the high demand, production figures for robotics in China exceeded pre-pandemic levels by June 2020. The common feature of these automation use cases is their correlation with high scores on physical proximity. The research finds that the work arenas with high levels of human interaction are likely to see the most significant acceleration in adopting automation and AI (McKinsey, 2021).

COVID-19 started to speed up the change process in the digital workplace. To establish a sustainable growth strategy and leverage the possibilities of technology, many companies have started to intentionally enhance their capabilities and resources to adapt to digital changes. During the pandemic, the shift in the digital workplace holds great promise for higher efficiency, productivity, sustainable growth and increased well-being.

The concept of digital workplace

In the last few years, companies have been experiencing an unprecedented transformation driven by technological advancements. The significant rise of mobile devices has changed people's attitudes and expectations toward the technology they use at work. The definition of office work has shifted from a single physical location with desk phones, fax machines and printers to a mixed-location, always-connected workplace in which information and people can be reached from any location with any device (Aaltonen et al., 2012; Attaran et al., 2019; Berland, 2016).

As technological innovations have changed the way we work and interact, the need for a digital workplace increased. Figure 17.1 highlights the evolution of the digital workplace. Both scholarly literature and practice-based literature have provided several definitions and approaches to the digital workplace regarding what it represents and how it can be implemented.

The term "digital workplace" was initially introduced as early as 1993 by Charles Grantham and Larry Nichols (Grantham & Nichols, 1993), but the term has since evolved and drew more attention. Marsh (2018) describes the digital workplace as "a way of describing the broad set of connected technologies that employees use daily to do their jobs and 'an integrative concept that reaches across enterprise tools" (Marsh, 2018, p. 16). According to Igloo (2017), industry and academia identify a digital workplace differently. The digital workplace creates networking and eliminates barriers between people and data. Breaking all barriers leads to more effective and efficient outcomes and, as a result, makes the business became more agile and competitive (Igloo, 2017). Dee Anthony, director at Stamford, Connecticut–based Information Services Group, highlights the understanding and interpretation of the digital workplace. From his point of view, the digital workplace comprises the service, innovation and technological advancements that workers apply daily as part of their routine work (Digital Workplace, 2021).

The digital workplace is defined as collecting all the digital tools in an organization that allow employees to do their jobs. Those tools include intranet, communication tools, email, CRM, ERP, HR systems, calendars and other enterprise processes or tools that assist in a business's general day-to-day functioning (Perks,

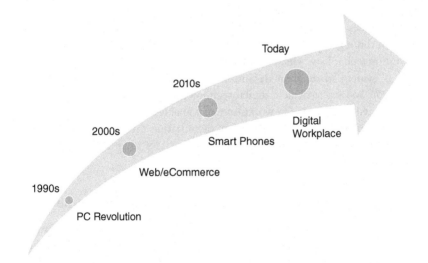

FIGURE 17.1   The Rise of the Digital Workplace

Source: Attaran et al. (2019).

2015). Intel defines technology, agile workplace and collaboration as pillars of a digital workplace (Constant, 2017).

The digital workplace is widely acknowledged for optimizing workers' productivity. While there are few research streams on the digital workplace, scholars have conducted intensive research on its advantages, such as collaboration, compliance, mobility, reduced stress and overload (Köffer, 2015; Haas et al., 2015; Perlow, 2012; Przybylski & Weinstein, 2013; Reyt & Wiesenfeld, 2015; Sykes, 2011; Turkle, 2016; Mazmanian et al., 2013; Aaltonen et al., 2012). According to the Deloitte study, the digital workplace encompasses the employee technology working environment. The study highlights the importance of adopting a digital workplace strategy and its benefits such as talent attraction, higher employee productivity and increased employee retention (Deloitte, 2014).

Digital workplace is a virtual equivalent to the modern version of the traditional workplace where an employee can work anywhere by using any device, browsing files and sharing knowledge. Schillerwein (2011) emphasizes that the digital workplace can be thought of as a master key that unlocks all resources an organization has to offer an employee to do his/her work. Those resources can include enterprise social platforms and communication tools (Attaran et al., 2019; Schillerwein, 2011; White, 2012). The interpretation of "digital workplace" goes beyond simply a continually evolving set of workplace technologies to a combination of physical, cultural and digital elements in the work environment (Dery et al., 2017) that lead to fundamentally new and complex configurations of human and technology relationships at work that reshape the very nature of work practices (Baptista et al., 2020; Orlikowski, 2016; Wajcman & Rose, 2011). The physical workplace is about much more than desks, calls, meeting rooms and other such artifacts, and the digital workplace is more than just the diverse technology environment that enables work. Both workplaces imply different practices involving organizational culture, working style, leadership approaches and cooperation with colleagues (e.g., Baptista et al., 2020; Coetzee, 2019; Dery et al., 2017; Köffer, 2015). In this regard, the term "digital workplace" differs in information and communication technology, which describes a set of technologies.

As is evident in different definitions, a digital workplace is more about the application and usage of new digital technologies, such as big data, social media and advanced analytics at the workplace, that enables significant business improvements. To unlock the full potential of an organization through digital changes and to get digital workplace transformation right is vital for sustainable business success in a new digital-first, consumer-centric business world.

A new normal: COVID-19 impact and working from home

In 2020, business trends and models changed drastically, and COVID-19 caused an acceleration of digital working trends, an essential way of working for knowledge workers in what has been referred to as "the world's biggest work-from-home experiment" (Banjo et al., 2020). WFH was an integral business model during the pandemic that helped most organizations keep their operations running while allowing the employees to do their jobs from home through the company-wide use of mobile and digital platforms. WFH was recently recognized as a priority approach for most governments to reduce the risk of COVID-19 infection. The concept of WFH is not new, it was introduced by Nilles (1988) as far back as 1973, and was referred to as "telecommuting" or "telework" (Messenger & Gschwind, 2016). According to the interpretation, it has been defined as remote work, flexible workplace, telework, telecommuting and e-working. The term describes the ability of employees to execute the tasks in flexible workplaces, particularly at home, through the use of technology (Gajendran & Harrison, 2007; Grant et al., 2019).

According to the survey conducted by Gartner (2020) of 229 human resources (HR) departments, approximately half of the companies had more than 80% of their employees working from home remotely from the early phases of the COVID-19 pandemic – and estimated substantial long-term increases for remote work after the pandemic.

The study of how the US labor force responded to COVID-19 by Brynjolfsson et al. in May 2020 shows that approximately half of the workforce in the United States shifted to a WFH model.

Another study called "Living, working and COVID-19", launched by Eurofound in April 2020 and conducted again in July, provides an overview of the implications of the pandemic for the way people live and work across Europe. The study has revealed the impact of the pandemic on people's living and working conditions and showed that in July 2020, nearly half of all employees in EU countries worked from home.

In response to COVID-19, the companies accelerated workplace digital transformation, impacting every aspect of the way we live and work. As a result, digital technologies and innovation became the primary way for employees to remain productive and connected (Ozimek, 2020).

Remote work has a broader interpretation since it can include work from anywhere (i.e., not necessarily home). We know that some – such as professionals who need to perform complex tasks that require little interaction with peers – actually prefer and are more productive if they WFH (Allen et al., 2014). However, several studies have argued that employees often find it challenging to maintain boundaries between work and non-work while working remotely (Ramarajan & Reid, 2013). While digital working brings great benefits, it is also acknowledged that it comes with an array of unintended negative consequences, such as technology-related stress and anxiety, which need to be understood in order for a digital work model that is optimal to both organizations and employees to be achieved. For many organizations, it is a transformation that will not be reversed – not least because early findings show improved productivity within specific industries and roles – with higher levels of remote working expected in the future (Bartik et al., 2020). The study conducted by OECD shows that WFH may lead to an increase in the welfare of workers and that the experience of WFH during the crisis may lead to growth in teleworking even after the crisis abates. However, the recent data indicates its impact still ambiguous on employee satisfaction since several studies have found worsened psychological well-being associated with WFH. This pandemic-driven WFH has significantly changed people's behavior and working styles, and it is crucial to sustain the operations during this ongoing crisis. Whether the new style will remain in our society depends on its effects on workers' productivity.

According to the research conducted during the pandemic by Rensselaer Polytechnic Institute, employees working from home on a regular basis may be considered for promotions but are likely to earn lower overall pay increases than those awarded to on-premises workers (Kaushik & Guleria, 2020b).

A recent study by FlexJobs concluded that, in the last few years, there was a 44% increase in the number of people working from home at least part time. Since the coronavirus outbreak, WFH has become the de facto practice for most office staff.

To shift to WFH practice has advantages and disadvantages. While the pandemic has a negative influence on business organizations and the economy, it has also forced businesses to look for new ways and tools to run operations through the deployment and application of digital technology at work. On the other hand, it has a positive impact since many employees have benefited from WFH to be productive while maintaining a work–life balance.

Another perspective from the study by Bloom et al. (2015) show that WFH had a positive effect on call center workers' productivity and reduced turnover. While the study reported evidence based on data collected before the COVID-19 pandemic, Emanuel and Harrington (2020) also found a positive effect on the productivity of call center workers during the COVID-19 crisis.

Several studies have reported both positive and negative effects of WFH on productivity, depending on skills, education, tasks or industry. For example, Etheridge et al. (2020) reported that women and those in low-paying jobs experienced the greatest average decrease in productivity. The study also showed that the decrease in productivity is strongly linked to declines in mental well-being (see also Bartik et al., 2020; Dutcher, 2012; De Sio et al., 2021; Escudero-Castillo et al., 2021; Oakman et al., 2020). Additionally, papers highlight the positive sides of teleworking, such as increased efficiency and a lower risk of burnout (see, for example, Baert et al., 2020). The changes in work style appear to have been accompanied by a transformation in behaviors, with entrenched resistance to remote working broken down for employees (Colley & Williamson, 2020).

Messaging tools, intranets, enterprise social networks, self-service portals, workplace mobility and, increasingly, smart technologies such as chatbots and sentiment analysis tools are among the workplace technologies that have enabled the shift to digital working (Dery et al., 2017).

The increase in productivity, cooperation, engagement and innovation, as well as waste reduction, have all been found to flow from the deployment of these technologies by many organizations (Attaran et al., 2019). Evidently, gaining such benefits is not only related to digital transformation. Having a clear strategy and business model, user-experience design, change management, conducive organizational culture, leadership support and end-user training is the key to success (Attaran et al., 2020; Hamburg, 2019).

Conclusion

The workplace was changed by COVID-19 and made companies redesign the post-pandemic workplace to think about the workforce again. Going digital in workplaces during the pandemic became large-scale business transformation, which affected the entire set of enterprise functions. The changes in work styles affect both the change in the operating model and the organizational setting of the enterprise. The new WFH business model will now be a permanent trend in corporations across the globe. While digital tools create opportunities to work in the new approach, the current pandemic has demonstrated that the companies need to support changes and workplace transformations in employee behavior. WFH, with the use of digital changes, has been shown to lead to greater work productivity if managed effectively. To be successful, the companies need to be agile and flexible. It is the successful workplace transformation and the change in the tasks that management is facing.

References

Aaltonen, I., Ala-Kotila, P., Järnström, H., Laarni, J., Määttä, H., Nykänen, E., . . . Nagy, G. (2012). State-of-the-art report on knowledge work. New Ways of Working. *VTT Technology, 17*.

Ahlstrom, D., & Wang, L. C. (2020). Temporal strategies and firms' speedy responses to COVID-19. *Journal of Management Studies, 58*(2), 592–596. https://doi.org/10.1111/joms.12664

Allen, T. D., Cho, E., & Meier, L. L. (2014). Work – Family boundary dynamics. *Annual Review of Organizational Psychology and Organizational Behavior, 1*(1), 99–121. https://doi.org/10.1146/annurev-orgpsych-031413-091330

Al-Mansour, J. F. & Al-Ajmi, S. A. (2020). Coronavirus' COVID-19'-supply chain disruption and implications for strategy, economy, and management. *The Journal of Asian Finance, Economics and Business, 7*(9), 659–672. https://doi.org/10.13106/jafeb.2020.vol7.no9.659

Ansell, C., Boin, A., & Keller, A. (2010). Managing transboundary crises: Identifying the building blocks of an effective response system. *Journal of Contingencies and Crisis Management, 18*(4), 195–207. https://doi.org/10.1111/j.1468-5973.2010.00620.x

Attaran, M., Attaran, S., & Kirkland, D. (2019). The need for digital workplace: Increasing workforce productivity in the information age. *International Journal of Enterprise Information Systems, 15*(1), 1–23. https://doi.org/10.4018/IJEIS.2019010101

Attaran, M., Attaran, S., & Kirkland, D. (2020). Technology and organizational change: Harnessing the power of digital workplace. In E. C. Idemudia (Ed.), *Handbook of research on social and organizational dynamics in the digital era* (pp. 383–408). IGI Global.

Baert, S., Lippens, L., Moens, E., Sterkens, P., & Weytjens, J. (2020). The COVID-19 crisis and telework: A research survey on experiences, expectations and hopes. *IZA Discussion Paper, 13229*, 1–39.

Banjo, S., Yap, L., Colum, M., & Vinicy, C. (2020, February 3). The coronavirus outbreak has become the world's largest work-from-home experiment. *Time*. Retrieved from https://time.com/5776660/coronavirus-work-from-home

Baptista, J., Stein, M. K., Klein, S., Watson-Manheim, M. B., & Lee, J. (2020). Digital work and organizational transformation: Emergent digital/human work configurations in modern organizations. *Journal of Strategic Information Systems*, 101618.

Bartik, A. W., Cullen, Z. B., Glaeser, E. L., Luca, M., & Stanton, C. T. (2020). What jobs are being done at home during the COVID-19 crisis? Evidence from firm-level surveys (No. w27422). *SSRN Electronic Journal*. National Bureau of Economic Research. https://doi.org/10.2139/ssrn.3634983.

Berland, P.S. (2016). *Berland, P.S. (2016). Dell & Intel Future Work Study Global Report*. [online] http://www.workforcetransformation.com/workforcestudy/assets/report/Dell-future-workfoce-study_GLOBAL.pdf.

Bloom, N., Liang, J., Roberts, J., & Ying, Z. J. (2015) Does working from home work? Evidence from a Chinese experiment. *The Quarterly Journal of Economics*, *130*(1), 165–218. https://doi.org/10.1093/qje/qju032

Brynjolfsson, E., Horton, J. J., Ozimek, A., Rock, D., Sharma, G., & TU. Ye, H.Y. (2020). *COVID-19 and remote work: An early look at US data* (No, w., 27344). National Bureau of Economic Research.

Cao, Y., Hiyoshi, A., & Montgomery, S. (2020). COVID-19 case-fatality rate and demographic and socioeconomic influencers: Worldwide spatial regression analysis based on country-level data. *BMJ Open*, *10*(11), e043560. https://doi.org/10.1136/bmjopen-2020-043560

Coetzee, M. (2019). Thriving in digital workspaces: An introductory chapter. In *Thriving in digital workspaces* (pp. 1–11). Springer.

Colley, L., & Williamson, S. (2020). *Colley, C. D. S. Williamson, Working during the Pandemic: From resistance to revolution?* University of New South Wales.

Constant, C. (2017). *Three steps to making the digital workplace a reality*. Gartner Symposium. http://www.slideshare.net/IntelITCenter/three-steps-to-making-a-digital-workplace-a-reality-chad-constant-at-gartner-symposium-2016.

Deloitte. (2014). *The digital workplace: Think, share, do transform your employee experience*.

Deloitte. (2021). COVID −19 Managing supply chain risk and disruption. https://bit.ly/3fcz8tD

Dery, K., Sebastian, I. M., & van der Meulen, N. (2017). The digital workplace is key to digital innovation. *MIS Quarterly Executive*, *16*(2).

De Sio, S., Cedrone, F., Nieto, H. A., Lapteva, E., Perri, R., Greco, E., et al. (2021) Telework and its effects on mental health during the COVID-19 lockdown. *European Review for Medical and Pharmacological Sciences*, *25*, 3914–3922. https://doi.org/10.26355/eurrev_202105_25961 PMID: 34109606

Dutcher, E. G. (2012) The effects of telecommuting on productivity: An experimental examination. The role of dull and creative tasks. *Journal of Economic Behavior & Organization*, *84*, 355–363. https://doi.org/http%3A//dx.doi.org/10.1016/j.jebo.2012.04.009

Emanuel, N., & Harrington, E., (2020). *"Working" Remotely? Selection, Treatment, and the Market Provision of Remote Work*. https://scholar.harvard.edu/files/eharrington/files/remote_work.pdf

Escudero-Castillo, I., Mato-D'ıaz, F. J., & Rodriguez-Alvarez, A. (2021). Furloughs, teleworking and other work situations during the COVID-19 Lockdown: Impact on mental well-being. *International Journal of Environmental Research and Public Health*, *18*(6), 2898. https://doi. org/10.3390/ijerph18062898 PMID: 33809017.

Etheridge, B., Li, T., & Wang, Y. (2020). Worker productivity during lockdown and working from home: Evidence from self-reports. *ISER Working Paper* Series No. 2020–12. https://www.iser. essex.ac.uk/research/publications/working-papers/iser/2020-12

Fong, M. W., Gao, H., Wong, J. Y., Xiao, J., Shiu, E. Y. C., Ryu, S., & Cowling, B. J. (2020). Nonpharmaceutical measures for pandemic influenza in nonhealthcare settings –

Social distancing measures. *Emerging Infectious Diseases, 26*(5), 976–984. https://doi.org/10.3201/eid2605.190995

Gartner. (2020). *Gartner HR survey reveals 41% of employees likely to work remotely at least some of the time post coronavirus pandemic* (Press Releases). https://www.gartner.com/en/newsroom/press-releases/2020-04-14-gartner-hr-survey-reveals-41--of-employees-likely-to-

Gajendran, R. S., & Harrison, D. A. (2007). The good, the bad, and the unknown about telecommuting: Meta-analysis of psychological mediators and individual consequences. *Journal of Applied Psychology, 92*(6), 1524–1541. https://doi.org/10.1037/0021-9010.92.6.1524

Grant, C. A., L. M. Wallace, P. C. Spurgeon, C. Tramontano, & M. Charalampous. (2019). Construction and initial validation of the e-work life scale to measure remote e-working. *Employee Relations, 41*(1), 16–33. https://doi.org/10.10.1108/ER-09-2017-0229

Grantham, C. E., & Nichols, L. D. (1993). *The digital workplace: Designing groupware platforms.* John Wiley & Sons, Inc.

Haas, M. R., Criscuolo, P., & George, G. (2015). Which problems to solve? Online knowledge sharing and attention allocation in organizations. *Academy of Management Journal, 58*(3), 680–711. https://doi.org/10.5465/amj.2013.0263

Hamburg, I. (2019). *Implementation of a digital workplace strategy to drive behavior change and improve competencies, Strategy and behaviors in the digital economy* (pp. 19–32).

Igloo Softeare (2017). *Ro-Why: The business value of a digital workplace.* https://www-cmswire.simplermedia.com/rs/706-YIA-261/images/RO_Why.pdf

Infocentric research AG [Online]. http://www.schillerwein.net/wp-content/uploads/The-Digital-Workplace-Whitepaper-Infocentric-Research.pdf

John Hopkins University. (2020). *New cases of COVID-19 in world countries.* Johns Hopkins Coronavirus Resource Center. https://coronavirus.jhu.edu/data/new-cases

Johns Hopkins Coronavirus Resource Center. (2021). *Mortality analyses web page.* https://coronavirus.jhu.edu/data/mortality

Kaushik, M., & Guleria, N. (2020a). The impact of pandemic COVID-19 in the workplace. *European Journal of Business and Management, 12*(15), 1–10.

Kaushik, M., & Guleria, N. (2020b). The impact of pandemic COVID-19 in workplace. *European Journal of Business and Management, 12*, 9–18.

Köffer, S. (2015). *Designing the digital workplace of the future – What scholars recommend to practitioners.*

Marsh, E. (2018). Understanding the effect of digital literacy on employees' digital workplace continuance intentions and individual performance. *International Journal of Digital Literacy and Digital Competence, 9*(2), 15–33. https://doi.org/10.4018/IJDLDC.2018040102

Mazmanian, M., Orlikowski, W. J., & Yates, J. (2013). The autonomy paradox: The implications of mobile email devices for knowledge professionals. *Organization Science, 24*(5), 1337–1357. https://doi.org/10.1287/orsc.1120.0806

McKinsey. (2021). *The future of work after COVID-19.* https://mck.co/3zKR08w

Messenger, J. C., & Gschwind, L. (2016). Three generations of telework: New ICTs and the(r)evolution from Home Office to virtual office. *New Technology, Work and Employment, 31*(3), 195–208. https://doi.org/10.1111/ntwe.12073

Nachit, H., & Belhcen, L. (2020). *Digital transformation in times of COVID-19 pandemic: The case of Morocco.* Retrieved from SSRN 3645084. https://doi.org/10.2139/ssrn.3645084

Oakman, J., Kinsman, N., Stuckey, R., Graham, M., & Weale, V. (2020) A rapid review of mental and physical health effects of working at home: how do we optimise health? *BMC Public Health, 20*, 1825. https://doi.org/10.1186/s12889-020-09875-z PMID: 33256652.

Orlikowski, W. J. (2016). Digital work: A research agenda. In Czarniawska, B. (Ed.). *A research agenda for management and organization studies* (pp. 88–96). Edward Elgar Publishing.

Ozimek, A. (2020, May 27). *The future of remote work.* Retrieved from SSRN. https://ssrn.com/abstract=3638597 or http://dx.doi.org/10.2139/ssrn.3638597

Perks, M. (2015). Everything you need to know but were afraid to ask: The digital workplace. *Unily.* http://www.unily.com/media/23747/the-digital-workplace-guide-white-paper.pdf

Perlow, L. A. (2012). *Sleeping with your smartphone: How to break the 24/7 habit and change the way you work.* Harvard Business Press.

Przybylski, A. K., & Weinstein, N. (2013). Can you connect with me now? How the presence of mobile communication technology influences face-to-face conversation quality. *Journal of Social and Personal Relationships, 30*(3), 237–246. https://doi.org/10.1177/0265407512453827

Ramarajan, L., & Reid, E. (2013). Shattering the myth of separate worlds: Negotiating nonwork identities at work. *Academy of Management Review, 38*(4), 621–644. https://doi.org/10.5465/amr.2011.0314

Reyt, J. N., & Wiesenfeld, B. M. (2015). Seeing the forest for the trees: Exploratory learning, mobile technology, and knowledge workers' role integration behaviors. *Academy of Management Journal, 58*(3), 739–762. https://doi.org/10.5465/amj.2013.0991

Schillerwein, S. (2011). *The digital workplace, redefining productivity in the information age.* Infocentric Research AG.

Shoss, M. (2021). Occupational health psychology research and the COVID-19 pandemic. *Journal of Occupational Health Psychology, 26*(4), 259–260. https://doi.org/10.1037/ocp0000292

Subramaniam, R., Singh, S. P., Padmanabhan, P., Gulyás, B., Palakkeel, P., & Sreedharan, R. (2021). Positive and negative impacts of COVID-19 in digital transformation. *Sustainability, 13*(16), 9470. https://doi.org/10.3390/su13169470

Sykes, E. R. (2011). Interruptions in the workplace: A case study to reduce their effects. *International Journal of Information Management, 31*(4), 385–394. https://doi.org/10.1016/j.ijinfomgt.2010.10.010

Turkle, S. (2016). *Reclaiming conversation: The power of talk in a digital age.* Penguin.

Wajcman, J., & Rose, E. (2011). Constant connectivity: Rethinking interruptions at work. *Organization Studies, 32*(7), 941–961. https://doi.org/10.1177/0170840611410829

Weiss, M., Schwarzenberg, A., Nelson, R., Sutter, K. M., & Sutherland, M. D. (2020). *Global economic effects of COVID-19.* Congressional Research Service.

White, M. (2012, December). Digital workplaces: Vision and reality. *Business Information Review, 29*(4), 205–214.

World Health Organization [WHO] (2020, August 4). Estimating mortality from COVID-19. *Scientific Brief.* https://www.who.int/news-room/commentaries/detail/estimating-mortality-from-covid-19

Zou, P., Huo, D., & Li, M. (2020). The impact of the COVID-19 pandemic on firms: A survey in Guangdong Province, China. *Global Health Research and Policy, 5*(1), 1–10. https://doi.org/10.1186/s41256-020-00166-z

18

MANAGING THE WORKPLACE IN THE NEW WORLD ORDER POST-COVID-19

Richa Sahay and Anupama Verma

Introduction

In the contemporary world, employees receive many services from their organizations to encourage them, to express their value, and for them to lead a more balanced life. It is because the job environment of today has become more unstable and uncertain. Even employees these days expect not only careers but also a healthy quality of work life (QWL) from employers. Hence, QWL has become a strategic means to attract and retain human resources. It originated from the total quality that was established in Japan (during 1980s) and later became prevalent in countries like the United States, Canada, and continents of Europe and Asia after its success in Japan. In India, the theme has been in the studies of management and psychology and got into practice at the operational systems at work context since the 1980s. QWL intends to upkeep and highlight the worth of employees as humans through taking care of their basic needs and the humanization of the work environment. Yet, a universal definition of QWL is still lacking since the varied cultures across countries have made researchers measure and modify QWL in different ways.

Definition of QWL

Among some of the earliest definitions of QWL, Boisvert (1977) has defined "QWL as a set of valuable consequences of work life affecting individuals, organization and society". Carlson (1980) defined

> QWL to be a goal (organization commitment to work improvement), a process (involvement of people within the organization for the realization of

DOI: 10.4324/9781003283386-21

these goals through individual and organizational developmental methods in the process), and a philosophy (acknowledging the individual's dignity within the organization.

QWL aims toward the creation of an appropriate working atmosphere for long-term organizational effectiveness and efficiency. Previous research has revealed that a good QWL provides positive outcomes for employees and the organization. However, "QWL" has little variance with the "quality of life" that embodies overall well-being and happiness in terms of health, work opportunities, comforts experienced by individuals or groups and "work–life balance" that reflects the manner in which the work affects the personal life of an employee. The early definitions on QWL might be of reduced relevance as per today's work settings. Hence, it is essential to discover factors that affect the present state of QWL during the COVID-19 pandemic that has transformed working patterns across the globe.

QWL of health care workers

Keeping in view the labor-intensive nature of health care services, QWL affects not only the quality of personal life but also the quality of health care services since QWL in health care is mainly influenced by unsuitable working hours, lack of accommodation facilities for nurses, inability to balance work and family needs, inadequate number of workers, inadequate vacations, poor management and supervision practices, lack of professional development opportunities, and an inappropriate working environment concerning the level of security, patient care supplies and equipment, and recreation facilities at health care systems (Almalki et al., 2021). Previous studies have also brought forth the fact that HCWs face excessive work pressure that can be transferred to their lives outside work, too. QWL is a complex concept for them and is influenced by and interacts with many aspects of work and personal life (Almalki et al., 2021).

QWL of health care workers during COVID-19

Many organizations offered a work-from-home structure to their employees since staying indoors became obligatory during the COVID-19 crisis, but the health care sector requires the physical presence of its workers. Thus, HCWs have been all out, faced directly with the infection by dealing with and treating COVID-19-infected patients at their workplace. Pandemics are proven to have enormous implications on health care systems, particularly on the workforce (Fernandez et al., 2020), and the COVID-19 pandemic represented a new working challenge for HCWs (Chatterjee et al., 2021). Therefore, in these uncertain times, the focus on QWL is important to health care organizations that aim to increase patient and employee satisfaction and produce quality health care services (Saygılı et al., 2020) because for the HCWs to continue to be working, they must learn to balance these obstacles to wellness while facing the unique challenges of a pandemic (Shreffer et al.,

2020). During a crisis similar to the COVID-19 pandemic, shortages of drugs and life-saving equipment may occur. This has overwhelmed the capacity of health care resources and has significantly changed the workplace rules of health care workers (Giannis et al., 2021). A positive work environment with the reassurance of personal safety are the two main factors that might be the key to encouraging medical staff to continue working. Previous research on outbreaks of such infectious diseases have revealed that such occurrences can have both short- and long-term effects on the professional outcomes of HCWs. Therefore, it is significant to look after the holistic welfare of the HCWs and find out the work factors and the personal factors to examine QWL during the COVID-19 pandemic.

Objectives

Thus, this study intends:

1 To study the work-related factors of HCWs during the COVID-19 pandemic
2 To study the personal factors of HCWs during the COVID-19 pandemic
3 To examine the correlation of QWL with work factors and personal factors of the HCWs during the COVID-19 pandemic

Review of literature (QWL)

A study conducted by Nayak and Sahoo (2015) suggested that QWL is the key to retaining and attracting motivated employees to achieve an enhanced quality of services in health care organizations. Samson and Sharma (2021) pointed out that QWL is as important as health or money. If an employee is dissatisfied in their QWL, frustration, boredom, and anger are common to any employee and can be costly or unhealthy to both the individual and organization in the long run. Sari et al. (2019) found out that QWL has a positive and significant influence on employee performance, motivation, and job satisfaction. QWL was found also to increase work satisfaction and work motivation. An increase in work motivation was followed by an increase in employee performance. In 2020, Saygılı et al. aimed to determine HCWs' QWL and burnout levels and investigate if any correlation existed between them. It was found that HCWs had good perceived QWL and a moderate level of burnout. A significant yet weak correlation was found between them. A study conducted by Lee et al. (2021) found that HCWs were challenged by working in critical situations and were overwhelmed by heavy workloads, fear of infection, and psychological and physical struggles during the COVID-19 pandemic.

Conceptual framework

The few earliest concepts of QWL come from Walton (1973) and Hackman and Oldham (1975). According to Walton (1973), regardless of their occupation, most of the employees are affected by dissatisfaction with life at work. However, it is a complex problem due to the difficulty to identify the responsible factors for the workers' quality of life in the workplace. In this sense, Walton proposed parameters that influence such issues to measure the interrelationship between them, like safe and healthy work conditions, the social relevance of work life, opportunity to grow, etc. Hackman and Oldham (1975) have linked QWL to internal motivation aspects, job satisfaction, and function enrichment. Thus, it can be established that QWL mostly depends on the concord between work and personal aspects and workplace social roles since while performing a job an employee gets acquainted with social contexts at the workplace, and this activity influences them in their personal life. From the organization's viewpoint, the importance of QWL is related to the understanding of the prevailing problems in routine working tasks. Thus, the QWL is indispensable for the improvement of internal processes and the relationship with people (Sirgy et al., 2001). So, the quality of life in its meaning to work may be a strategy to increase the market value of the company (Karthik, 2013).

It is also proven that the work conditions, such as reasonable working hours, a safe and healthy physical environment, and an absence of unhealthiness, directly affect the work output of an organization (Fernandes et al., 1996). Safe and healthy working conditions aim to ensure the employees' good health, safety covers the physical conditions, and working hours as overtime payment, situations that reduce the risk of accidents and health problems (Fernandes et al., 1996). It is related to the healthiness of the work environment (Timossi et al., 2009).

Another factor that influences the QWL is motivation. It serves as a useful way to retain employees and improve competitiveness for the company (Ogbuabor & Okoronkwo, 2019). Thus, taking measures to improve QWL is expected to increase employee motivation, ultimately leading to the enhancement of performance and productivity (Nanjundeswaraswamy & Swamy, 2013). If motivation is high, it will increase job satisfaction, leading to better results for employees in the organization. If the employee feels that the needs of the workplace are available or exceed expectations, then they feel a better level of QWL, which will increase their level of job satisfaction, and a higher level of job satisfaction will cause employees to be engaged in their workplace (Park & Gursoy, 2012). Social belonging to a social group has also been reported as an important indicator of QWL in work-related performance. That corresponds to aspects of self-esteem and personal relationship, incorporating the sense of community, fellowship, social equality, social mobility, prejudice, and information exchange (Walton, 1973). It is also related to acquaintanceship within the organization and equal opportunities (Timossi et al., 2009) and the social ability to maintain positive relationships concerning assistance taken by family, friends, neighbors, and society/community. Thus, among the main aspects worked in the organizations are the enrichment of the role and tasks, motivation, personal satisfaction, commitment, achievement of leisure, and physical and cultural activities (Kirby & Harter, 2001).

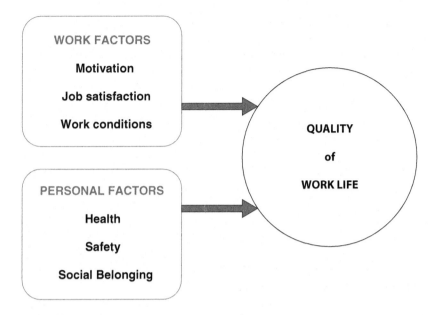

FIGURE 18.1

Source: (primary) Conceptual model for study.

Proposed model for study

Based on the review of the literature and conceptual framework, some variables have been identified to design and propose a model for the present study where the subjective matter of QWL shall be determined by examining work-related factors, like motivation, job satisfaction, and work conditions, and personal factors, like the health, safety, and social belonging of HCWs. Several previous studies have identified that factors like motivation, job satisfaction, work conditions, good health, safety, and social belonging from social groups at work and non–work areas have a significant influence on the QWL of employees, which also benefit the organization. The proposed model for the study shall examine the work factors and personal factors of HCWs through the data obtained from an online survey via a Google questionnaire designed to access the different parameters of work and personal factors, and their impact on QWL shall be verified.

Methodology

Sample instrument and data collection

This study was conducted for 60 days in two phases during wave 1 and wave 2 of the COVID-19 pandemic. A cross-sectional survey using the snowball sampling technique was performed using Google Forms that were disseminated via email and WhatsApp to HCWs working in three different regions of India: Delhi, State of Maharashtra, and Jharkhand. A total of 612 received responses were found complete in all respects and were included for the study. The investigated population refers to all the HCWs from the three chosen locations. The 19-item questionnaire comprised the dependent and independent questions in addition to the control questions inserted to draw out a brief demographic profile of the HCWs. The questionnaire was meant to explore the demography (age, gender, qualification, profession, and place of work), work factors (motivation, job satisfaction, and work conditions), and personal factors (health, safety, and social belonging) to access the QWL of HCWs using a five-point Likert scale. "Job satisfaction" as a work factor was determined with questions based on job security and adequate staffing. "Work conditions" was accessed with work overload and workplace infection-control measures. "Safety" was accessed with the workplace safeguard protocols against COVID-19 infection. Data on "social belonging" was accessed in context of support/discrimination from colleagues, family, and society as experienced by HCWs during wave 1 and wave 2 of COVID-19. "Motivation" was accessed with the fears faced by HCWs working amidst the infection and mortality threats of COVID-19. "Health" was accessed with the HCWs testing positive for COVID-19. For analysis of demography, work factor and personal factor descriptive statistics were applied using Microsoft Office Excel 2010, and Pearson's correlation coefficient was applied to analyze the correlation between work factors and QWL, and personal factors and QWL, via Minitab version 19.

Results and discussion

The study was conducted in two phases: a) during wave 1 of COVID-19 in India (January 2021) and b) before the rise of the second wave of COVID-19 in India (March 2021). The demographic details (descriptive analysis) of the HCWs, like age, gender, qualification, profession, and place of work are represented in Table 18.1.

Out of the total 612 HCWs, 61% were male and 39% were female. The majority (48%) were postgraduates belonging to the age groups ranging from 31 to 60 years. Observing at the profession, it was found that 62% of the HCW respondents were doctors, 21% were nurses, and 5% were lab technicians. Twelve percent from other categories consisted of the community health workers and Aayush workforce.

For descriptive statistical analysis of work factors like motivation, work conditions, and job satisfaction, the mean and percentage of their tabulated data were taken. "Job satisfaction" was determined by the mean of data based on job security and adequate staffing. Similarly, "work conditions" were determined by the mean of work overload and workplace infection control measures. "Motivation" was calculated with data based on the fears of HCWs working amidst the infection threat and mortality rates of COVID-19. The descriptive statistical analysis revealed that 63% of the total investigated population of HCWs were motivated

TABLE 18.1 Demographic details of HCWs (N = 612)

Demographic variables of HCWs		Total number	Percentage %
Age	20–30 years	98	16%
	31–40 years	232	38%
	41–50 years	232	38%
	51–60 years	25	4%
	More than 60 years	25	4%
Gender	Male	374	61%
	Female	238	39%
Qualification	Graduate	184	30%
	Postgraduate	294	48%
	Super specialization	67	12%
	Others	67	11%
Profession	Doctor	380	62%
	Nurse	129	21%
	Lab technician	30	5%
	Others	73	12%
Place of work	Delhi	159	26%
	Mumbai State	86	14%
	Jharkhand State	367	60%

TABLE 18.2 Descriptive analysis of work factors

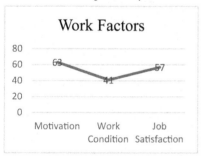

enough to work during the pandemic. Forty-one percent of the HCWs were found satisfied with the work conditions, and 57% were found satisfied with their jobs despite the COVID-19 crisis. The analysis of work factors is represented in Table 18.2.

For descriptive statistical analysis of personal factors like health, safety, and social belonging, mean and percentage of the data were taken after tabulation. Data on "health" was calculated by the number of HCWs testing positive for COVID-19. "Safety" was accessed with the level of workplace safeguard measures. "Social

TABLE 18.3 Descriptive analysis of personal factors

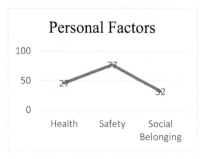
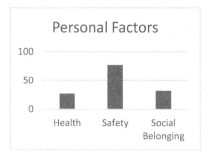

TABLE 18.4 Pearson's correlation coefficient matrix between work factors and QWL using Minitab 19

Method	
Correlation type	Pearson
Number of rows used	612
Correlations	**Work factor**
QWL	0.557

belonging" was calculated with support/discrimination from colleagues, family, and society during wave 1 and wave 2 of the COVID-19 pandemic. The overall statistical analysis of personal factors revealed that only 27% of the investigated population of HCWs reported good health, 77% of the HCWs found their workplace safe and following appropriate safeguard measures as per COVID-19 norms, and 32% reported adequate social belonging from their social groups. Thus, it can be concluded that working during COVID-19 impacted the personal factors (health and social belonging) of HCWs. The analysis of personal factors is represented in Table 18.3.

The Pearson's correlation coefficient value for work factors and QWL of HCWs received on the statistical analysis using Minitab 19 was found to be 0.557. This indicates a strong correlation between both the variables and demonstrates that the work factors have a positive impact on the QWL of HCWs. This value received specifies that the decrease in any factor at work shall lead to a low QWL of HCWs.

The Pearson's correlation coefficient value received for personal factors and QWL of HCWs on statistical analysis using Minitab 19 was found to be 0.742. This indicates a strong positive correlation between both variables and demonstrates that the personal factors have a strong positive impact on the QWL of HCWs. The value received specifies that the decrease in personal factors shall lead to a low QWL of HCWs.

TABLE 18.5 Pearson's correlation coefficient matrix between personal factors and QWL using Minitab 19

Method	
Correlation type	Pearson
Number of rows used	612
Correlations	**Personal factor**
QWL	0.742

Conclusion

The study found out that QWL is having direct implications during the COVID-19 pandemic for HCWs. The findings also suggest that QWL is impacted due to work factors since the influence from work factors redirects toward personal factors for leading a good quality of work life. The results revealed that there was significant positive correlation between QWL and work factors (0.557) and QWL and personal factors (0.742) among HCWs during the COVID-19 pandemic. This study instituted that QWL suggestively impacts the personal factors of HCWs due to the infection of COVID-19. This calls for appropriate actions by policymakers and administrators concerned with health care. The studies in this area are limited and need consideration for uninterrupted quality of health care services by providing HCWs with well-adjusted QWL. This study also gives out indications to keep up with the changes that are taking up due to the COVID-19 pandemic in the health care sector. These can be achieved by high QWL of HCWs and a robust health care system.

Limitations

Due to the ongoing pandemic and restrictions on visiting the HCWs personally, difficulties were faced in getting responses from HCWs. The response rate was found to be lower from the expected because of this. A bigger sample size with the usage of better sampling techniques can produce better results in the future. The findings from two different waves of COVID-19 have been clubbed for statistical analysis in this study; hence, reliability of the results can be differed.

Significance

This study will find relevance to the policymakers, organizers, and HCW administrators finding resolution for improved QWL management of HCWs in the continuing COVID-19 pandemic. This study can also provide a platform to develop strategies for the upkeep of HCWs in future pandemics. Researchers can also use this study as future reference.

Scope of the study

This study can be furthered to envisage QWL of HCWs based on single different waves and also for the predicted forthcoming waves of COVID-19. QWL can be additionally evaluated based on different demographic factors like age, gender, occupation, and work experience. Research in the area concerning HCWs is negligible and needs to be instigated. The present research is based on a cross-sectional study; effects of change in the long term could also be studied.

References

Almalki, A. H., Alzahrani, M. S., Alshehri, F. S., Alharbi, A., Alkhudaydi, S. F., Alshahrani, R. S., Alzaidi, A. H., Algarni, M. A., Alsaab, H. O., Alatawi, Y., Althobaiti, Y. S., Bamaga, A. K., & Alhifany, A. A. (2021). Impact of COVID-19 on HCWs in Saudi Arabia: A year later into the pandemic. *Frontiers in Psychiatry*, *12*, 797545. https://doi.org/10.3389/fpsyt.2021.797545

Boisvert, M. P. (1977). The quality of working life: An analysis. *Human Relations*, 30(2), 155–160. https://doi.org/10.1177/001872677703000204

Carlson, H. C. (1980). A model of quality of work life as a developmental process. In W. W. Burke & L. D. Goodstein (Eds.), *Trends and issues in OD: Current theory and practice* (pp. 83–123). University Associates.

Chatterjee, S. S., Chakrabarty, M., Banerjee, D., Grover, S., Chatterjee, S. S., & Dan, U. (2021). Stress, sleep and psychological impact in healthcare workers during the early phase of COVID-19 in India: A factor analysis. *Frontiers in Psychology*, *12*, 473. https://doi.org/10.3389/fpsyg.2021.611314

Fernandes, R. B., Martins, B. S., Caixeta, R. P., Da Costa Filho, C. G., Braga, G. A., & Antonialli, L. M. (1996). Quality of work life: An evaluation of Walton model with analysis of structural equations. *Revista Escapios*, *38*(3), 5.

Fernandez, R., Lord, H., Halcomb, E., Moxham, L., Middleton, R., Alananzeh, I., & Ellwood, L. (2020). Implications for COVID-19: A systematic review of nurses' experiences of working in acute care hospital settings during a respiratory pandemic. *International Journal of Nursing Studies*, *111*, 103637. https://doi.org/10.1016/j.ijnurstu.2020.103637

Giannis, D., Geropoulos, G., Matenoglou, E., & Moris, D. (2021). Impact of coronavirus disease 2019 on healthcare workers: Beyond the risk of exposure. *Postgraduate Medical Journal*, *97*(1147), 326–328. https://doi.org/10.1136/postgradmedj-2020-137988

Hackman, J. R., & Oldham, G. R. (1975). Development of the job diagnostic survey. *Journal of Applied Psychology*, *60*(2), 159–170. https://doi.org/10.1037/h0076546

Karthik, R. (2013). A study on work life balance in Chennai port trust, Chennai. *Advances in Management*, *6*(7).

Kirby, E. L., & Harter, L. M. (2001). Discourses of diversity and the quality of work life: The character and costs of the managerial metaphor. *Management Communication Quarterly*, *15*(1), 121–127. https://doi.org/10.1177/0893318901151008

Lee, J. Y., Lee, J. Y., Lee, S. H., Kim, J., Park, H. Y., Kim, Y., & Kwon, K. T. (2021). The experiences of health care workers during the COVID-19 pandemic in Korea: A qualitative study. *Journal of Korean Medical Science*, *36*(23), e170. English. https://doi.org/10.3346/jkms.2021.36.e170

Nanjundeswaraswamy, T. S., & Swamy, D. R. (2013). Review of literature on quality of worklife. *International Journal for Quality Research*, 7, 201–214. Google Scholar.

Nayak, T., & Sahoo, C. K. (2015). Quality of work life and organizational performance: The mediating role of employee commitment. *Journal of Health Management*, *17*(3), 263–273. https://doi.org/10.1177/0972063415589236, Google Scholar.

Ogbuabor, D. C., & Okoronkwo, I. L. (2019). The influence of quality of work life on motivation and retention of local government tuberculosis control programme supervisors in South-Eastern Nigeria. *PloS One*, *14*(7), e0220292. https://doi.org/10.1371/journal.pone.0220292

Park, J., & Gursoy, D. (2012). Generation effects on work engagement among U.S. hotel employees. *International Journal of Hospitality Management*, *31*(4), 1195–1202. https://doi.org/10.1016/j.ijhm.2012.02.007

Samson, Sarita. & Sharma, D. (2021). To study the quality of work life in higher education institutions with reference to PCMC area, Pune. *Psychology and Education Journal*, *58*(2). https://doi.org/10.17762/pae.v58i2.3438

Sari, N. P. R., Bendesa, I. K. G., & Antara, M. (2019). The influence of quality of work life on employees' performance with job satisfaction and work motivation as intervening variables in star-rated hotels in Ubud tourism area of Bali. *Tourism and Hospitality Management*, *7*(1). https://doi.org/10.15640/jthm.v7n1a8

Saygılı, M., Avci, K., & Sönmez, S. (2020). Quality of work life and burnout in healthcare workers in turkey. *Journal of Health Management*, *22*(3), 317–329. https://doi.org/10.1177/0972063420938562

Shreffler, E. et al. (2020, September). The impact of COVID-19 on healthcare workers wellness: A scoping review. *Western Journal of Emergency Medicine*, *21*(5), 1059–1066. https://doi.org/10.5811/westjem.2020.7.48684

Sirgy, M. J., Efraty, D., Siegel, P., & Lee, D. (2001). New measure of quality of work life (QWL) based on need satisfaction and spill over theories. *Social Indicators Research*, *55*(3), 241–302. https://doi.org/10.1023/A:1010986923468

Timossi, L. da S., Pedroso, B., Pilatti, L. A., & de Francisco, A. C. (2009). Walton's model adaptation for quality of work life evaluation. *Journal of Physical Education*, *20*(3), 395–405. https://doi.org/10.4025/reveducfis.v20i3.5780, Retrieved from https://periodicos.uem.br/ojs/index.php/RevEducFis/article/view/5780

Walton, R. E. (1973). Quality of work life: What is it? *Sloan Management Review*, *15*(1), 11–21.

INDEX

Note: Page numbers in *italics* indicate a figure and page numbers in **bold** indicate a table on the corresponding page. Page numbers followed by "n" indicate a note.

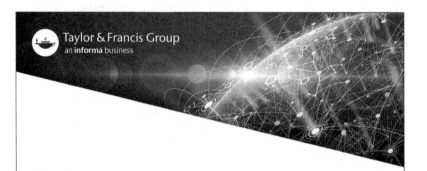

Printed in the United States
by Baker & Taylor Publisher Services